Do it

The Lazy Way

alpha books

1. Aren't sure it's worth it? Read why knowing Spanish is a valuable asset—both personally and, possibly, financially.

2. Spanish is pronounced and spelled logically. Once you know the rules, you'll know how to say it and spell it. Always!

3. Use gestures and body language to get lots of mileage out of just a few basic phrases.

4. Learn to recognize the words that are common to both Spanish and English. Increase your vocabulary ten-fold overnight.

5. Gato got your tongue? No problem. A few well-placed courtesies and polite phrases can work wonders in any situation.

The Lazy Way
alpha books

*One luxurious
bubble bath*

The Lazy Way
alpha books

*Access to most comfortable
chair and favorite TV show*

The Lazy Way
alpha books

*One half-hour massage
(will need to recruit spouse, while...*

The Lazy Way
alpha books

*Time to recline and listen to a favorite CD
(at least one song)*

cut

6. Masculine vs. feminine? Don't worry—gender can actually be your friend.

7. Need a verb fast but aren't ready to conjugate? Create excellent sentences with "Yo quiero" to tell people what you want.

8. Don't know what it is or how to say it? Relax—you can use "esto" and "eso" for "this" and "that" all day.

9. Trust yourself. You don't need anyone else to tell you how to learn. Enjoy the freedom of creating your own exercises to fit your personal learning style.

10. Stressed about grammar and syntax? Finally: Explanations are both easy and enjoyable to read!

The Lazy Way

alpha books

COUPON

The Lazy Way

alpha books

COUPON

The Lazy Way

alpha books

COUPON

The Lazy Way

alpha books

COUPON

cut

Learn
Spanish

Learn
Spanish

Steven R. Hawson

Macmillan • USA

To my loving wife Kristin and newborn son, Kieran. With love, all things are possible.

Macmillan Publishing books may be purchased for business or sales promotional use. For information please write: Special Markets Department, Macmillan Publishing USA, 1633 Broadway, New York, NY 10019.

International Standard Book Number: 0-02-862650-8
Library of Congress Catalog Card Number available upon request.

01 00 99   8 7 6 5 4 3 2 1

Interpretation of the printing code: the rightmost number of the first series of numbers is the year of the book's printing; the rightmost number of the second series of numbers is the number of the book's printing. For example, a printing code of 99-1 shows that the first printing occurred in 1999.

Printed in the United States of America

Book Design: Madhouse Studios

Page Creation: Carrie Allen and Heather Pope

You Don't Have to Feel Guilty Anymore!

IT'S O.K. TO DO IT *THE LAZY WAY!*

It seems every time we turn around, we're given more responsibility, more information to absorb, more places we need to go, and more numbers, dates, and names to remember. Both our bodies and our minds are already on overload. And we know what happens next—cleaning the house, balancing the checkbook, and cooking dinner get put off until "tomorrow" and eventually fall by the wayside.

So let's be frank—we're all starting to feel a bit guilty about the dirty laundry, stacks of ATM slips, and Chinese takeout. Just thinking about tackling those terrible tasks makes you exhausted, right? If only there were an easy, effortless way to get this stuff done! (And done right!)

There is—*The Lazy Way*! By providing the pain-free way to do something—including tons of shortcuts and timesaving tips, as well as lists of all the stuff you'll ever need to get it done efficiently—*The Lazy Way* series cuts through all of the time-wasting thought processes and laborious exercises. You'll discover the secrets of those who have figured out *The Lazy Way*. You'll get things done in half the time it takes the average person—and then you will sit back and smugly consider those poor suckers who haven't discovered *The Lazy Way* yet. With *The Lazy Way,* you'll learn how to put in minimal effort and get maximum results so you can devote your attention and energy to the pleasures in life!

THE LAZY WAY PROMISE

Everyone on *The Lazy Way* staff promises that, if you adopt *The Lazy Way* philosophy, you'll never break a sweat, you'll barely lift a finger, you won't put strain on your brain, and you'll have plenty of time to put up your feet. We guarantee you will find that these activities are no longer hardships, since you're doing them *The Lazy Way*. We also firmly support taking breaks and encourage rewarding yourself (we even offer our suggestions in each book!). With *The Lazy Way*, the only thing you'll be overwhelmed by is all of your newfound free time!

THE LAZY WAY SPECIAL FEATURES

Every book in our series features the following sidebars in the margins, all designed to save you time and aggravation down the road.

- **"Quick 'n' Painless"**—shortcuts that get the job done fast.

- **"You'll Thank Yourself Later"**—advice that saves time down the road.

- **"A Complete Waste of Time"**—warnings that spare countless headaches and squandered hours.

- **"If You're So Inclined"**—optional tips for moments of inspired added effort.

- **"The Lazy Way"**—rewards to make the task more pleasurable.

If you've either decided to give up altogether or have taken a strong interest in the subject, you'll find information on hiring outside help with "How to Get Someone Else to Do It" as well as further reading recommendations in "If You Really Want More, Read These." In addition, there's an only-what-you-need-to-know glossary of terms and product names ("If You Don't Know What It Means, Look Here") as well as "It's Time for Your Reward"—fun and relaxing ways to treat yourself for a job well done.

With *The Lazy Way* series, you'll find that getting the job done has never been so painless!

Series Editor
Amy Gordon

Editorial Director
Gary Krebs

Director of Creative Services
Michele Laseau

Cover Designer
Michael Freeland

Managing Editor
Robert Shuman

Development Editor
Matthew X. Kiernan

Production Editor
Scott Barnes

What's in This Book

Introduction: *¡Así es la vida!* That's Life

Some people would rather face the stampeding bulls of Pamplona than learn Spanish—the idea of having to study grammar and memorize vocabulary lists seems even more frightening. But fear not! Now there's a way to learn Spanish that is specifically geared to your lifestyle. Forget those tedious language classes that you had (or heard horror stories about) in high school or college—the endless memorization of useless words, the failed tests, the boring dictations, the unforgiving teacher. This book proves that no matter how lazy (or more likely, busy) you are, you can learn Spanish. You might even find yourself enjoying it, too!

With *Learn Spanish The Lazy Way*, you won't have to feel guilty because you're too busy to put in long hours of study time. You'll learn all the shortcuts and time-saving tools you'll need to maximize your language acquisition with minimal effort. So let everybody else run with the stampede … while you kick back, relax, and learn by working smarter, not harder.

WHAT YOU'LL NEED TO GET STARTED

The intention of this book is to have you speaking and understanding Spanish as quickly as possible with the least amount of effort. Why? Because you're too busy to do it any other way. With this in mind, *Learn Spanish The Lazy Way* won't require you to go out and purchase a lot of expensive equipment or craft supplies. This book has been designed to provide you with most of what you'll need.

However, to get the most out of this *Lazy* book, you will need a decent Spanish/English dictionary, since many of the practice sessions require you to find new words. *Learn Spanish The Lazy Way* is not designed to give you all the vocabulary that you'll ever need. That would be impossible. Every language student must feel comfortable using a dictionary; strong dictionary skills will help you tremendously in the long run.

Currently there are many Spanish/English dictionaries on the market, with new ones coming out all the time. Some are definitely better (and more expensive) than others. At this stage, you need not be too picky. Still, your dictionary should be relatively new (no more than 10–15 years old). If you have an older dictionary, I'd advise replacing it with something more up-to-date. And, as they say, size does not matter. I have one large hardback dictionary that is absolutely useless, and a small cheap paperback that is excellent. So don't go spending a lot of money. You can always buy that gilded $250 hardback with CD-ROM and action figures later.

If you can't get your own dictionary right now, there are several "virtual dictionaries" on the Internet. Simply search for "Spanish Dictionary" and surf around until you find one that works for you. Just make sure that you're accessing a general-reference dictionary and not a technical glossary.

In addition to the dictionary, you should find a few texts written in Spanish. You'll need them for some of the practice sessions. These texts don't have to be long, and the subject matter is not important (though you might want to stay away from particle physics). The Internet is one of the *laziest* places to find written Spanish. Simply search for "Spanish" or "Español" and you'll be up to your *orejas* (ears) in *palabras* (words). Print a few of these out and you'll be all set. If you're not online, check your local library, bookstore, or see if there are any Spanish-language publications available in your area. Even your telephone directory may have a Spanish section. If you're really hard up for a Spanish text, call your long-distance phone company, utility company, or even the IRS, and ask them to send you an information packet in Spanish.

I also recommend that you keep a notebook (it could be on your computer, if you like). Even though I have endeavored to keep the busy work to a minimum, you'll still need paper and pencil (or a word processing application) for many of the exercises. You may also want to create your own word list. Keep your work together, and arrange the information to suit your personal style.

The Internet is also used as a resource in this book. I have included a few Web addresses to help you learn more about selected topics. But Internet access is not a requirement. You'll find much of the same information at your local or college library.

Keep in mind that Web sites come and go all the time. If you can't log on to a site that I've listed in this book, it's possible their server is down or the Web page is out of commission entirely. If you can't find what you're looking for, just perform a search under the topic at hand with your favorite search engine and surf through the links it generates.

WHAT TO EXPECT FROM THIS BOOK

After you've digested *Learn Spanish The Lazy Way*, you should be able to express and understand all but the most complex ideas in Spanish (possibly with the aid of a dictionary for specific words). Nonetheless, *Learn Spanish The Lazy Way* is by no means the definitive reference work on Spanish syntax and grammar. To be honest, I'm far too lazy to write that kind of book right now. So, some of the finer points of Spanish grammar have been purposefully left out for the sake of brevity. As a beginner, you don't really need to worry about them right now. *Learn Spanish The Lazy Way* will show you creative ways to communicate and teach you the rules of the language. Spanish is very logical—understand the rules, and you understand everything.

The *Lazy Practice* sections in this book are designed to help you understand the logic behind the concepts being presented and to make suggestions as to how to practice them. However, keep in mind that everything will need to be "practiced" in some way, even when no *Lazy Practice* section is given. Simply use the examples (and your own creativity) as your guide, and try to construct similar sentences.

Learning a new language is like going to the doctor: It's always a good idea to get a second opinion. At some point, you may wish to consult additional Spanish instructional references. There are many other "Teach Yourself Spanish" books on the market today. Some are excellent resources, while others aren't fit to wrap *pescado* (fish). Check your local library and see what's available for free before spending any more money on new books. Additional references are listed in Appendix B.

This book should be fun to read as well as a good reference for the future. If something doesn't click, don't dwell on it. Move on and come back to it later. And while some of the *Lazy Practice* sections do involve you putting pen to paper (something that you may find "un-lazy"), I guarantee that these activities will ultimately save you time once you understand the concepts being discussed. My goal is for you to work smarter, not harder. *¡Buena suerte!* (Good luck!)

Part 1

Spanish at a Glance

Are You Too Lazy to Read "Spanish at a Glance"?

1 The only Spanish you understand is *taco*, *burrito*, and *el Niño*.
☐ sí ☐ no

2 If someone asks *"¿Cómo está usted?"* you respond with "Same to you."
☐ sí ☐ no

3 You think that taking a *siesta* on your couch counts as a cultural experience. ☐ sí ☐ no

¡*Vamos!* What You Should Know Before We Start

Let's begin with an overview of this strange new tongue you're about to wag. In this chapter, the crucial differences (and similarities) between Spanish and English will be revealed at last!

I'll compare and contrast the two languages. Then I'll discuss a bit of history and why studying Spanish is a worthwhile endeavor. I'll also give you some hints on how to make your Spanish work equally well from Tijuana to Madrid to Tierra del Fuego.

SPANISH VS. ENGLISH

At first glance, Spanish and English may seem very different (though not quite as different as, say, Chinese and English). While it's certainly true that Spanish and English are not mutually intelligible, you may be surprised to learn that they have several things in common.

Care must be taken when saying that something or someone is "Spanish." Technically, "Spanish" refers to Spain. If you say "I am talking to a Spanish person," that means that this person is from Spain. Just because you speak English, doesn't mean that you are English. If you're not sure where someone is from, say "Spanish-speaking" instead.

Common Ground

Let's take a look at the similarities between Spanish and English:

- Both Spanish and English are Indo-European languages. That means that many thousands of years ago they had a common linguistic ancestor. Although much has obviously changed since then, you can at least take some comfort in knowing that Spanish and English are distant cousins. So, while there are numerous differences in syntax and vocabulary, there are also many words and structures in Spanish that will be familiar to you as an English speaker.

- Both Spanish and English use the same Roman alphabet (with a few extra letters in Spanish). Yes, I know that you already knew that. But other languages such as Hindi or Thai use a vastly different writing system from the one you already know, so count your blessings!

- Spanish, being a *Romance* language, is made up mostly of words that started as Latin. English also contains a large number of words that originally came from Latin. I don't just mean *ipso facto* those high-brow phrases that lawyers use *ad nauseum* on an *ad hoc* basis for their *quid pro quo*. I'm talking about words that you use every day. In fact, in almost every English sentence, you'll find common words that were born in ancient Rome. Later, I'll teach you how to recognize these words.

Basic Differences

Now, let's look at how Spanish and English are different. Don't worry if you don't understand all the terminology yet. I'll go into greater detail later. For the moment, just take mental notes.

Spanish nouns work differently than English nouns

In Spanish, all nouns have a "gender." In English, unless we're talking about living things, nouns don't have a gender classification. Although the concept of a gender for non-living nouns may seem rather odd to you at first, it will eventually make sense. Gender is not just some bizarre way of trying to see the universe in terms of masculine or feminine. This gender thing actually helps to hold Spanish sentences together. When dealing with inanimate nouns, don't think of them as "boys and girls," but rather as words with similar endings that belong to two different classes. You'll see later how gender will actually be very helpful to you.

Spanish verbs change more than English verbs

The ways Spanish expresses time and aspect ("do," "will do," "was going to do," "might do," "could do," "would do," "will have done," "did do but my dog ate it") are different from English. While English tends to use other "helping" words before the verbs such as *will*, *would*, *might*, and *could*, Spanish usually indicates these differences at the end of the verb with suffixes such as *–ó*, *-ía*, *-aba*, and *–ría*. More about these later.

IF YOU'RE SO INCLINED

Have some fun learning a bit more about Latin. On the Web, visit www.ancientsites.com/as/Latin/. There are several other Web sites about Latin and ancient Rome as well. No, they won't help you much with your Spanish at this point, but they might give you an idea of what was going on in the world back when Spanish was being born.

Many people worry about all those funny áccent márks and upside-down punctuation marks such as ~ ¡ ¿ ' ¨ Don't stress about them. In fact, these marks actually make sense if you know the rules. The problem is that both textbooks and Spanish teachers have traditionally been unable to adequately explain the logic behind why and when these marks are used. I promise you that I am about to establish a new tradition ....

In Spanish, you don't always have to use the words *I, he, she, we, they*, etc. with the verb

Unless you're sending a telegram, English sounds odd and confusing if you don't indicate who is doing what. We must say "*I* want to go" and "*They* like to play" and "*He'll* take out the garbage tonight." If you leave out the *I*, *They*, and *He'll* parts ("want to go," "like to play," "will take out garbage"), you'll start sounding like Tarzan. In Spanish, however, the verb by itself can indicate *who* is doing the wanting or liking or taking by its ending (conjugation). Thus the pronouns (I, he, she, we, etc.) may often be omitted without sounding as though you were raised by wolves.

Verbs in Spanish don't have a "to" part at the beginning (to do, to want, to live, to love)

English verbs in the infinitive form (more about that later) need the word "to" at the beginning, as in "I like *to* eat ice cream." In Spanish, the "to" part of the verb is at the end of the word in the form of *-ar*, *-er*, and *-ir*. These three endings will influence the way verbs behave.

The order of the words in a Spanish sentence is usually different

The placement of the words in a Spanish sentence is usually not the same as it would be in the same sentence in English. For example, in English I say, "I gave it to him," while in Spanish I say, "I to him it gave" (*Yo se lo di*). Also, when something in Spanish is being described, we usually put the adjective after the noun rather than before it. Instead of "I see the red car," I say, "I see the car red" (*Yo veo el carro rojo*).

Spanish words have to "agree with each other" more than English words

Although Spanish speakers themselves may vehemently disagree about many things, agreement within their language is mandatory. In English, we also have situations where words must "agree." For example, according to the rules of standard English usage, it is grammatically incorrect to say "I wants" or "He know" or "We done" or "I is," and sentences like "Jane is my boyfriend and he is a nice girl" don't make much sense.

In Spanish, the need for words to agree is much greater. Not only do the pronouns and verbs have to correspond, adjectives must also agree in gender and number with the things they describe. The word we use for "it" must have the same gender as the thing it refers to. This isn't true in English because we don't classify our nouns by gender (except for living things when we use "he" and "she"). For now, don't worry about all this agreement stuff. It will make sense to you later.

Spanish pronunciation differs from English pronunciation

Naturally, you will find yourself producing some sounds in Spanish that you never make in English. But the good news is that Spanish is actually easier to pronounce than English. There are at least eleven distinct vowel sounds in standard English, while in Spanish there are only six. Spelling rules in Spanish are logical and fixed with virtually no exceptions. Once you know how to read and spell, you will always know how to pronounce a word. Wouldn't it be lovely if this were true in English as well?

IF YOU'RE SO *INCLINED*

The word that Spanish uses for all this agreement is *concordancia*. You don't need to learn this word, but you may want to keep it in the back of your mind.

A COMPLETE WASTE OF TIME

The 3 Worst Things to Do When You First Decide to Learn Spanish:

1. Spend extra money on additional Spanish language resources when you haven't exhausted what's available for free at your library and on the Web.

2. Feel overwhelmed by all this information. Read it through once, then review it later.

3. Forget that there are only two ways to speak Spanish: You can speak it well, or badly. People in one country don't speak it better than another—just differently.

WHY STUDY SPANISH?

Since you've already bought or borrowed this book, you probably don't need me to convince you that Spanish is important stuff. Maybe you've always wanted to study a second language and have decided that Spanish would be a good one to start with. Or perhaps you're studying Spanish for professional reasons. You might be getting ready to travel to a Spanish-speaking country and want to make sure you'll get the most out of your trip. You might not even want to learn Spanish at all, and are only doing so to fulfill a requirement for school. But whatever your reasons for studying this language, you still might be interested in knowing a few facts:

- Spanish is relatively simple and logical in its structure and pronunciation.

- Spanish is one of the most important languages in the world. It is an official language of many international organizations such as the United Nations, the European Union, and the Organization of the American States.

- The purchasing power of Hispanics in the United States reached $350 billion in 1997, up 66 percent since 1990.

- Over 300 million people speak Spanish. It is spoken in Spain; in North, Central, and South America; in parts of northwest Africa; in the Canary Islands; and in Equatorial Guinea. There is even a small Jewish community (Sephardim) in Istanbul, Turkey, where an old Spanish dialect is spoken; and Spanish is still understood by some people in the Philippines.

The United States of America is one of the largest Spanish-speaking countries in the world. Being able to speak Spanish is becoming a very important skill, and can even increase your earning potential! The number of jobs in the United States for which some knowledge of Spanish is required is increasing every year, and there are people in the United States who are *not* being hired for certain jobs because they *can't* communicate in Spanish.

Spanish-language radio, television, and advertising in the United States is a multi-billion dollar industry (and is growing fast).

The Commonwealth of Puerto Rico (population about 3 million) has a "Free Associated State" relationship with the United States. Puerto Ricans are U.S. citizens. Spanish is the official language of the island. Puerto Ricans have the same rights as all U.S. citizens, but they don't vote in presidential elections (oddly, they do vote in the primaries) or pay income taxes while they live on the island. However, they may move to the U.S. mainland (and start paying income tax!) whenever they wish. Puerto Rico *could* someday become the 51st state of the Union.

The United States shares a 2,000-mile-long border with Mexico, the most populous Spanish-speaking country. There are many Spanish-speaking communities located along the border, and in cities such as New York, Miami, Chicago, Denver, Washington D.C., Los Angeles, and others. Spanish is an official language of the state of New Mexico.

YOU'LL THANK YOURSELF LATER

Hispanics in the United States already constitute the largest single ethnic minority. Currently estimated at about 35 million (both legal and illegal immigrants), the number of Hispanics in the United States is expected to reach 50 million by the year 2005. This makes the United States one of the largest Spanish-speaking countries in the world. The number of Spanish speakers in Canada, Australia, and the United Kingdom is also on the rise.

- The Spanish-speaking world has produced great literature, art, film, and music. Both Spain and Latin America have been home to some of the world's finest artists, authors, musicians, actors, poets, and dancers.

- The possibilities for travel, personal development, and research in the Spanish-speaking world are practically endless. Whatever floats your boat: history, arts, music, archeology, architecture, philosophy, rain forests, wildlife, Native American cultures, international development, beaches, food. It's all there … somewhere in Latin America or Spain.

Some Very Basic History

As I've mentioned, Spanish is a Romance language. This has nothing to do with love, but rather with the language of the ancient Romans. Spanish developed as a Latin dialect in the Roman province of Iberia. That's why the peninsula on which Spain is located is called the Iberian Peninsula. Portuguese and Catalan are closely related to Spanish, as are French, Italian, and Romanian.

From about A.D. 800–1400, Spanish was influenced by the Arabic of the Moors. While Arabic had little influence on the grammatical structure of Spanish, it did introduce many new words and place names. For example, the name *Guadalajara* comes from the Arabic *Wadi alhayara,* which means "River of Stones."

Before the arrival of the Europeans, the native peoples of the Americas (don't forget that "America" includes both North *and* South America) spoke hundreds

IF YOU'RE SO
INCLINED

On the Web, check out www.puertorico.com for all the statistics on this lovely island nation. The site is in English and Spanish.

of different languages. As the Native Americans learned to speak Spanish, they brought their own syntax and pronunciation to the new European language. Spanish, in turn, accepted many new words from the Native American languages. Words like "chocolate," "tomato," and "potato" are New World words that entered English by way of Spanish.

Immigration from countries other than Spain also had an influence on Latin American Spanish. Many people don't realize that Latin America has welcomed immigrants from around the world, including people from such unexpected countries as the United Kingdom, India, Japan, Germany, Lebanon, and Korea. Alberto Fujimori, the current president of Peru, is of Japanese ancestry. When the Ottoman Empire fell apart in the 1920s, some immigrants from the Middle East headed for Latin America. Large-scale immigration from Italy to Argentina during the early twentieth century influenced how Spanish developed in that country. And in the Caribbean, West Africans brought many words, idioms, and customs to the area.

More recently, Spanish has borrowed hundreds of new words from English, especially in the areas of technology, food, and entertainment. Words like *modem, monitor, sandwich,* and *show* are all common in contemporary Spanish.

Lazy Practice

Listening to Spanish will help you to familiarize yourself with the sounds of the language, even if you understand *nada* (nothing). Try doing the following:

IF YOU'RE SO INCLINED

Check out the Internet for info on the countries you found in the atlas. Every Spanish-speaking country maintains a Web page. Just search for the country or subject that interests you. If you don't have Internet access, try the local library. This stuff is also available in print. The more you know about the Spanish-speaking world, the more excited you'll be about learning the lingo, and the faster you'll learn it.

In Brazil, Portuguese, not Spanish, is the official language. But many Brazilians can understand some Spanish, since the two languages are similar. If you learn Spanish, you *may* be able to make yourself understood in Brazil, Portugal, and other Portuguese-speaking countries in *some* basic situations. Knowing Spanish will nevertheless speed up your acquisition of Portuguese, should you ever decide to study that language.

Check your television and radio for any Spanish-language broadcasts. You may be surprised to learn that there are Spanish-language programs in your area. In the United States, Univisión, Telemundo, Galavisión, and some local networks broadcast in Spanish. These channels may be part of your cable TV service.

If you can't find anything on the airwaves, there are Spanish-language news and information Web sites on the Internet. If you have a computer with speakers and audio playing capability, you can find lots of Spanish to listen to. Just do a search for "Spanish Radio" or "Spanish News" and surf away.

If all else fails, there are Spanish-language tapes available. But before you spend any money, check your public library. Once you find something, spend 15 minutes or so a few times a week just listening to the sounds of the language.

VARIETY: THE SPICE OF LIFE

Spanish, like English, is spoken by millions of people living in many different places around the world. Just as folks in Mississippi speak differently from those in Manhattan—who in turn, speak nothing like the good citizens of Manchester or Melbourne—it only stands to reason that the way Spanish is spoken varies greatly from place to place.

Mexicans speak differently from Chileans. Cubans speak differently from Bolivians. Each country has its own way of saying things. There can even be differences in pronunciation within the same country. People who live in the mountains speak differently from those living in the valleys or along the coast. The accents of some regions are so strong that others can immediately identify someone as being from a particular area from the very first word they utter.

You don't need to worry about this issue at this stage. But you will notice differences in pronunciation as you increase your exposure to the language. Spanish is a rich language, and I've always found regional speech variations to be quite fascinating.

Pronunciation

There are two principal varieties of Spanish: the Spanish of Spain (known as *Peninsular* or *Castillian Spanish*) and the Spanish spoken in that country's former colonies. The chief difference between Peninsular Spanish and Latin American Spanish is the pronunciation of the letters *C* and *Z*. Most people in Spain pronounce the letter *C* (when written before the letters *E* and *I*) and the letter *Z* something like our "th" as in "fif*th*" and "*th*ink." Thus, *zapato* (shoe) sounds like "*th*ah-pah-toh" and *ciudad* (city) as "*th*ee-oo-dahd." But people in southern Spain and everywhere else pronounce these letters as the "*s*" sound in "street" and "smarts." So, in most of the Spanish-speaking world, *zapato* is "sah-pah-toh" and *ciudad* is "see-oo-dahd."

Another issue that you should be aware of has to do with the letter *S* at the end of a word. Some Spanish speakers do not pronounce the letter *S* at the end of words. As a general rule, people living in coastal areas of

QUICK ● PAINLESS

Find a good world atlas. Look up Mexico, Central and South America, Cuba, and Puerto Rico. Now find Spain. South of Spain you'll find Morocco. Along Morocco's Mediterranean coast there are two small cities that belong to Spain (Ceuta and Melilla). Now go down to West Africa and locate Equatorial Guinea (between Gabon and Cameroon). Next, find the Canary Islands. Finally, go over to Asia and check out the Philippines. Though Spanish is not the official language there, some Filipinos still understand it.

Latin America and in Southern Spain tend to drop or "swallow" the final *"s"* sound, especially when talking rapidly. People in the Caribbean are famous for this. So, the word *zapatos* sounds like *zapatoh,* even though there should be an *"s"* sound at the end.

Though this may sound odd to you, don't forget that many Americans say *goin'* for "going," *talkin'* for "talking," and *whutchagonnadoo* for "what are you going to do." In Boston, folks say *"pahk the cah"* for "park the car." And in the Cockney English of London, people drop the letter *h* from the beginning of words and say *'ere's 'is 'at* for "here's his hat."

For now, just keep this information in the back of your mind. If you aren't at least partly aware of the dropped *S* phenomenon, you may spend a lot of time wondering what's wrong with you and why you can't understand people. Trust me, it ain't you!

Regionalisms

Pronunciation is not the only thing that varies from place to place. Sometimes certain words and phrases that are used in one country may be entirely unknown elsewhere (although television and films are changing this somewhat). There are even words that are perfectly acceptable in one country that have an entirely different meaning in another. So, though a particular word may have worked very well in Spain, it may provoke blank stares in Puerto Rico, unbridled laughter in Argentina, and righteous indignation in Mexico. Just think of all the different words and phrases used in Britain that are practically unknown in the United States.

Such issues are known as *regionalism.* In reality, you shouldn't be too concerned about this issue as you begin to study the language. The Spanish covered in this book will work everywhere, and when regional considerations arise, I'll do my best to point them out to you.

Good Spanish vs. Bad Spanish

Now and then you may hear someone say that Castillian is the "real" or "pure" form of Spanish. They say, "I don't speak Spanish, I speak Castillian," as if this should somehow impress. Nonsense! Don't believe them. As I've said, there are only two ways to speak Spanish: You can speak it well, or you can speak it badly. One variety of Spanish is not better than another, just different. Remember that not everyone in Spain speaks "Castillian," and that some people in Spain don't even speak Spanish at all.

What Should You Do About All This Spice?

Well, you basically have two choices. If you know that you'll be staying in a particular country for an extended period of time, then you might wish to fully adopt the Spanish pronunciation and usage of that country. When you return home, you will most likely feel a certain kinship with the people from that nation and you will want to reflect that in the way you speak your Spanish (unless you had a bad time there—if so, there's still hope!). If you're in Spain for an extended stay, please learn Castillian. If you're in Mexico, learn Spanish the Mexican way. In Argentina? Learn to speak it as they do. Later on, other Spanish speakers will detect your regional accent and you'll have a great way to break the ice at parties.

YOU'LL THANK YOURSELF LATER

Lucky you! English borrowed thousands of words from those old Romans, too. We'll use this to our advantage later on.

On the other hand, if you're one of those free-spirited individuals who hates being associated with a specific place, you'll probably want to adopt a Spanish that travels well and is place-neutral. If you plan to travel a lot through the Spanish-speaking world, I would *not* recommend that you adopt a Castillian or Peninsular accent. A "standard" Latin American Spanish will be far more useful to you in the long run, and people in Spain will still understand you without difficulty.

My Spanish tends to change depending on the situation. As a professional translator and interpreter, I talk to Spanish-speaking people from just about everywhere. My solution? I speak Mexican Spanish with Mexicans, Caribbean Spanish with Puerto Ricans and Cubans, and Argentine Spanish with people from Argentina. However, it would be equally valid for me to choose one way of speaking and stick to it all the time no matter who my audience is. This is an entirely personal choice.

Being Understood Everywhere

The key to communicating effectively in Spanish is simple. No matter where you are—Mexico, Spain, Central or South America, Equatorial Guinea—the rules are the same. Make sure that you always speak at a reasonable pace and are enunciating your words clearly. Don't worry if you have a strong accent. People *will* understand you and appreciate your efforts to speak their language. Avoid regionalism from other countries (unless you don't know any other word). And don't forget to smile.

YOU'LL THANK YOURSELF LATER

Once you feel comfortable with your Spanish, you can always change the way you speak it depending on your surroundings.

ACTIVITY: SPANISH AND LATIN MUSIC

Spain and Latin America produce some of the most exciting music in the world. Depending on where you live, you may be able to listen to Spanish music simply by turning on your radio or television.

Most large music stores have a section of Latin or Spanish tapes and CDs. You may want to check out what's available. New groups and performers come and go. To see what's hot, check out **www.lamusica.com** on the Web or do a search for Latin Music or Spanish Music. For Spain, visit **flamenco-world.com**. Both these sites are in English. If you can't listen to the music on your computer, you can at least visit the sites and see what's available. Then you can go to the CD stores and ask for specific titles. Some libraries also have tapes and CDs that you can borrow.

Listening to music is also a great way to get into the rhythm of the language. Research has shown that students learn a foreign language faster if they are exposed to music sung in the language they are studying.

Chapter two

A-B-Cs and 1-2-3s

In this chapter, you'll begin to unlock the secrets of the Spanish language. First, you'll learn how to pronounce *el español* accurately. Luckily, Spanish uses the same alphabet as English (with a few extra letters thrown in for taste). My new *Lazy* method makes pronunciation, spelling, and accentuation easy and logical with a common-sense phonetic system based on sounds and concepts you already know. You'll also learn how to count, so that later—when you're haggling over the price of a blanket in the *mercado*—you'll know just how much money is at stake.

THE LAZY WAY TO THE SPANISH ALPHABET

Let's start by looking at the Spanish alphabet in (what else?) alphabetical order. You should know the names of the letters in Spanish so if you're unable to say a particular word or need to clarify something, you can at least spell it out.

In the following list, the word or words after the "=" approximates the Spanish pronunciation for the *name* of each letter. Remember, we're still using English here as a phonetic

tool. If you already know some Spanish, be careful not to read the text after the "=" as Spanish. When pronunciation is indicated in this book, *"ay"* sounds like "day," "way," "say" (and "the rain in Spain falls mainly on the plain"); and *"eh"* sounds like the *E* in "Edward" and "elf."

A = *ah*. Think Dr.'s office ("Open wide and say *Ahhh*"). Or, "Ah ha! I've caught you at last!"

B = *bay*. As in the San Francisco Bay or the Bay of Pigs.

C = *say*. As in, "What did you *say?*"

CH = *say ahchay*, or just *chay*.

D = *day*. The opposite of *noche* (night). How about Doris Day?

E = *ay*. Same as *"day"* but without the *d-* or *"Able"* without the *-ble*. The character "Fonzie" of *Happy Days* fame used to say this a lot.

F = *ehfay*. The *"eh"* part is like the *"E"* in Edmond; the *"fay"* like the actress Faye Dunaway.

G = *hay*. As in "Hey you!" or "Hay is for *caballos* (horses)." Say the *"h"* sound with a little scratch in your throat, a wee bit like the *"ch"* sound among the Scots (as in "Loch Ness").

H = *ahchay*. Dr.'s office (Open wide and say, "ah") plus Cuban Revolutionary (Ché Guevarra).

I = *ee*. As in *"sleep"* and *"peep."* Stop thinking of this letter as the English *"eye."* From now on, it's *"ee."* Some people call it *"I latina"* (*ee lahTEEnah:* "Latin I").

J = *hotah.* *"Ho"* as in Santa Claus ("Ho! Ho! Ho!"), or *"ta"* as is in the "Ta da!" a magician says at the end of a trick. Again, say the *"h"* part with a slightly scratchy throat, as in *Achtung!* in German.

K = *kah.* As in the sound one might use to describe an explosion: "Kaaaa boom!" Not a common letter except for *"kilo."*

L = *ehlay.* The largest city in California.

LL = *ayyay* or *ehlyay.*

M = *ehmay.* Just say the English letters *M* and *A*. Think graduate degree.

N = *ehnay.* Say the English letters *N* and *A*.

Ñ = *ehnyay.* Say the English letter *N* and cheer for your team again.

O = *oh.* As in "Oh boy" or "Yoko Ono," but not quite as long.

P = *pay.* What the person did who bought this book (I hope).

Q = *coo.* Think pigeons and babies.

R = *air ay.* What you breathe plus *"ay."* Think Scotland—the *R* is trilled like the sound of a propeller or a cat purring. But not too much.

RR = *ehrrrray.* Also *dohblay ehray.* Think about Scotland even more, and purrrrr as much as you like.

S = *essay.* What one writes in English class.

T = *tay.* Like *"tame"* without the -*m*. If you still can't get Scotland out of your mind, there's the *Firth of Tay* near Dundee.

QUICK ⬛ PAINLESS

Depending on the region, the name and pronunciation of the letter *LL* can vary. But it's nothing to worry about. For now, just learn the first name: *ay + yay:* "ay" plus what you say when your favorite team scores points. People will still understand you in the countries where it's called *ehlyay.*

The Lazy Way

U = *oo*. As in *boo hoo,* and *who.*

V = *vay* (*oovay* in Spain). Also known as *V corta* and *V chica* (*vay KOHRtah, vay CHEEkah* = short V, small V) or *V de vaca* (*vay day vahkah* = "v as in *cow*"). "Vich *vay* did he go?" "He vent zata *vay.*"

W = *dohblay oo; vay dohblay* (depending on region).

X = *ehkeess.* You may have heard of the beer that has *"dos"* of these letters in its name.

Y = *ee gree ay gah* (*I griega*).

Z = *sayta.* Say *"say"* and *"Ta da"* but don't say the *"da"* part.

Lazy Practice

Choose an English text at random. Anything will do: today's paper, last year's paper, the telephone directory, or if you're too busy to go searching, just use this book. Read each letter in the text using its Spanish name. For example, the sentence "See Spot run" would be: *essay ay ay essay pay oh tay ehray oo ehnay.* Choose different sentences and refer to the earlier section if you're in doubt. Do it until you get tired (or until you start speaking Pig Latin). Don't forget to review *ñ, LL,* and *RR.* When you think you've got it, move on to the next section.

THE LAZY GUIDE TO PRONOUNCING SPANISH

Now that you've learned the Spanish names for the letters, let's look at the sounds they actually make by associating them with words, sounds, and concepts that are familiar to you. Fortunately, Spanish spelling is very logical: The way the word is written will always indicate its pronunciation. This certainly can't be said of English, where "daughter" rhymes with *water,* and "laughter" sounds like *after.* Why, one Spanish letter is soooo lazy, it doesn't make any sound at all (we like this guy). So this can't be too bad. Let's take a look:

The Consonants

We'll begin by looking at the letters that make the exact same sounds as they do in English:

F, K, L, M, N, P, T

No need to worry about these. Just follow your instincts.

Now, the letters in this next group are almost exactly the same as English. You don't need to agonize over them too much, since your instincts will usually be close enough. Nonetheless, they will require a few words of explanation:

B, V, C, D, G, Q, R, RR, S, W, X, Y, Z

B and V

The sound of the Spanish *B* and *V* is distinctive. It's not exactly like the *B* in "boy," which sounds a bit like our *"p"* to Spanish speakers. To make this sound, say your *"b"* as in English, but don't close your lips all the way. Rest your bottom lip under your upper front teeth. The correct sound lies somewhere between the English *B, V, W,* and *M.* If this sounds too confusing, try pronouncing both *B* and *V* like the English *V* in "Victoria" and "velvet"

A COMPLETE WASTE OF TIME

The 3 Worst Things to Worry About at This Point:

1. Trying to sound like a native from the beginning.

2. Trying to memorize all this stuff the first time you read it.

3. Being afraid that there may be some sounds that you simply cannot produce. Don't worry. Do the best you can and people will understand you.

QUICK 🐷 PAINLESS

One of the most common spelling errors that Spanish speakers make is to write the letter *B* when a word actually requires a *V* and vice versa. Don't stress too much over this one. Technically, there's a slight difference in pronunciation between *B* and *V*, but it's only observed in some countries. You can say it like the English *V* until your ear can tell the difference.

(as some Chileans do) until your ear becomes more attuned to the actual sound.

C

As in English, this letter can sound like *"k"* as in *"car"* and *S* as in *"city."* When the letter is written before an *E* or *I*, it's pronounced like *"s."* Thus, *ciudad* is *"see oo dahd."* When *C* is written before *A, O,* or *U,* it is hard as in *"carro" (Kahrroh).*

In Spain, most people pronounce *C* like the *"th"* in *"think"* and *"fifth"* when written before *E* and *I*. So, in Spain, *ciudad* is *"thee oo dad."* The advantage to pronouncing the *C* (and *Z,* as you'll see in a moment) this way is that many spelling errors can be avoided. For example, in Latin America, the verbs *casar* (to marry) and *cazar* (to hunt) sound exactly the same. However, unless you're actually going to be in Spain, I suggest you not use the Castillian pronunciation. It is, however, up to you.

D

Almost the same as English, but softer and closer to the *"th"* in *"that"* and *"these."* The hard English *D* in words such as *"dandy"* and *"dime"* sounds like *T* to Spanish speakers. Try to soften your *D*.

G

Like *C, G* has two sounds. Before *A, O,* and *U* it is hard, like *gone, gate,* and *gun.* But before *I* and *E* (and *Y*) it's soft and sounds like a raspy *"h."* The name of the letter helps you on this one. So, *gente* (people) sounds like *"hehn tay,"* but *gato* (cat) sounds like *"gah toh."* The letter *G* never sounds like the English *"j"* sound as in *"gentleman"* or *"Ginger Rogers."*

Q

Spanish could have lived without this letter. It sounds like "k" and is always followed by *U* (just like English). However, Q is not pronounced like "kw" as in "quick" and "quack." The word *queso* (cheese) is pronounced "kay soh" and never "kway soh." Spanish uses the letters *QU* to indicate a "k" sound before the vowels *I* and *E*. That's its main job. The letter *Q* is not written before other vowels. The letter *C* is used for that.

R

Trilled (rolled) as in Scotland. But not too much when the letter is by itself. Just a wee bit. At the beginning of a word, you can flutter your tongue more if you like, but be careful not to overdo it. Save that for the next letter.

RR

See previous (now you can overdo it).

S

In most of the Spanish-speaking world, the letter *S* sounds exactly as it does in English. But in Spain, it's much more buzzy, a little bit like the "zh" sound in "plea*s*ure" and "trea*s*ure" but softer. If you're in Spain, try to imitate the locals. Otherwise, stick to the same old "s" sound that you use now ("silver" and "stress") and you'll be fine. Spaniards will have no problem understanding you either way.

W

Used only in foreign words. Usually maintains the same pronunciation as the original word. Thus: "Washington" and "William" have the same pronunciation as they do in

QUICK 🔲 *PAINLESS*

You probably already know if you can make the trilled "rrrr" sound or not. Try as they might, some people just can't make this sound (my mother is from Denmark and couldn't say "rrrr" if her life depended on it!). If this sounds like you too, don't worry. Just pronounce the *R* and *RR* the same as you normally do in English, but with as much emphasis as you can. You might never sound like a native, but people *will* understand you.

English. But "Wagner" (Richard) and "Wilhelm" (Schmidt) maintain the German *"v"* sound.

X

Knowing how to pronounce the X can be tricky, since its sound can vary (as it can in English: xylophone). Basically, *X* usually sounds like the *"ks"* sound that we have in "excellent" and "axe." It almost never sounds like the *"z"* sound in "examine." Until the letter *J* was invented, the Spanish used *X* to represent the *"h"* sound. That's why we see *"México"* (MEH-hee-koh) instead of *"Méjico."* (In Spain, you see the word spelled *"Méjico,"* which irritates the Mexicans to no end.) When the Spanish arrived in the New World, *X* was used to represent certain indigenous sounds (with varying degrees of success). For example, *X* sounds like *"s"* in "Xochimilco" (Sohch-ee-MEEL-koh), the water gardens in Mexico City. In Mayan regions, *X* sounds like our *"sh"* in "shell"; for example, "Uxmal" (OOSH-mahl). Elsewhere, ask the locals.

Y

Pronounce it like the *Y* you grew up with, but be aware that its pronunciation varies within the Spanish-speaking world. In Argentina and Uruguay especially, the letter *Y* sounds like the *"zh"* sound in "trea*s*ure." It may also act as a vowel, as in *gymnasio,* where it sounds the same as its Latin cousin *I.*

Z

Sounds more like our *"s"* than *"z."* Just treat it as *S* and you'll be fine. In Spain, it sounds like the *"th"* in *these*

Given the similarities in pronunciation between *B* and *V,* this letter is often referred to as *B larga* (*bay LAHrgah* = "long B") or more colloquially as *B de burro* (*bay day booroh* = "B as in *burro*"), the Spanish equivalent of saying "*B* as in boy."

and *those* before *A, O,* and *U.* The letter *Z* is almost never written before *I* and *E.* The letter *C* is used for that.

Finally, here are the consonants that act quite differently than their English cousins:

H, J, LL, Ñ

Both Latin and Greek gave Spanish a letter called *"ee."* To differentiate between them, *Y* was called the "Greek *I.*" It's important to distinguish between *Y* and *I.* If you just say "ee," people will assume that you mean *I,* but some last names can be spelled with either letter, so you should always say "ee greeaygah" when you mean *Y.*

H

Our partner in laziness. This letter is NEVER pronounced. No sound. Zip, zilch, *nada* (think *'enry 'iggins* rather than "Henry Higgins"). If you really must make an *"h"* sound, please use the letters *J* and *G.*

J

Pronounced like a raspy *"h"* (same as the soft *G*). Think "Loch" or even *"Achtung!"* in German. However, if you find this difficult, you may pronounce it (and the *G* for that matter) just like the English *"h"* in "Hillary" and "hall" and people will understand you. Many people in Central America say it that way, so you can too. The letter *J* spends most of its time written before *A, O,* and *U,* while *G* (when sounding like an *"h"*) is used before *E* and *I.*

LL

Usually pronounced like the letter *Y* in English: *llama* ("yahmah"). In some regions (Spain, Columbia, parts of Bolivia, and among purists), this letter is pronounced like the *"l + y"* sound in "million" and "Wi*ll* you." You can pronounce it this way if you like, but it's not necessary. If you do, call the letter *"ehlyay."* In Argentina and Uruguay especially, this letter sounds like the *"zh"* sound in "trea*s*ure."

QUICK  PAINLESS

Ñ

Don't let this one throw you off. It's just the Spanish way of writing the *N + Y* together in one letter. It's not a sound that English speakers tend to make in words. One place you find it is the word "canyon"—from the Spanish *cañon.* The only other one I can think of is "onion." It also comes up between words, such as "Joh*n y*elled at his brother," and "Da*n y*anked the weeds from the ground." Don't forget *el Niño (el NEEN-yo).*

Finally, the Vowels: *A, E, I, O, U*

Vowels are generally pronounced just like their names.

A

This letter is always pronounced like its name, *"ah."* It is never pronounced like the *"a"* in words such as *wait, Amy, able, ant, aunt, at, apple.* Thus, the Spanish word *amar* (to love) sounds like *"ahmahr"* and "blah blah blah" is written as *"bla bla bla"* in Spanish and sounds exactly the same.

E

The letter *E* is generally pronounced like its name *"ay."* However, *E* is pronounced like the *E* in "Edward" when it begins a word. Thus, *esto* (this) is not *"aystoh"* but *"ehstoh."* "Eduardo" (Edward) is not *"Aydwahrdoh"* but *"Ehdwahrdoh."* It can also take this sound in the middle of a word when it isn't stressed and the word has more than two syllables: *exelente* = *"ehksehlehntay."* You may find that the actual sound in such cases is somewhere between *"ay"* and *"eh."*

I

Always like the *"ee"* sound in "sleep" and "cheap."

O

Always long, never like "pop" or "too." Sounds like its name. Pronounce as in "pope" or "toe," but don't round your lips.

U

Always pronounced like its name in Spanish. Never as in "cut" or "put."

Lazy Practice

Here's a list of Spanish words. Read them aloud and practice your pronunciation. Don't worry yet about what they mean. In some cases, you can probably guess. If you have a Spanish-speaking friend, you might ask him or her for guidance. If not, just refer to the previous section for help. Remember, don't be too hard on yourself. After the first time reading through this list, review the section on pronunciation and see how you did.

apartamento	cariño
burrito	olé
casa	puerto
cielo	quepo
dedo	quito
excelente ("X" = ks)	quieto
entre	reina
franco	carro
gato	sapo

QUICK ⊙ PAINLESS

Spanish occasionally uses a *U* with an umlaut on it: *Ü*. It is used when we want the *G* to sound like *"gw"* when it is written before A, I, or E. Thus, *pingüino* (penguin) is pronounced "peengweenoh." Without the *ü*, it would have been "peengeenoh." In other words, the *U* would be silent if the dots weren't there.

gesto	tierra (say it slowly first, then say it quickly)
hambre	Uruguay (stress the "-guay" part)
iglesia	victor
jarro	Washington
kilo	xilofón (*x* = "ss")
lampa	yanqui
llamada	zebra
calle	Tegucigalpa (Honduras)
mapa	Montevideo (Uruguay)
nido	

These last three are places in Mexico. Good luck!:

Oaxaca (*x* = "h" as in "Henry" but raspy)

Tlaxcala (*x* = "s")

Coatzacolacos

STRESS AND THOSE WEIRD ÁCCENT MÁRKS

So what's with all the squiggles? Well, I'm gonna tell you. While the following is a bit of an oversimplification, this system will work for you 99 percent of the time. I'm going to outline some rules for Spanish pronunciation and accentuation. Skip this part at your own peril! Bear with me until we get to the end.

IF YOU'RE SO INCLINED

Take one of your Spanish texts and try reading a few sentences. Don't worry about the áccent márks yet (we'll talk about those next). Just have fun and see what the language feels like on your tongue.

Stress (No, Not That Kind of Stress)

Accentuation (stress) refers to the part of a word that is the loudest. We say that the stress or accent falls on this or that syllable. We do it in English all the time. Usually, stress in English seems to fall on the first syllable of a word:

TELephone

AMbulance

BAby

CATegory

SYLLable

COMfort

ELephant

Sometimes, the stress can fall on an internal syllable:

comPUter

reUNion

hippoPOTamus

inSTINCtive

associAtion

Stress in English usually doesn't fall on the last syllable, but it can happen:

enDOW

reMAIN

reBOOT

IF YOU'RE SO
INCLINED

Use one of your Spanish texts (or turn to a later chapter in this book) and pick ten Spanish words at random. You can skip over any words that have vowels with accent marks *á, é, í, ó, ú.* Read the words slowly and count the number of syllables of each word. Refer to the previous explanation if you get stuck: *perro = pe-rro; libro = li-bro; interesante = in-te-re-san-te; amigo = a-mi-go; iglesia = i-gle-sia; Chihuahua = Chi-hua-hua; milla = mi-lla.*

There are some additional spelling rules (also known as "orthographic conveniences") that we'll discuss later on. They'll make more sense to you after you've worked through more of the material in the book.

Now for some Spanish rules about stress.

First, let's define what a syllable is in Spanish. A Spanish syllable is formed by the combination of a consonant and a vowel: *ba, pi, chu, que, mo, ño,* and so on. If a vowel begins a word, it is usually considered a syllable by itself: *amistad = a-mi-stad.* The clusters *pr, br, cl,* stick together: *pri, bro, cla.* In one-syllable words, the syllable may also end in a consonant: *dan, sin, mis, pez, miel.*

Diphthongs such as *ia, ei, ue, ie,* and *io* count as one syllable unless there is an áccent márk over one of the vowels (more on that in just a second). So, *pue, cie, fei, pia,* and so on count as one syllable, not two. And if the vowel or diphthong is followed by an *n* or *s,* that letter stays with the first syllable and not the following one: *puente = puen-te; pasta = pas-ta; presidente = pre-si-den-te.*

OK. Great. Now, hold on to your *sombrero …*

The accent (stress/emphasis) in EVERY Spanish word that ends in a vowel, or with the letter *–n* or *-s,* no matter what kind of word (or form of word) it is, falls *naturally* on the penultimate (second-to-last) syllable. It doesn't matter how many syllables the word may have. If it has ten syllables, the rules still apply. The same is true of those short two-syllable words. The first syllable of a two-syllable word is *still* the second to the last. Examples:

SApo

CArro

EsTEban (Eh STAY bahn)

ele*FAN*te (Eh lay FAHN tay)

*MU*cho

*HA*bla

*HA*blan (the -*n* doesn't change anything)

congre*SIS*ta

presi*DEN*te

presi*DEN*tes (the -*s* at the end makes no difference)

mexi*CA*nos

intere*SAN*te

But, if the word ends in a consonant which is NOT -*n* or -*s*, the stress falls *naturally* on the last syllable:

ha*BLAR*

be*BER*

ciu*DAD*

re*LOJ*

man*TEL*

Para*GUAY*

fu*GAZ*

Now, here's where things seem tricky. *Every* time the previous rules DO NOT apply, an áccent márk will be required. To illustrate this point, let's look at some examples:

▨ Let's say that you know the Spanish word for "number" is *numero*. According to the rules of Spanish stress, since this word ends in a vowel, it should be pronounced "noo-MEH-roh," with the accent on the penultimate (second-to-last) syllable. However, let's say we also know that the correct pronunciation for this word is "NOO-meh-roh," with the accent on a syllable other than the one on which it would *naturally* fall. So, in order to indicate that the rules have been broken, an áccent márk must be written over the *U*. So, the word is written as *número*.

- The surname *Calderon* ends in an *-n*. The letters *N* and *S* at the end of a word still allow the stress to fall *naturally* on the penultimate syllable: "Kahl-DEH-ron." But we know that this person's name is pronounced "Kahl-deh-RON," with the accent on the last syllable. So, we need to put an áccent márk on the final *O: Calderón*.

- The word *alcazar* (castle) ends in a consonant. We checked it out and, no, it's not *-n* or *-s*. This means that the stress falls *naturally* on the last syllable, "ahl-kah-SAHR." But the word that we are trying to write is actually pronounced "ahl-KAH-sahr," so we must write an áccent márk over the middle *A* to show that the rules have been broken and the accent falls there: *alcázar*.

Lazy Practice

Go back to your Spanish text and try to read it again. Select some words that have áccent márks. Pretend that they aren't there. Pronounce the words according to the rules, letting the stress fall naturally where it's supposed to. Now, re-read the Spanish words, paying attention to those áccent márks. See how your Spanish sounds now.

Dippity Diphthongs

And finally, we have those diphthongs. Here's the deal. The vowels *I, U,* and sometimes *Y,* are considered weak with respect to accentuation. The others (*O, A, E*) are strong. Any combination of vowels, EXCEPT when both vowels are strong, will form a one-syllable diphthong: *ia, oi, oy, ue, eu,* and so on. If both vowels are strong, they will be read as two syllables (and thus are not technically diphthongs): *ae = "aheh," oe = "oheh," eo = "ehoh," oa "ohah."*

Now, if we want two weak vowels (or one weak and one strong) NOT to form a one-syllable diphthong, we must write an áccent márk. For example:

- *García = Gahr-SEE-ah.* Without the áccent márk, this person's name would have only two syllables: *GAHR-syah.*

- The name *María = Mah-REE-Ah.* It would sound like "MAH-rya" without the áccent márk.

- The word *cortesía ("courtesy") = kohr-teh-SEE-ah.* Without the áccent márk it would be "kohr-TEH-syah."

However:

- *maestro*   = mah-EH-stroh
- *poema*   = poh-EH-mah
- *paella*   = pah-EH-yah
- *proa*   = PROH-ah

QUICK ⬭ PAINLESS

The longer numbers can also be written as one word: *"dieciseis," "veintiuno,"* etc. But personally, I find the longer form less confusing, even though it may be a bit old-fashioned in the eyes of most Spanish speakers. In practice, you probably won't be spelling out the numbers, anyway.

LOS NÚMEROS: THE NUMBERS

You may already know some of these, but here are the numbers from 1–99. We'll deal with numbers over 100 in Chapter 14:

1 = *uno* ("OO-noh"). I played this card game when I was young.

2 = *dos* ("dohss"). A measure used for medicine (possibly your own if you've been mean).

3 = *tres* ("trayss"). Place thin paper over picture and draw. Or, just a "little bit left behind."

4 = *cuatro* ("KWA-troh"). Audi makes this car.

5 = *cinco* ("SIN-ko"). Where you wash your hands. Or, what happens to a boat when it fills with water.

OK! Enough silliness ....

6 = *seis* ("sayss")

7 = *siete* ("see-EH-tay")

8 = *ocho* ("OH-choh")

9 = *nueve* ("noo-AY-vay")

10 = *diez* ("DEE-yess")

11 = *once* ("OHN-say")

12 = *doce* ("doh-say")

13 = *trece* ("TRAY-say")

14 = *catorce* ("kah-TOHR-say")

15 = *quince* ("KEEN-say")

After *quince* the pattern changes. It actually gets easier. It's just basic addition. The Spanish word for "and" is *y* ("ee"). So now, start with ten and add until you get to twenty:

16 = diez y seis (dee-yess ee sayss) = "ten and six."

17 = *diez y siete* ("ten and seven")

18 = *diez y ocho*

19 = *diez y nueve*

And finally:

20 = *veinte* ("VAYEEN-tay")

Now instead of "*diez y #,*" use *veinte* and work up:

21 = *veinte y uno* ("vayeen-tay ee oo-noh")

22 = *veinte y dos* ("twenty and two")

23 = *veinte y tres*

… and so on. Then continue:

30 = *treinta* ("TRAYN-tah")

31 = *treinta y uno* ("trayn-tah ee oo-noh")

40 = *cuarenta* ("kwah-REHN-ta") Follow same pattern …

50 = *cincuenta* ("seen-KWEHN-tah")

60 = *seisenta* ("say-SEHN-tah")

70 = *seitenta* ("say-TEHN-tah")

80 = *ochenta* ("oh-CHEN-tah")

90 = *noventa* ("no-VEN-tah")

99 = *noventa y nueve* ("no-ven-tah ee noo-ay-vay")

QUICK PAINLESS

Lazy Practice

Look at the page numbers of this book from 1 to 99. Flip through randomly and try to say the number in Spanish. If you're not sure, refer to the previous number section. The pattern is logical and should help you to figure out the right answer.

ACTIVITY: A TONGUE-TWISTER

Say the following 10 times fast:

Erre con Erre cigarro
("rr" with "rr" cigar)

Erre con Erre barril
("rr" with "rr" barril)

Rápido corren los coches,
(quickly run the cars)

Coches del Ferrocarril
(cars of the railroad)

This is a well-known nonsense tongue-twister and is good practice for your *rrrr* sounds. See, even Spanish speakers need to learn how to do it.

Part 2

Shortcuts to Spanish

Are You Too Lazy to Read "Shortcuts to Spanish"?

1 Your idea of a real shortcut would be to skip this section altogether.
☐ sí ☐ no

2 You plan to teach everyone else English during your next trip to a Spanish-speaking country. ☐ sí ☐ no

3 The last time you took the "shortcut" in Mexico you got hopelessly lost.
☐ sí ☐ no

Chapter three

Pointers for Success: The Art of Nonverbal Communication

The Italians aren't the only people who gesture when they speak. With the help of a few key words and phrases to get someone's attention, you too can learn to communicate effectively "in Spanish" by using body language. In this chapter, you'll learn some very important introductory phrases and how to get extra mileage out of them by pointing and gesturing. Get ready to let your body do the talking!

GESTURING: THE INTERNATIONAL LANGUAGE OF LAZY PEOPLE

In addition to verbal language, we humans also use body language to indicate our wants, feelings, desires, and opinions. In fact, the meaning of many gestures is so obvious as to be practically universal. If you hold your stomach and make a face indicating pain, people will realize that you have an bellyache.

As a warm-up to this chapter, you might spend a few minutes observing the various gestures that people use while talking. Look for hand movements, pointing, head emphasis, smiles, frowns, and any other form of body language that helps them to express or clarify their ideas. Oddly, some people seem to gesture the most while talking on the telephone. Go figure ....

If you shrug your shoulders, bend your elbows, and turn your palms skyward while your face indicates bewilderment, people will understand that you don't know the answer to a question. If you put your left hand in your right pocket, hop up and down on one leg, grab your nose, and stick out your tongue repeatedly, everyone will think you're crazy and leave you alone.

This is all well and good, but what does it have to do with Spanish? I knew you'd ask. Well, you can use gestures to express ideas when you don't quite have all the Spanish words you need. And as long as your gestures appear courteous, people will understand that you are doing your best to communicate something important. Of course, if you are not courteous and polite, you'll have people indicating their feelings about *you* with a few choice gestures of their own.

Pointing

Generally, most of the pointing gestures that you use naturally will convey a similar meaning to Spanish speakers. If you point to your open mouth, people will understand that you're hungry. You can point to your wrist to ask what time it is. You can point at something that's for sale, and someone will probably sell it to you. And you can indicate a dish on the menu with your finger and the waiter will assume that you want to order it.

While pointing can get you pretty far, you should avoid pointing at people with your index finger, even if that person is far away. It's considered rude. Instead, use your open palm, or perhaps your thumb if your hand is closed. People in some Latin American countries (such as Mexico) sometimes use their head to point at someone.

Never use your index finger to tell someone to "come here." That gesture is reserved for pets. To indicate that someone should approach you, open your palm and face your open hand toward the person you are addressing. Then quickly close your fingers in an grabbing motion as you move your wrist downward (This gesture is best seen with your own eyes before you attempt it yourself. It can vary from country to country.)

Other Gestures

Moving your head up and down means "yes" and from side to side means "no," but there are differences in the gestures used to indicate height and length:

- Don't indicate the length of something with two hands facing one another as you might do naturally. Indicate length by extending your forearm and using your other hand to show how long something is.

- To indicate height (my friend is "this" tall), use an upturned palm and your index finger, not your down-turned palm.

- In some countries, especially Mexico, waving an index finger from side to side (as we might do to scold a naughty child) is a reasonably polite way of saying "no" or "No, I don't want any." It takes some getting used to, because it seems rather rude to us. Still, after a few weeks, you may find it a very expedient way to say "no." But don't let this gesture

IF YOU'RE SO
INCLINED

Sit down with a friend and try to express as many ideas as you can without saying a word. Try to be as polite as possible in your pointing and gesturing, treating your friend as if she were someone whom you just met. Make a note of any gesture or movement that really gets an entire idea across. Resist the temptation to be vulgar.

replace *"No, gracias"* as your primary way of saying "No, thank you."

Get Their Attention First

While it's true that gesturing can express basic ideas when you don't have enough words to say what you want, I find that it's usually a better idea to gesture in conjunction with a few simple words or phrases of introduction. Unless you're desperately trying to inform someone that his house is on fire, you'll want to pleasantly greet people and politely get their attention *before* you start all your pointing and gesturing. Below are some common words and phrases to help you do just that.

The actual cut-off between *días, tardes,* and *noches* is not written in stone and may vary slightly from place to place. If you use the explanation here as a general guide, you should be fine most of the time. These "hello" phrases usually work best if you have already made eye contact with someone. If the person whom you are about to

Ways to Say "Hello"

Phrase	Definition	When to Use
Buenos días	Good day	From dawn 'til noon
Buenas tardes	Good afternoon	From 12:01 'til dark
Buenas noches	Good night	From dark 'til dawn
Hola	Hello	Any time; best used in conjunction with one of the previous three

address is staring off into space, it might be a bit of a shock for you to appear out of nowhere and exclaim *"¡Hola!"* at them.

Lazy Practice

Over the next few days, practice greeting people (quietly to yourself if you like) with the time-appropriate *buenos/as* phrase. Don't just think *"hola"* all the time. No need to be shy—they won't hear you if you just think it. But if you know anyone who speaks Spanish (or who doesn't care what you say), practice out loud.

THE MAN/WOMAN ON THE STREET

If you're walking down the street, or in a situation where you need to get someone's attention, you can use one of the following phrases in conjunction with the four we just learned. Yes, "Hey you!" does exist in Spanish too, but remember that you are an ambassador of goodwill from *your* country while visiting theirs.

If you approach someone who is not paying attention to you already, you can say: *"Señor, disculpe ... "* or *"Señora, perdone ... "* or *"Disculpe, señorita ... ."* There are countless variations on this theme. You can combine them with the "hello" phrases that you learned previously: *"Hola, señor, buenos días. Disculpe ... ,* (your question goes here)."

Lazy Practice

Study the following phrases. Then create as many new combinations as you can. Imagine the situations in which

A COMPLETE WASTE OF TIME

The 3 Things to Watch for When Gesturing:

1. Unless you are indeed unable to speak, don't assume that you can gesture your way through everything. Try it at home first and see what happens.

2. Don't use "slangy" gestures until you have been in the country for quite awhile. You could get yourself into a lot of trouble.

3. Never point directly at someone. It's very rude. Your mother should have taught you this.

you might say them, and try to think of gestures that you
may want to use at the same time:

> *Disculpe, señor …*
> "Excuse me, sir … "
> *Señorita, perdone …*
> "Miss, excuse me … "
> *Hola, señor. Buenas tardes …*

Getting Someone's Attention

Phrase	Definition	When to Use
Señor	Sir	Any time you wish to address a man (especially if he's older than you or in a respected position)
Señora	Madam	Any time you wish to address a married woman (especially if she's older than you or in a respected position)
Señorita	Miss	Any time you wish to address an unmarried woman (regardless of professional status)
Disculpe	Forgive me; sorry	Any time; can be used in conjunction with top two
Perdone	Pardon; excuse (me)	Any time; same as above

Buenas noches, señor. Disculpe …

Hola. Buenos días. Disculpe …

Señora, hola. Buenos días. Perdone …

Señora/Señorita

Don't anguish too much over the *señora/señorita* debate. Yes, sometimes you can't know before you open your mouth if a woman is married or not. As a general rule, if the woman you are addressing is obviously young (up to 24ish), say *señorita.* If she is older or with a husband or child, use *señora.* If you get it wrong, she may correct you, but it's unlikely that any offense will be taken (unless it's really obvious that she is one or the other and you miss the cues). Hint: Native speakers make this mistake, too.

THE ONE-WORD QUESTION: THE LAZY PERSON'S BEST AMIGO

Now that you have people's attention, they'll be expecting you to do or say something else. Assuming for the moment that you don't yet have a large Spanish vocabulary, the best thing to do is to simply state the subject of your concern in a rising tone while shrugging your shoulders, pointing, and/or indicating a question with your facial expression. For example:

1. You've looked in your dictionary and found that *el baño* means "the bathroom." You really need to go, but you don't know how to say "Where is … " yet. So, you approach a gentleman nearby and say:

QUICK ⬤ PAINLESS

If the person whom you are addressing does not respond, raise your hand, politely wave, and repeat your phrase in a courteous but confident tone.

QUICK ✏ PAINLESS

"Hola, señor. Buenos días (tardes/noches). Disculpe, ¿el baño?" Say *el baño* in a rising, questioning tone. The entire "do-you-happen-to-know-where-the-closest-*baño*-is" part is implied in your tone. If you think that the *baño* may be located inside a building or in a specific direction, you can gesture to the place you think the bathroom might be while saying *¿el baño?* to ask "is it over there?" The gentleman whom you asked will understand exactly what you mean and (hopefully) lead you to relief.

2. Later on you're in a restaurant. Somehow you've managed to point to the menu and order something. Thirty minutes later, your food still hasn't arrived. You want to flag down the waitress, but you don't know how to say "Could you please tell me what's happening with my meal and when it should be arriving?" But you can communicate this idea easily and painlessly simply by following the previous model. Just look up the word for "food" and you're in business. After politely flagging her down, you say: *"Señorita, perdone. ¿La comida?"* You gesture by raising your hands, turning your palms upward, and shrugging your shoulders. She'll know exactly what you mean.

3. After dinner you go to the store. There's an item behind the counter, and you want to know how much it costs. You don't know how to ask this question, but thanks to your dictionary, you do know that the word for "price" is *el precio.* So you

approach the woman at the register and politely say: *"Hola, señora. Buenas noches. Disculpe, ¿el precio?"* You point to the object with an inquisitive smile on your face. She will understand exactly what you're asking about.

Naturally, you wouldn't want to spend your entire life talking like this. But this pattern is entirely acceptable (even among native speakers) and can really help you to express yourself when you don't quite have all the words. The "Where is … ," "What about … ," "What happened to … ," "Do you know anything about … " parts are all implied, and context (and a gesture on your part) will usually indicate what you're asking about.

The Conjunctions: and, but, or

To say "and" in Spanish, say *"y"* (sounds like "ee"). The word for "or" is simply *"o."* And to say "but," the word is *pero* (be sure not to trill the *R* too much; the word *perro* means dog). You can use these to add new ideas to your one-word questions: *¿y, la cuenta?* ("And what about the check?"); *¿o el cine?* ("Or how about the movies?"); *¿pero, mi dinero?* ("But what about my money?").

Lazy Practice

Here's a list of some basic things that you might want to inquire about. Imagine that you're in a Spanish-speaking country (if you aren't already). Following the previous model, practice greeting various people and asking them for information about these subjects. Remember to add

YOU'LL THANK YOURSELF LATER

Spanish speakers expect you to maintain eye contact while you're talking to them. If you keep looking away or at the floor, they may feel that you're rude or that you don't care about what they're saying. Try to maintain a reasonable level of eye contact, unless you want to be left alone or feel that you may be in danger. When speaking to superiors, however, Spanish speakers may lower their eyes out of respect.

a gesture and a rising tone at the end of your sentence. Don't be afraid to vary the word order of the "hello" phrases. After you practice this list, consult your dictionary for more words. You'd be amazed at the number of questions you can ask with only a few words and a gesture:

¿el avión?	the airplane?
¿el autobús?	the bus?
¿el tren?	the train?
¿la hora?	the time? (hour)
¿mi amigo?	my friend? ("mi" means "my")
¿mi dinero?	my money?
¿y el hotel?	the hotel? (don't pronounce the "H")
¿o el museo?	the museum?

ACTIVITY: SPANISH MOVIES

Most larger video stores have a foreign film section. Check out their selection of Spanish language films. Some of these films have won prestigious international awards. You may want to check the Internet under "Spanish Films" to get a list of available titles. Rent two or three of these films and study the body language used by the actors. Remember to make popcorn, too.

IF YOU'RE SO
INCLINED

Consult your dictionary and look up any subjects that you think you might need to ask about. Continue to practice as shown here.

Chapter four

If You Can't Join 'Em, Beat 'Em: Circumventing the System

Until you've had the chance to study the language for awhile, there'll be times when you just won't know enough Spanish to say what's on your mind. Though this can be frustrating, you can't let it stop you from practicing and communicating with Spanish speakers. In the previous chapter, you learned how to use gestures and body language to communicate some basic ideas. Now you'll learn even more techniques to help you express yourself while your Spanish is still getting off the ground.

BETWEEN A ROCK AND A HARD PLACE

Experts say that best way to learn a new language is to start speaking it right away—even if you can only say a few words. Sounds great! Too bad these "experts" forgot to mention the frustration you'll feel as you realize that you don't know

When traveling abroad, you should always carry the address and phone number of your country's embassy or consulate. If your Spanish is still weak or rusty, you may also want the number of an office or agency where there's someone available to interpret for you in case of an emergency. Even if you never use these phone numbers, it's better to have them and not need them, than to need them and not have them.

enough Spanish yet to say what you want. Welcome to the rock and hard place of learning a new language: The more eager you are to start speaking and practicing the language, the quicker you'll figure out how much you don't know how to say. Far too often, many talented students of Spanish give up because they feel overwhelmed by all the things they can't say yet.

That's definitely not *The Lazy Way.* My hope is that the techniques in this chapter, as well as those introduced in Chapter 3, will help you to get your ideas across, keep your spirits up, and make your stay between that rock and hard place just a bit more comfortable as you continue to improve your Spanish skills. Don't give up. Help is on the way!

¿HAY ALGUIEN AQUÍ QUE HABLE EL INGLÉS?

"Does anyone here speak English?" If you're faced with a difficult (or emergency) situation and don't have the vocabulary to communicate your needs, you may be forced to turn to someone who speaks English. In the larger cities and tourist spots of Spain and Latin America, finding someone who understands at least some English shouldn't be too tough. In fact, you'll probably be amazed at how well some Spanish speakers can speak English. Nonetheless, I suggest that you consider falling back on your English only as a last resort.

I've always felt uncomfortable with the idea of English speakers using English as their sole means of communicating while traveling in the Hispanic world.

Except when talking to young children, who will always giggle and smile when you speak English to them, relying on English exclusively while you're in a Spanish-speaking country is a bad idea and, frankly, makes us look bad. The all-too-familiar image of the loud American tourist who makes no attempt to speak Spanish has always caused me embarrassment. Nonetheless, I'm forced to admit that even in the case of languages, every coin has two sides.

Since English is the international language of trade and commerce, you'll meet many Spanish speakers who are studying English and who would be delighted to practice it with a native speaker. That's where you come in. In many areas, English-speaking travelers are few and far between. You'll be a welcomed guest if you can help someone who is struggling to learn English and has no one to talk to. Just put yourself in their *zapatos.* Doesn't if feel good to understand and effectively express yourself in another language?

Your attitude and demeanor are the key to successfully using English in a non-English environment. If you must use English (and I do mean *must*), consider being an ambassador of linguistic goodwill by providing others with the opportunity to practice their English skills with you. Follow these tips to ensure that your use of English results in a positive experience for everyone:

- Begin with whatever Spanish courtesies you already know. Ask in Spanish *"¿Habla usted el inglés?"* If the answer is no, then ask *"¿Hay alguien aquí que hable el inglés?"*

No matter how frustrated or overwhelmed you may feel by the process of learning Spanish, please don't give up. Yes, you can and should aspire to eventually being able to speak Spanish perfectly, but having fun and learning how to communicate should be your primary focus for now.

The Lazy Way

- Always speak English clearly and slowly, but never so slowly as to give the impression that you think the person you're talking to is incompetent.

- Avoid slang and words that you know are only used in your neck of the woods.

- Try to speak a standard international English that everyone can understand.

- Be careful not to speak louder than normal. Some people seem to think that shouting will translate into increased comprehension. Believe me, most of the people you'll meet will be able to hear just fine (unless the tourists keep yelling at them).

THE "PICASSO" METHOD

A picture doesn't have to be worth a thousand words—it can be worth as few as one or two. When you don't know how to say something, you might be able to get your idea across by drawing a simple picture.

Obviously, this technique won't work for complicated or abstract concepts (unless, perhaps, you're an abstract artist!). But you'd be amazed at the number of ideas you can communicate with a simple line drawing. Yes, I admit that this technique can sometimes be a long shot—especially if you're like me (couldn't draw myself out of a paper bag). But in a pinch, it's worth a try.

QUICK 'N' PAINLESS GUIDE TO LONG NUMBERS

In Chapter 2 you learned the numbers from 1 to 99, but it still may take awhile before they come naturally to

IF YOU'RE SO
INCLINED

Find a friend who's willing to be your guinea pig for a few minutes. Practice speaking to her as if she only knew a little English. Monitor how your voice and speech changes to accommodate the situation. Keep in mind some of the points raised here.

you. In fact, most people instinctively count in their native language, even if they're fluent in a second language and have been living abroad for decades.

Here's a trick that will help you to express long numbers in Spanish until you feel more comfortable with them. The word for number in Spanish is *"número"* (*NOO-mair-oh*). To say "the number," you put *el* before it. If you're in a bind with a long number, simply say *"el número"* and then read out the numbers one by one. Granted, it's not the most eloquent Spanish, but if you say *"el número: uno ocho cero ocho cinco nueve dos,"* people will understand that you mean 1,808,592.

IF YOU'RE SO *INCLINED*

Write down a list of ten relatively long numbers. Now, say *"el número"* and read the numbers one by one.

TWELVE *"LAZY"* FRIENDS IN SPANISH

Here's a list of twelve words and phrases that you just gotta have. Some may already be familiar to you. But perhaps I can tell you a little more about them:

Word or Phrase	Definition
1. *Sí*	Yes
2. *No*	No
3. *Y*	And
4. *Pero*	But
5. *O*	Or
6. *Por favor*	Please (literally, "as a favor")
7. *Gracias*	Thank you
8. *Ya*	Now; already

YOU'LL THANK YOURSELF LATER

If you're headed to a particular country, do a bit of research on the Internet or in a travel guide before you go and see if you can locate and write down some of the telephone numbers and addresses you'll need in case of an emergency. *Sombreros* off to you if you already did this!

Word or Phrase	Definition
9. *A ver …*	"To see … "
10. *Así*	Thus
11. *¿Se puede … ?*	May one … ? (Is it possible or allowed?)
12. *Con permiso*	With (your) permission

Sí

Yes, this means "yes." It may also mean "Sure," "Of course," "I understand," "That's fine," "You bet." With a rising tone, it can mean: "Really?" or "Is that right?" If someone indicates something to you that you find acceptable, you can agree to it by saying *"sí."*

Sí can also be translated as "do" or "does" in sentences such as *Juan no quiere comer, pero Julio sí* = "Juan doesn't want to eat but Julio does." It also works as an intensifier: *Juan sí quiere comer* = "Juan really does want to eat."

No

Yes, this means "no." It also means "not." In some situations, it can mean "I don't believe it," "I hope not," "Oh my gosh!" "Stop it!" "You are wrong," "I don't want it," "You've got to be kidding," "I'm so sorry to hear that," "Help!" and other negatives. The context and your tone of voice will indicate what you mean.

No can also be translated as "don't" or "doesn't" in sentences such as *Juan quiere comer, pero Julio no* = "Juan wants to eat, but Julio doesn't."

Y

This means "and." But with a rising tone, it can also mean "Well?" "So now what?" "What about that?" Be careful when using *y* outside of its meaning as "and," however, since *¿y?* can be a little brusque. When written before a word starting with *I, Y,* or *Hi,* "y" becomes "e."

Pero

It means "but." Be careful not to trill the *"r"* too much since *perro* means "dog." During a conversation, you'll sometimes hear *pero* used to introduce a sentence: *¿Pero, no me puedes dar ni un poquito?* = "But couldn't I have just a little bit?"

O

O means "or." It's a good way to give people options: *¿Sí o no?* = "Yes or no"; *¿Así o así?* = "Like this or like that?"; *Más o menos* = "More or less." When written before a word beginning with *O* or *Ho,* "o" becomes "u."

Por Favor

Por favor means "please." You should use it as often as you can. Saying *por favor* is also a polite way to indicate that you want someone to do something. If, for example, you're on a bus and you wish to give up your seat to someone older than yourself, gesture to the seat and say *por favor* for "Please take my seat." In Spanish, Dirty Harry's famous "Go ahead, make my day" line might have been *"Por favor, haz mi día."*

IF YOU'RE SO INCLINED

Depending on your tone of voice, *por favor* can also mean "Come on!"; "Hang on!"; "You've got to be kidding!"; "Leave me alone!"; "Be quiet!"; "The price is too high"; "The price is too low"; "Try to understand my point of view."

If someone does something not so nice (like drive by and spray mud all over your new clothes with his tires), you could say *gracias* to mean "Gee, thanks a lot, buddy."

Gracias

Yes, *gracias* means "thank you." And *no gracias* means "no thanks." Use *gracias* any time someone does something nice for you. However, if someone offers you something that you don't wish to accept, *gracias* all by itself will be understood to mean "No, thank you" if your tone of voice clearly indicates that you don't want it. Say *sí gracias* for "yes please."

Ya

Ya means "already," but it's also commonly used for "now." If you're waiting for something to happen (to get on a bus, for permission to enter a museum, to start eating, etc.), you can simply ask "*¿Ya?*" for "Can I get on the bus now?"; "Are we (Is it) ready?"; "Do I have to keep waiting or can I do this now?"

A Ver ...

Literally, *A ver* means "to see." It's probably the second half of *"vamos a ver"* (Let's see) or some similar phrase. It can be translated as "May I see/hear/touch/smell/taste the thing we are talking about?"; "Hand me/Show me the thing we are talking about"; "Tell me more about your idea."

If someone wants to show you something, you can say *"A ver"* for "OK, let me see it." The thing in question need not be a physical object or place. If your friend comes to you and says "I've got a great idea for a book," your response could be simply *"A ver,"* meaning "Great, tell me all about it."

Así

The tiny word *así* ("ah-SEE") is extremely useful. It can mean "This way"; "That way"; "Like this"; "Like that"; "Thus"; "That's true." When said with a rising tone, *así* means "Really?"; "You don't say"; "Is that right?"; "Oh yeah?"; "Is that really true?"

Así is the best word to use with gestures and drawings. It's also good when you want to show someone the manner in which you want something done. If you point to something and say *"así,"* you are essentially saying that what you have in mind is just like the thing you're pointing to. Here are a few examples for *así:*

1. You walk into a barbershop in Mexico for a haircut. You smile, then point to your head making a scissors-like gesture with your fingers. The barber now understands that you want a haircut. Next, you point to a picture of the hairstyle you want and say *"así."* The barber understands exactly how you want your hair to look.

2. Someone runs into your hotel room and yells *"¡Hay un incendio!"* ("The place is on fire!"). You respond *"¿Así?"* which means "Really?"; "Are you serious?". He responds *"¡Así!"* ("Yes, it's true!"). You're now convinced that you should quickly exit the building.

3. After trying in vain to explain something to someone in the best Spanish you can muster, you whip out a piece of paper and pen, draw a simple picture, point to it and say *"así."* If your drawing is clear, the person will understand what you mean, because *así* means "Just like this."

¿Se Puede ... ?

Literally, *¿Se puede ... ?* means "Can one ... ?" or "Is (whatever) permitted?" Another translation might be "Am I allowed to do this thing that I'm talking/drawing/gesturing about?"

Use this when you want to know if something you intend to do is permissible or not. The response could be either *"Sí, se puede"* or *"No, no se puede."* Here are some examples:

1. You're at an international crossing point along the U.S.–Mexican border and you want to make sure that you have the border guard's permission to drive into Mexico. You indicate with a gesture that you wish to pass and you ask *"¿Se puede?"*. The guard will understand that you're asking for permission to cross.

2. You're in the International Airport in Madrid. You think your plane is about to board, and you want to pass through a door toward your gate. But you're not sure if passengers are being allowed to walk through yet. You approach the attendant and say: *"Hola, señor. Disculpe. ¿Se puede ... ?* indicating with a gesture that you wish to pass through this door. He will surely respond *sí* or *no.*

3. While getting into a taxi, you decide that you want to sit in the front seat, rather than the back seat where the driver has indicated he wants you to be. You open the front passenger-side door and say *"¿Se puede?"* The driver will understand that you would rather sit up front.

You can also use *así* with the little word *de* (of) plus an adjective to say "This ... (big, small, bright, etc.)." For example: *Así de grande* = "This big"; *Así de fácil* = "This easy"; *Así de blanco* = "As white as this." Naturally, to make this work you must indicate what the *así* is referring to. If it's not already understood from the context, point to something of equivalent value and say *"así de ...."*

Con Permiso

Literally, *con permiso* means "with (your) permission." In reality, its meaning is closer to "excuse me." *Con permiso* can be used in a variety of ways. It's the best expression to use when you wish to walk past someone or leave the room (you needn't use *"perdón"*). For example:

1. You're sitting on a crowded bus in Lima. The vehicle stops and it's time for you to exit. But in order to reach the door, you have to pass in front of the person sitting next to you, and then inch your way through the crowd of standing Peruvians. So you say *"Con permiso"* to the person at your side as you move past, and continue with *"Con permiso"* as you squeeze by everyone else. If you step on someone's foot, then you can say *"Perdón."*

2. You're back at the border crossing. You got through the first time, so you're confident that you'll be let through again without delay. You lean out of the window and say: *"Hola, señora. Buenas tardes. Con permiso."* For emphasis, you gesture that you wish to keep going forward. She understands and lets you through.

3. Now you're in a restaurant in Guatemala (boy, you sure get around). A local family has invited you to sit at their table. After an hour, you need to leave the table and find *"el baño."* You stand up, smile at your hosts, and say *"Con permiso."* You may now leave the room.

English speakers say "Uhhhh" or "Ummm" when hesitating or trying to think of what to say: "So, ummm, do you like ... " or "Uhhhh, want to go out sometime?" These utterances are known as fillers. In Spanish, people don't tend to use "Umm" or "Uhh." Rather, they say *"este ... "* (in Spain *"esto ... "*). To make your Spanish sound more natural, try incorporating these fillers into your speech pattern when you're searching for just the right word.

The difference between "¿Se puede?" and "Con permiso" is subtle but important. The first is a question where you are actually asking for permission to do something. The second is a statement, ("with your permission") suggesting that you already know that what you're about to do is all right, and are simply confirming this fact as a courtesy to others.

ACTIVITY: TALKING AND DRAWING CHARADES

Using the information you've learned so far, it's time to play charades. But the rules for this version are a little different than the charades you grew up with.

In this game, you may talk. However, you may only use the Spanish words and phrases that you have learned up to this point. You can also draw pictures (don't take more than a minute per picture). No English will be allowed! Focus on communicating situations you're likely to encounter during a trip to a Spanish-speaking country.

You'll need at least two people for this activity. If you're the only one around who is learning Spanish *The Lazy Way,* make a list of the words and phrases you've memorized so far and hand it out to everyone. They'll be able to look up the Spanish expressions as you use them.

A Method to the Madness: How to Make It All Stick

Knowing a second language is sort of like owning a pet. If you don't take good care of your dog (cat, horse, marmot, python) she will not thrive and may even die. If you want to keep your Spanish in good form, you'll have to feed it, pet it, and take it out for walks. So, how do you "pet" your Spanish? I'm glad you asked. This chapter gives you some helpful hints as to how you can improve and maintain your Spanish skills once you've mastered this *lazy* course.

KEEPING YOUR SPANISH ALIVE

The best way to learn Spanish is to go to any country where Spanish is spoken and stay there for as long as you can. But even if you aren't able to travel at this point in your life, there's a lot you can do for your Spanish. The suggestions and activities that follow can help you maintain and perfect your *español*—right from the comfort of your own home town.

Surf the Internet

Outside of actually being in a Spanish-speaking country, the World Wide Web is one of the best places to find up-to-date Spanish. The Internet allows you free access to an endless number of Spanish texts and tutorials. And if your computer has audio and video capability, you can even watch and listen to Spanish-language programming. Anything and everything you ever wanted to know about the Spanish language and Latin culture is as close as a click on your *ratón*.

Bookmark the Web sites that strike your fancy and visit them often. A great Web site about Spain and Spanish is **www.el-castellano.com**. You could spend days exploring this Web site and still not see it all. For details on Latin America, you can't beat **www.mundolatino.org**. For more sites, search for "Español," "Spanish," "gente," or some other random Spanish word and you'll find lots of material to choose from. Some search engines, such as **www.altavista.com**, give you the option of searching by language.

Print out some Spanish texts and study them carefully. With dictionary in hand, read the same passages several times over a week or so, and write down any new words or expressions. Each time you read the text, you'll understand it a little better. This is a great way to improve and maintain your Spanish skills.

The Internet can also hook you up with Spanish speakers through Spanish chatrooms. The Web site **www.mundolatino.org** is one place where you'll find a Spanish chatroom. America Online, CompuServe, and

Some of these activities aren't for everyone. If you live on a remote Aleutian Island, for example, you won't have quite the same opportunities for contact with a Hispanic community as someone who lives in Miami. And if you're in college, you're obviously not going to be hosting a foreign exchange student in your dorm. In some cases, you'll need to modify these activities to fit your own lifestyle and situation.

The Lazy Way

several other Internet service providers also maintain language-specific chatrooms and bulletin boards. Try sitting in some time. Don't worry if you feel shy or self-conscious … they can't reach through your modem and grab you. Just type *Quiero practicar mi español* ("I want to practice my Spanish"), and get ready to learn.

Read Books, Magazines, Newspapers

Most urban areas have at least one out-of-town newsstand where a variety of Spanish language newspapers and magazines can be found. Larger bookstores may also carry Spanish and Latin American newspapers. If you don't see any, ask. University libraries usually have Spanish-language newspapers available to their students and faculty. Ask the librarian if you can take home a few older editions that might otherwise be headed for the recycle bin. If you're interested in receiving a Spanish-language newspaper by mail, you may be able to subscribe to a Spanish daily or weekly paper from a city with a large Hispanic population, such as Los Angeles, Miami, or New York.

Spanish-language magazines are also readily available in the United States. *Newsweek* and *Reader's Digest* have been publishing Spanish versions of their magazines for years (*Newsweek en Español, Selecciones de Readers Digest*). Many other "mainstream" English-language magazines such as *Cosmopolitan* and *People* have also begun to publish in Spanish. If you'd like to subscribe, contact the publishers of these magazines to find out how.

QUICK 🎮 PAINLESS

On an IBM-compatible keyboard running a Windows operating system, make the letter ñ by pressing the Ctrl + Shift + ~ keys. Then release the keys and hit "n." Or, with your number lock on, hit Alt + 0241 on your number pad. On a Macintosh computer, make the letter ñ by pressing Option + "n" and then "n" again.

In neighborhoods with a sizable Spanish-speaking population, you should have no trouble buying books in Spanish. There may be a *librería latina* in the area. Check your local telephone directory under "bookstores." But before you spend a lot of money, see what's available for free at the public library. Depending on the size and clout of the Spanish-speaking community, you may find Spanish-language books on the shelves. Libraries run by colleges and universities will certainly have books in Spanish.

Used bookstores offer another excellent (though sometimes unpredictable) resource for Spanish-language materials. You'd be amazed at what can turn up at a used book store—especially in a university town. I've found Spanish-language reference materials, teaching texts, and several volumes of Spanish and Latin American literature for a fraction of their original price. While there's no guarantee that you'll find what you need, it's always worth a try. You may have to ask the manager if there are any Spanish books in stock.

Rent Movies

Your local video rental store or library may carry a few movies in Spanish. Though the selection may be limited, only the best foreign-language films tend to make it to the mainstream English market. Thus, the Spanish-language movie you chose will probably be reasonably good (there are exceptions). Read the jacket to make sure that the movie is subtitled and not dubbed into English.

Having your own copy of at least one film in Spanish can be a great way to work on your language skills, since it gives you the opportunity to watch the same movie over and over whenever you have the inclination. Each time you see it, you'll pick out and understand new words and phrases. Try watching the images and avoiding the subtitles and see how much you understand. Have your dictionary and notebook on hand, and keep your finger on the pause button to give yourself a moment to write things down. If you look at the experience as a Spanish lesson rather than entertainment, you're less likely to get bored with the plot.

Find a Pen Pal

For the last twelve years, I have maintained an active correspondence with a friend I met in Argentina. During that time, I've learned far more Spanish from his letters than I could have possibly learned in a classroom.

With the speed and ease of e-mail, you might think that the days of the traditional pen pal are about over. But you can still have it the old-fashioned way. Contact International Pen Friends Representatives at 758 Kapahulu Avenue, #101 Honolulu, Hawaii 96816. You can get the addresses of other Pen Pal organizations over the Internet. Just search for "Pen Friends" or "Pen Pals." But do be careful, as some of these "organizations" are actually fronts for "male-order" marriage services.

If you prefer e-mail to regular mail, you're in luck. Finding Spanish-speaking "e-pals" is easy. Visit **www.mundolatino.org** to start your search. America

When I started studying Spanish in junior high school, my exposure to the language and culture of Spain and Latin America was limited to an ancient textbook, black-and-white filmstrips, and a few tattered Mexican *sombreros* dangling on the wall. BORING! Today, things are much different. The student of Spanish has access to so many resources that learning the language doesn't have to be as painfully dull as it used to be.

The Lazy Way

QUICK ◉ PAINLESS

Online, CompuServe, and other such providers are also good places to hook up with Spanish-speaking "virtual friends."

Attend a Class at a Community College or Adult Learning Center

You probably bought this book because you didn't want to sit in a classroom. But someday you may want to take a class, if for no other reason than to hook up with other people who are studying the language. If there's a community college or learning center in your area, find out what Spanish classes are being offered. Tuition is usually reasonable, and there may be both day and night classes to fit your schedule.

Use Flash Cards

You can purchase Spanish instructional flash cards at college bookstores and over the Internet. You can also make your own, by writing the English word on one side and the Spanish word on the other. Go through a stack of 15 to 20 cards whenever you have a free moment. Practice Spanish to English first. Then go from English to Spanish. Once you have learned a word well enough to produce it in both languages, put the card in the "I know these" pile. If you make your own cards, make sure that you include nouns, verbs, adjectives, adverbs, prepositions, useful phrases, and idioms.

Watch Spanish Television

Check to see what Spanish-language programming is offered in your area. In the United States, *Univisión,*

Telemundo, Galavisión, and in certain areas local Spanish-language broadcasters may already be available on your TV. Most cable companies offer at least one of these stations as part of their expanded basic cable service. If you have a satellite dish, you definitely have Spanish TV at your disposal. Both *Univisión* and *Telemundo* have quality news programs every evening. Or you could start with something easier, such as *Plaza Sésamo,* the Spanish-language version of *Sesame Street.* For a more "mature" approach, try getting hooked on a Latin American soap opera (*tele-novela*).

Listen to Audio Cassettes

Many bookstores sell "teach-yourself" audio tapes for Spanish and other languages. The in-flight magazine on your favorite airline may advertise similar (though probably more expensive) products. You can also purchase these packages over the Internet. Before you spend any money, see if your local library has Spanish instructional tapes that you can check out for free.

Most people find it difficult to learn the language from audio cassettes alone. Tapes usually throw a lot of words at you without any grammar or context. But cassettes can be an excellent way to hear the language pronounced correctly. They can also help you to expand your vocabulary.

Listen to the Radio

Spend a few minutes roaming through the FM and AM bands of your radio. Depending on your location, you may be able to find Spanish-language programs. Many

IF YOU'RE SO
INCLINED

Worried about your written Spanish? There are Spanish spell-checking software programs available. Call your local software store or search the Internet for "Spanish proofing tools" if you're interested in purchasing such a program.

major U.S. cities, as well as Toronto and Vancouver, have at least one station that broadcasts in Spanish. Listening to the radio can be a great way to keep your Spanish active.

You'll definitely be able to find Spanish programming on a short-wave radio. Of the many programs you'll hear, Voice of America seems to come in the strongest. Unfortunately, the audio quality on short-wave radios usually isn't very good. But if you're unable to find any Spanish-language stations on the FM or AM frequencies, you can at least find something to listen to over the short-wave. Don't expect to hear anything during the day. Nighttime is always best for short-wave reception.

Buy Instructional Software

Spanish instructional software is readily available at your local software or computer store. In-flight magazines advertise it. And of course, you can purchase lots of language software over the Internet.

Some of these computer programs are excellent; others are not so excellent. As with audio tapes, those programs that simply throw words at you randomly, even if they do have those cute little graphics, may not actually teach you the language. Knowing a lot of words is great, but if you can't put them together in a sentence, you won't really be speaking Spanish.

Though some of these software programs seem quite reasonably priced, be careful. Far too many of us have purchased a cheap "Teach Yourself Spanish" software package only to discover that it's practically useless

YOU'LL THANK YOURSELF LATER

A great way to take advantage of the radio is to record an hour or so of a Spanish-language program that appeals to you. Try to record some music, an announcer, and maybe even the news. Listen to the tape over and over until you practically have it memorized. I promise that it will do wonders for your Spanish.

because of its dull and uninspired format. Read the box carefully before you open your wallet, and make sure that the program's presentation really appeals to you. Be prepared to spend a little extra *dinero* for the best software.

Host an Exchange Student

If you can't actually *be* an exchange student, you may be able to invite a Spanish-speaking student into your home. The International Rotary Club, American Field Service (AFS), and other exchange organizations place foreign students with host families. Contact AFS at **www.afs.org** and the Rotary Club at **www.rotary.org**.

If you're not in a position to have someone staying with you, contact your local high school or college to inquire about the possibility of arranging to meet with a Spanish-speaking exchange or foreign student attending classes in your area.

Find Someone to Talk To

If you're in college, there may be foreign students in your dorm. And there will certainly be a foreign students' organization. Also, the Spanish Department may have a program to link students with Spanish-speaking students. See if you can hook up with other students who speak Spanish.

If this isn't a possibility for you, ask around to see if there's someone who speaks Spanish in your neighborhood. Mexican restaurants are a good place to start (though I once came upon a Mexican restaurant that was owned by a Chinese family who didn't speak a word of

QUICK ⚬ PAINLESS

On an IBM-compatible keyboard running a Windows operating system, the ! and ? symbols can be made using a combination of the following keys: "Ctrl + Alt + Shift + ?" and "Ctrl + Alt + Shift + !" On a Mac, hit Option + Shift + ? or !. You may also use the Key Caps menu.

Spanish!). How about a retirement home? You may meet a Spanish-speaking senior citizen who would greatly appreciate your company. Call the local Catholic church or diocese. They'll probably know if there are any Spanish speakers in the area. Put up posters on public bulletin boards and at colleges with a phone number where you can be reached: *Quiero practicar mi español con usted* ("I want to practice my Spanish with you"). See if there are any charitable organizations working with Spanish speakers that are looking for volunteers.

Still no luck? Well, desperate times may call for desperate measures. Open the phone book and look under last names such as García, González, Hernández, López, or Martínez, and start calling around. You may find that there's someone out there who would love to help you with your Spanish (perhaps in exchange for English lessons). It's a bold step, but if you're really stuck, it's worth a try.

Marry Someone Who Speaks Spanish

No doubt about it, if you form a romantic relationship with someone who speaks Spanish, you'll get lots of practice. Now, I'm not trying to play matchmaker here. And I'm not saying that falling in love with someone just because you can practice your Spanish with that person is a strong foundation for a long-term relationship. But hey, who am I to stand in the way of *el amor?*

Talk to Yourself

If you can't hook up with someone who speaks Spanish, you may have to talk to yourself. But don't panic, I'm not

QUICK 🔘 PAINLESS

Your VCR may have a bilingual menu option. Try changing the menu language to Spanish (this is assuming that you, unlike myself, actually know how to program your VCR). You'll quickly become familiar with the Spanish equivalents for words such as "record," "play," "date," "time," and "program." As long as everyone else in your home doesn't mind, this is another good (and free) way to introduce more Spanish into your life.

suggesting that you walk around town all day mumbling Spanish under your breath.

We all think about things. Sometimes we think too much. Ever have one of those days when your mind just won't shut up? Why not harness some of that energy and put it to good use by privately translating your thoughts into Spanish?

When you look at your watch, say the time to yourself in Spanish. If you suddenly remember that you need to take out the garbage and put out the cat, think *basura* and *gato*—even if you don't know how to say "to take out" or "to put out."

Whenever I have trouble falling asleep, it's usually because my mind is working overtime reviewing the day's events, planning for the future, or analyzing some childhood memory. If you find yourself doing too many mental gymnastics at night, try thinking your thoughts in Spanish instead of English. Even if your vocabulary is limited, you can still fill in Spanish here and there. At least this activity might get you to sleep a little faster.

ACTIVITY: DO ONE OF THE ABOVE

You don't have to wait until you're finished with this book to start finding ways to practice your Spanish. Pick the activity that most appeals to you from this chapter and see how far you can take it.

Everyone has their own learning curve. Most people experience a "three steps forward, two steps back" progression. You may make great gains one day, only to find that you can't even say *"Hola"* the next. Your brain needs time to process the new information before you can use it on command. Don't measure your improvement on a daily basis. Take stock every week or so instead.

The Lazy Way

El Español: Clear and Simple

Are You Too Lazy to Read "El Español: Clear and Simple"?

1 You hope that reading Spanish grammar will work better than counting sheep when you can't get to sleep. ☐ sí ☐ no

2 Every time you think about learning Spanish your stomach feels like you've just eaten five burritos with extra hot sauce. ☐ sí ☐ no

3 You gave up learning the subjunctive because you felt it was all too "subjective." ☐ sí ☐ no

You Already Speak Spanish: Cognates

"**W**hat?!" you say, "I don't speak Spanish." Well, actually, you already know a lot more Spanish than you think you do, because English and Spanish share many common words (and I'm not just talking about Mexican food). In this chapter, I'll show you how to recognize the Spanish words that you already know, and suggest some low-impact projects to help you get a head start on building your Spanish vocabulary. Think of them as "free words" (just what the *Lazy* doctor ordered).

COGNATES: WORDS SO LAZY, THEY HARDLY CHANGE AT ALL

Spanish and English share many words. These words are known as *cognates* (as in the word "cognizant," meaning you're already aware of them). For example, the word for "television" in Spanish is *televisión*. Such words are also known as "friends" or "amigos." Some of these amigos look exactly the same in both languages, while others require you

The word lists in this chapter serve two purposes. First, they illustrate the points I'm trying to make. Second, they passively introduce you to words you'll want to know later. Don't worry about learning all these words the first time you read the chapter. But later on, when you're ready, reread the chapter and work on memorizing the words. You'll be glad you did.

to work a little harder. You'll see what I mean in a minute.

Latin: Your Dead Amigo

You may not be "cognizant" of the fact that your English vocabulary contains words and phrases *ad infinitum* that were born in Rome centuries ago. And since Spanish is a Romance language, the vast majority of the Latin words we use in English exist in Spanish, too. You don't need to have studied Latin to benefit from all this. Believe it or not, you already have a Spanish vocabulary (by way of Latin) of several hundred words at least—words that you use every day without missing a beat.

Some amigos are identical in both languages. The only difference is in their pronunciation (consult the pronunciation rules in Chapter 2 if you're unsure):

popular	(poh-poo-LAHR)
tropical	(troh-pee-KHAL)
natural	(nah-too-RAHL)
radio	(RAH-dee-oh)
hotel	(oh-TEHL)
motor	(moh-TOHR)
horrible	(oh-RREE-blay)
terrible	(etc.)
actor	
monitor	
capital	
alcohol	

tumor

violín   (vee-oh-LEEN)

conga

oboe   (oh-BOH-ay)

Although there are many words in Spanish and English that look identical, there are even more that are nearly the same except for a slight change in spelling. In many cases, the only difference between the Spanish word and the English word is the addition or change of a vowel at the end, or the use of one consonant where there are two in the English word. A *th* in English may be written as a *t* in Spanish, and *ph* as *f.* There may also be other internal changes to compensate for the bizarre way we spell English:

teléfono

presidente

autor

calandario

fotographía

carro

rata (yes, a rat)

senador

democrata

republicano

crema

vitamina

aspirina

IF YOU'RE SO
INCLINED

Browse through the Spanish side of your dictionary. Notice how many words look very familiar to you.

excelente

guitarra

grupo (group)

americano

droga (drug)

medicina

lampa

aniversario

confortable

automóvil

banco

catedral

diferente

elegante

elefante

famoso

computadora

IF YOU'RE SO
INCLINED

Look over one of your Spanish texts and high-light any words that you recognize as *amigos.* See if you can guess their meaning. Spend about 15 minutes doing this exer-cise with other texts as your energy permits. Don't worry too much about learning these words right now. This is just an exercise. If you do want to memorize them at this point, be sure to confirm their meaning in your dictionary. Some may be "false amigos"—more on that later.

Some cognates don't always jump out and bite you on the nose. You may need to study such words a bit before you recognize can them:

champú	shampoo
silla	seat
humedad	humidity
ejecutar	to execute

Some Spanish words are cognates with English words that are uncommon in our daily speech. For example, the Spanish verb for "to end" is *terminar.* It is a cognate with "to terminate," a word that you know but might not use every day. The Spanish word for someone who walks in his sleep is *sonámbulo.* The word "somnambulist" exists in English and means "one who walks in his sleep." It's not a common word, but if you already knew it, you're in luck. When you hear a Spanish word, you may have to go through several synonyms of the English word before you actually locate the cognate.

In the following sections I'll give you more clues to help you recognize your Spanish amigos.

–ción, es- and -um

Most words that end in "–tion" in English exist in Spanish as *-ción* or *–sión.* The meaning of such words is often the same in both languages:

> *terminación*
>
> *información*
>
> *constitución*
>
> *navegación*
>
> *decisión*
>
> *indecisión*
>
> *posición*
>
> *contaminación*

YOU'LL THANK YOURSELF LATER

The number of words that end in *–ción* and *–sión* in Spanish is quite large. If you've decided to keep a list of cognates in your notebook, you could start with these to get a head start. Every page in your Spanish dictionary should have at least one of these.

Many Spanish words that begin with *es-* have an English friend. If you remove the *e* (and possibly the final vowel), the cognate becomes even clearer:

espacio	space
especia	spice
especial	(shame on you if you can't guess)
espía	spy
esquí	ski
estudiar	study
estimado	esteemed (careful, some times the e stays)
estupendo	stupendous
estúpido	not-so-stupendous

Words that end in *-um* in English tend to end in *-o* in Spanish:

gymnasio	gymnasium
acuario	aquarium
auditorio	auditorium

Lazy Practice

Write down all of the English words that you can think of in ten minutes that end with *–tion* or *-um.* Change the "t" in *–tion* to *c* and write an accent mark on the *–ó*, making *-ción.* You have just created a list of words that are likely candidates for Spanish. Now, take your dictionary and verify some of the words that you have created.

IF YOU'RE SO
INCLINED

Start keeping a list of cognates in your notebook. Just partition a section off to use only for words that are cognates in both languages. This will really help you to increase your vocabulary quickly.

Although some may not have worked out (or may have needed *s* instead of *c*), this exercise is extremely valuable and will dramatically increase the number of Spanish words that you know. There may be some variances in spelling and meaning here and there, but even so, this exercise is still worthwhile.

-dad, -ity, and -a

There are many Spanish words (nouns) that end in *–dad* (sometimes *–tad* or *-tud*). These are usually abstract concepts or intangible things. This suffix corresponds to *–ity* or *-tude* in English. You can learn a lot of new nouns this way. Check this out:

comunidad	community
intensidad	intensity
mentalidad	mentality
vecindad	vicinity
ciudad	city
libertad	liberty
sociedad	society
longitud	longitude

The ending *–a* is common in Spanish and may correspond to *–e* (or nothing) in English:

persona	person
agricultura	agriculture
causa	cause
dama	lady

disciplina	discipline
gasolina	gasoline/petrol
forma	form
planeta	planet
idiota	idiot
mapa	map

FALSE AMIGOS: CLOSE BUT NO *CIGARRO*

Now, before you get too excited, hold on! Yes, it is true that there are many words in Spanish and English that look similar and mean the same thing, but cognates can also lead you astray. Some "amigos" may have the same general meaning, but in the other language they may have a long list of secondary meanings that don't exist in the first language. Other false friends can have entirely different (or even opposite) meanings in each language. You must always verify either by way of a context or your dictionary that a cognate really does mean what you think it does. Observe:

asistir	to attend (not "to assist")
caro	expensive (not "car")
comer	to eat (not "to come")
fábrica	factory (not "fabric")
flor	flower (not "floor")
librería	bookstore (not "library")
joya	jewel (not "joy")

pan	bread (not "pan")
sopa	soup (not "soap")
familiar	having to do with family (not "something you already know a lot about")
colegio	elementary school (not "college")
horno	oven (not "horn")
luz	light (not "loose")
curioso	strange (not "curious" like a cat)

So, Now What ... ?

At this point, you're probably feeling both elated and frustrated. First I tell you about all these cool free words, and then I say that you can't always trust them and should always look them up just to make sure they aren't false amigos. Well, I know it's frustrating. Tell you what ... here's my *Lazy* advice.

When you speak Spanish, you can figure that about 70 percent of the time, your instincts about cognates will lead you in the right direction (at least close enough for you to get your idea across). So go ahead and use a cognate when it occurs to you. If you need to say "communication" and haven't learned the Spanish word yet, try *comunicación* and see what happens. If someone doesn't understand you, they'll let you know. And even if the cognate you choose isn't 100 percent correct, it may be a lot better than saying nothing at all. I don't care how

A COMPLETE WASTE OF TIME

The 3 Biggest Warnings About Cognates:

1. Don't assume that a cognate always means the same thing in both languages. Use cognates as a tool, not as a way to fumble through the language.

2. Don't forget that although a cognate may look the same, it is pronounced very differently.

3. Don't forget what it's like to have strange tourists in your country. Think how you would react if a Spanish-speaking person went around trying to speak English by removing the *–o* from the end of all of his Spanish words.

good your nonverbal skills have become, there are just some concepts that you can't get across by pointing or gesticulating.

Nevertheless, when it's *your* turn to understand Spanish rather than produce it, you might want to be a bit more cautious. Don't assume that you know exactly what's meant by a word just because you think you recognize it. You may indeed be right, but too many people have gotten into a lot of trouble by blithely using cognates as a way to muddle through Spanish. If the subject at hand is important, make sure that you really understand what the words mean. Follow your instincts, but let your dictionary be your guide.

A Final Word About Cognates

You may have heard or seen people (Hollywood movies are famous for this) who take this amigo concept a bit too far, believing that they can somehow conjure up Spanish by making their English sound Spanish: *"I want-o to buy-o a Mexicano blanket-o. How much-o cost-o?"*

Nice try, but that ain't Spanish, and talking like that is a bad idea and an embarrassment to those English speakers who are really trying to learn the language correctly. Lazy or not, I will personally slap anyone vigorously with a wet tortilla who goes around talking like that after having read this book.

Linguists divide cognates into several subcategories depending on how similar the words are to each other. But for the purposes of this book, let's define a cognate as any word that looks reasonably similar in both languages that means about the same thing. Cognates will help you to understand many Spanish words with minimal effort. They'll also help you to produce new Spanish words practically out of thin air.

ACTIVITY: CREATE A STORY

Create a Mad Lib story using some of the cognates that you learned in this chapter. Feel free to create more Mad Libs to check your dictionary for additional cognates:

"Once upon a time there was a ___ who was very interested in ____ and ____. Unfortunately, her/his/its ____ didn't like the ____ of the ____. One day, the ____ left home and went to the ____, which was full of ____ and ____. All of a sudden, the ____ came and said that she/he/it wasn't going to ____ the ____ until the next ____. This was bad news for the ____, who cried all the way home."

For more Mad Libs, you can visit **www.needham. mec.edu/NPS_Web_docs/High_School/Menu/madlib. html**, or do an Internet search on your own for "Mad Libs."

IF YOU'RE SO
INCLINED

Check out these two Web sites for more info on how to learn more about cognates: mwn.net/ infomac/app/ss/emeec. html and www.opengroup. com/open/labooks/ welcome.shtml. If these don't work out, use your favorite engine and search for "Spanish Cognates." I know that you'll find some excellent leads.

Nouns: *Gente, Lugares, y Cosas* (People, Places, and Things)

Now we'll start to unlock the structure of Spanish grammar. But before you break out into a cold sweat over the "g" word, remember that you are among *lazy* friends here. The only reason that I'm discussing grammar now is to save you time later. I've made it as painless as possible. You might even find yourself enjoying it. What's more, instead of dealing with words that you'll probably never use, like "chalkboard," the examples contain many words that you use every day. This means that we can kill two *pajaros* with one *piedra:* You'll learn how the language works while you simultaneously start building a vocabulary filled with useful things to say. As I said before, we're working smarter, not harder.

There's a lot of info in this chapter. Don't try to learn everything in one sitting. Read the chapter through once. Then read it again by sections as needed. Slowly but surely, everything *will* start to make sense.

THE SPANISH NOUN: ¿BOY MEETS GIRL? NOT EXACTLY ...

As I mentioned in Chapter 1, Spanish nouns are classified as either masculine or feminine. But before you start to criticize those Spaniards for their folly, you should know that centuries ago, English also used masculine and feminine nouns. It was only due to historical events that inanimate-gendered nouns in English were discarded. Had Britain not been settled (invaded?) by so many different peoples over the centuries, each noun that I'm writing on this page might well have been either masculine, feminine, or (heaven forbid!) even neuter.

Still, the concept of masculine and feminine words often confounds English speakers. Yes, we can accept the idea of gender when it comes to living things: people, cows, dogs, horses, sheep, goats, even plants and insects. But inanimate objects? Cars, walls, houses, doorknobs, money, clouds, patriotism, and so on are all obviously neither girls nor boys. So what gives?

Well, good question. Let's take a look. It's actually not that bad ....

Lazy-Noun Rules

In *general* terms, Spanish nouns that end in –a are feminine, while those that end in –o are masculine. There is no neuter gender in Spanish, so your "fixed" cat is still a *gato,* even though he may not be quite as *macho* as he once was.

Most *living* things have both a masculine and feminine form. Usually, the final letter is the only difference between the two forms.

YOU'LL THANK YOURSELF LATER

A noun is a person, place, thing, or idea. You've heard it before. But I sometimes find it easier to think of a noun as any "thing," whether that thing is animate (living), inanimate (not alive), believed, or conceived. Thus, Mr. Gómez, his hometown, the plants in his backyard, and anything he thinks about or believes in, are all just "things."

As you can see, the only difference between these words is the final letter. Those ending in –a indicate a female, and those ending in –o indicate a male. So far, so good.

Lazy Practice

Here are some masculine animals. Make them all feminine (they won't mind). The answer is at the beginning of the alphabet:

mono	(monkey)
perico	(parrot)
oso	(bear)
cocodrilo	(crocodile)
zorro	(fox)
novio	(boyfriend)

OK. You probably can accept that Spanish indicates girls with –a and boys with –o. But what about all those

QUICK ⟨▪⟩ PANLESS

Relax. Close your eyes and breathe deeply. Now, every time that you breathe in, think to yourself: "A" is feminine. As you exhale, think to yourself: "O" is masculine. Repeat until you have come to accept this rule. Quit if this starts becoming a profound or spiritual experience.

Masculine		Feminine	
niño	(boy)	niña	(girl)
vecino	(neighbor)	vecina	(neighbor)
maestro	(teacher)	maestra	(teacher)
amigo	(friend)	amiga	(friend)
gato	(tomcat)	gata	(female cat)
perro	("tom" dog)	perra	(female dog)

If you look up a noun in the dictionary, its gender should be indicated by an *m.* or *f.* somewhere close to it. (The "A" and "O" class concept was my idea. Don't go looking for it in your dictionary. I'm thinking of getting it patented.)

things that can't be male or female because they aren't alive? How is that going to work?

Well, those nouns are also divided into masculine and feminine, and the –*a* and –*o* rules apply just the same. But try *not* to think of non-living Spanish nouns as male or female per se. If the masculine/feminine thing doesn't work for you, try thinking of inanimate Spanish words as belonging to one of two grammatical categories: "A" class words and "O" class words. Sort of like blood types. Usually it's just the spelling of the word—rather than any latent masculine or feminine qualities—that determines the gender of inanimate nouns.

Unlike animates, non-living nouns usually do not have an equivalent in the opposite gender. For example, the word for "beer" is *cerveza*. There is no such thing as *cervezo*. It doesn't matter if a man or a woman is drinking it. The word *cerveza* never changes. It ends in -*a,* so it's feminine (or "A" class if you prefer).

"O" Class (Masculine)		"A" Class (Feminine)	
edificio	building	casa	house
micrófono	microphone	música	music
libro	book	revista	magazine
plato	plate	comida	food
dinero	money	pérdida	loss
cuchillo	knife	pobreza	poverty
palo	stick	cama	bed

Spanish uses all this gender stuff to help hold the language together once you start building sentences. You'll see why later. For now, just relax and check this out:

Remember that if the word refers to something that is not alive, "maleness" and "femaleness" have nothing to do with it; gender is merely a method of classifying nouns. Keep this in mind as you read on. It gets even more interesting.

The Definite Article

One of the most important differences between masculine and feminine words in Spanish is how we say the word "the." "The" is known as the *definite article*, because it indicates that the thing we're talking about is specific and defined, not just any old noun. The word for "the" in Spanish is *el* for masculine words, and *la* for feminine (or, if you prefer, *"A" class* and *"O" class* for inanimates). Observe:

el niño	the boy
la niña	the girl
el señor	the gentleman
la señora	the married woman
el perro	the dog
la lluvia	the rain
el teléfono	the phone
la planta	the plant
el caballo	the horse
la manzana	the apple

Good job! If you've come to terms with the concept that *-a* is for feminine and *-o* is for masculine, you deserve a reward. Ask a friend or loved one for a five-minute neck rub. As they massage you, say "Ahhh" and "Ooohhh," being sure to recognize the grammatical significance of these utterances. If you can't find someone to massage you, give yourself a well-deserved pat on the back instead.

The Lazy Way

IF YOU'RE SO
INCLINED

Whenever you come across a new Spanish word in this book, I highly recommend that at some point you also look it up in your dictionary. Why? Because most words have several uses or meanings. Unfortunately, I can only give you the principal uses and definitions of the Spanish words in this book. But you will learn a lot more Spanish if you spend a little extra time researching other ways that a particular word may be used.

Lazy Practice

Go back to previous word lists and read the words again, being sure this time to add the correct definite article (*el* or *la*). So far, there are no exceptions. Everything follows the rules, so all this should be a no-brainer!

An Indefinite Article

When we want to be less specific and say "a man" or "a bridge" instead of "the man" or "the bridge," we use *un* for masculine nouns and *una* for feminine. This is known as the *indefinite article,* because it indicates that the noun that follows is not very specific. Any old one of these will do. It corresponds to *a, an,* and sometimes *one* in English:

un niño	a male child
una niña	a female child
una taza	a cup (tea, coffee)
un negocio	a business
una tienda	a store
un insecto	a bug
una hoja	a leaf; a sheet of paper
un vaso	a glass (drinking)
una bandera	a flag
una palabra	a word
un momento	a moment
un grupo	a group
un puente	a bridge

Lazy Practice

Go back to previous word lists. Read the words again, and this time add the indefinite article *un* or *una*. Make sure you use the article that corresponds to the gender of the noun.

Nouns With Other Endings

So far this has been pretty easy. Now for the bad news. Not all Spanish nouns end in *–a* or *–o*. Sorry to disappoint you. But don't panic. Even though the endings may not always be *–a* or *–o,* there are still many useful guidelines that will help you to know what the gender of the word is.

Nouns ending in consonants such as *r, l, s, z, j,* and *n* tend to be masculine, as do words that end in the vowels *-i* and *–u* (there aren't too many of these). Those that end in *–e* can go either way. Generally, you can guess masculine for these nouns, but be careful. You'll often learn the gender of a new word when you learn it in a sentence. But if you come across the word by chance or out of context, it's usually a good idea to check your dictionary just to be sure:

un reloj	a watch
el arbol	the tree
un balcón	a balcony
el pañal	the diaper
el francés	French (language)
el alemán	German (language)
un hotel	one hotel

You can give yourself a big pat on the *espalda* every time you recognize a new Spanish word as a noun. But don't be too hard on yourself if you guess wrong. As you learn more Spanish, you'll soon develop a sense for which words are nouns and which are not, just by the way they look and where they are placed in the sentence.

The Lazy Way

el esquí	the ski; skiing
un restaurante	a place to eat
el bote	small boat; tin can (Mexico)
el hindú	a language of India

But:

la flor	the flower
la gente	the people
una nube	a cloud

Now, remember all those words ending in *–dad, -tad, -tud, -ción,* and *–sión* from the previous chapter? Well, they are ALL feminine. Always! No extra guesswork is required. And words ending in *–umbre* (*costumbre* = habit) and *-ie* (*serie* = series) are nearly always feminine.

"Wrong-Ending" Words

There are some words that end in *-a* that are actually masculine (*"O" class*) words. Most words that end in either *–ama, -ema, -ota,* or *-eta* are actually masculine:

el planeta	the planet
un idiota	a male idiot (for a female, use *una*)
un mapa	a map
el programa	the program
el problema	the problem
el clima	the climate

But not always:

la forma	the form; the manner
la paleta	the Popsicle (Mexico)

Nouns that end with the suffix *-ista* (the equivalent of "–ist" in English) also fall into this category when they refer to a male person (can be *la* when referring to a woman):

un socialista	a male socialist
el capitalista	the capitalist
un villista	a follower of Pancho Villa

But:

una comunista	a female communist

Masculine nouns that end in *-és, -r,* or *-n* will add *-a* to form the feminine equivalent. áccent márks may disappear (see Chapter 2 if you don't understand why):

un francés	a male French person
una francesa	a female French person
un autor	a male author
una autora	a female author
un alemán	a male German person
una alemana	a female German person
un traductor	a male translator
una traductora	a female translator

QUICK ⬤ PAINLESS

The word for "day" is *día*. It is always masculine. Never say *"la día."* Also, the word for "problem" is *el problema*. Never say *"la problema."* The word for "hand" is *mano* which is also feminine.

Sometimes, though, there are specialized words:

un actor	an actor
una actriz	an actress

Some nouns are the same for both masculine and feminine. These are usually living things. However, the article does change according to the gender of the person in question:

el estudiante	the male student
la estudiante	the female student
el/la joven	male/female teenager
el/la interprete	male/female interpreter
el/la artista	male/female artist
el/la modelo	male/female model (fashion)
el/la dentista	male/female dentist
el/la guía	male/female guide
el/la tigre	tiger/tigress

Some nouns change gender according to their meaning. For example, *el capital* refers to money, while *la capital* is a country's center of government. Other nouns retain their specific gender even if they refer to a person of the opposite sex. For example, *persona* and *víctima* (person, victim) are always feminine, even if they refer to a man.

la persona	the person (never becomes "*el persona*")
la víctima	the victim (never becomes "*el victima*")

YOU'LL THANK YOURSELF LATER

Although the Spanish word *macho* does mean "manly" or "brave" when talking about people, it also means "male" in a general sense when talking about animals or hardware (the male end of a plug or socket). The word for "female" is *hembra*. If you need to inquire about the gender of an animal, ask *¿Es macho o hembra? Masculino y feminino* are more suited to questions of a grammatical nature.

There is also a small class of feminine words that take *el* in the singular form. These words begin with a stressed *"a"* sound (could be written *"ha"*). The most important word in this class is *agua* ("water"). The idea is that *"la agua"* is tough to say. You need to say *el agua,* even though *agua* is a feminine word. In all other respects, these words are treated as feminine (and will take feminine adjectives … more on that in the next chapter).

The good news about all these exceptions is that after awhile, even they seem to make sense and follow a logical pattern. You'll eventually see that these words aren't really exceptions at all, but are just following the beat of their own *conga.* With a little practice, you'll actually be able to guess the gender of a word from its form (and be right about 95 percent of the time).

Lazy Practice

Guess the gender of the following words, applying the rules that I have just outlined. There are no exceptions here. If you're not sure, reread the rules:

pluma	feather; pen
comunidad	community
comunicación	communication
marco	frame
dinero	money
esquema	outline
computadora	computer
monitor	monitor
impresora	printer

YOU'LL THANK YOURSELF LATER

Occasionally, there can be two versions of the same inanimate word, one masculine and one feminine. For example, both *cesto* and *cesta* mean "basket." But such words usually mean approximately the same thing. It may be simply a matter of personal or regional preference. Don't let this trouble you.

QUICK ☜☞ PAINLESS

More Lazy Practice

To say that a singular noun "is here" in Spanish, you can say *"X" está aquí* ("ehs-TAH ah-KEE"). *Aquí* means "here" and *está* means "is." You can also say *Aquí está "X,"* which means "Here is … " If everyone already knows what's being talked about, you can simply say *Aquí está,* which means "Here it is." The "it" is understood. Look at the following examples:

Aquí está el hombre.	Here is the man.
Una mujer está aquí.	A woman is here (has arrived).
El arbol está aquí.	The tree is here.
Aquí está el teléfono.	Here's the phone.
Aquí está mi hotel.	Here's my hotel.
¿El perro?	And what about the dog?
Aquí está.	He's here.

If you put *no* before *está,* it means *not:*

Aquí está mi amigo.	Here is my friend.
¿El gato?	And what about the cat?
No está aquí.	The cat is not here.
¿El tren?	And what about the train?
Aquí no está.	It's not *here* (could be elsewhere).

Now, use these formulas to create some very useful sentences on your own. Choose ten of your favorite nouns, either from this chapter or from elsewhere, and start making sentences that express the idea that "X" is here, or that "X" isn't here.

PLURALS: WHEN THERE'S *MÁS* THAN *UNO*

In English, we put an *-s* on the end of nouns to indicate plurality: one car, two car*s;* one telephone, two telephone*s;* one house, two house*s;* one mouse, two mouse*s* (OK, not always). Spanish also uses the *-s* at the end of a noun to indicate more than one.

But in English, the word "the" never changes. We say "the houses" and "the cars," not "the*s* houses" or "the*s* cars." And here's where Spanish differs. The plural of *el* is *los* and the plural of *la* is *las*. When a word is plural, the article must also be pluralized:

el sombrero	the hat	*los sombreros*	the hats
la camisa	the shirt	*las camisas*	the shirts
la casa	the house	*las casas*	the houses
el camino	the road	*los caminos*	the roads
el libro	the book	*los libros*	the books

For the words that end in a vowel (such as the previous examples), all we need to do is to add an *–s* at the end. If the word ends in a consonant (including *y*), *-es* is added:

el rumor	the rumor	*los rumores*	the rumors
el ratón	the mouse	*los ratones*	the mice
el pañal	the diaper	*los pañales*	the diapers

IF YOU'RE SO INCLINED

If you haven't thought about grammar in a long time, you may want to visit www.dsoe.com/explore/english for a basic grammar review. Or search for "English grammar" and visit other grammar-related sites on the Web. Several universities maintain such sites as a resource for their students. Your local library should also have some basic English grammar books for your reading enjoyment.

If an áccent márk appears on the last syllable of a noun ending in a consonant (such as –ón), it will probably disappear when you add a plural –es ending. The syllable with the áccent márk has just become the penultimate (second-to-last) and thus no longer requires a special mark: *balcón* becomes *balcones.* The *-ón* now gets stressed naturally. Go back to Chapter 2 if you feel you need a review.

la sesión	the session	*las sesiones*	the sessions
el rey	the king	*los reyes*	the kings
la tienda	the store	*las tiendas*	the stores

When a noun ends in –z, the -z becomes -c in the plural:

la voz	the voice	*las voces*	the voices
el avestruz	the ostrich	*los avestruces*	the ostriches

If a noun or family name already ends in –s or –z in the singular, there is no change in the plural, except for the article:

el lunes	Monday
los lunes	Mondays
los González	the González family

You can add a number before the plural article to indicate a specific quantity (don't use the number 100 just yet):

los tres amigos	the three friends
las cuatro hermanas	the four sisters
los cuarenta ladrones	the forty thieves
las noventa y nueve botellas de cerveza	the ninety-nine bottles of beer

Note that the number never changes. If the number ends in –o (cuatro) it does not change to "cuatra" just because the noun is feminine. However, when the number is one, you must use *un* or *una* according to the gender of the noun:

un muchacho	a boy
una muchacha	a girl
un hospital	a hospital
una decisión	a decision

In this construction, the indefinite articles are really acting like adjectives (the subject of our next chapter). *Un* and *una* may also take a plural: *unos* and *unas.* The concept of a pluralized number one may seem strange, but it's a good way to express the idea of "some," as in "There are some (whatever) here." Check these out:

los amigos	the friends
unos amigos	some friends
las piramides	the pyramids
unas piramides	some pyramids
los problemas	the problems
unos problemas	some problems

Lazy Practice

Let's go back to the "X" *está aquí* model. Now that we're dealing with more than one of something, we need to say … *están aquí.* Note the *-n* at the end of *está.* I'll explain why it's there in Chapter 9. For now, just try to follow this pattern: *Las personas están aquí* ("The people are here"). Practice pluralizing some of the words that you have learned in this chapter or in previous chapters.

YOU'LL THANK YOURSELF LATER

The word for "motorcycle" is *moto.* The word for "photograph" is *foto.* Both are always feminine, in spite of the *–o* ending (they are actually short for *motocicleta* and *fotografía*).

Use the *están aquí* model and practice aloud or in your notebook. Use your dictionary to look up new words.

YOU ARE NOUN NÚMERO UNO

We'll be looking more at pronouns in Chapter 9. But as this chapter comes to an end, I want you to learn one important pronoun: *Yo* (as in "Yo! I'm talkin' to you!"). *Yo* means "I." The "am" part in Spanish is *soy,* as in "bean." Therefore: *Yo soy Steven* = "I am Steven."

ACTIVITY: CAT IN THE HAT GAME

Get a small group of people together (at least two). Take some 3 × 5 cards and cut them in half (or use other pieces of paper). Then think up about 30 to 40 nouns, writing the English on one side and the Spanish (with article for gender) on the other. There are almost enough nouns in this chapter, but you'll have to look elsewhere for more (later chapters, or even better—your dictionary!)

Now put all of these in a hat (box, bucket, can, pot) and mix them up. Close your eyes and pull out a word combination from the container. Hand it to someone on the other team. The other team reads one side of the paper, and you give the same word in the other language. If you do, you get a point. If you can't, the other team gets a point. When the words are all gone, tally up the score to see who wins.

QUICK ⬤ PAINLESS

Say: *Yo soy* (insert *your* name here). Repeat 100 times. (OK, fine! Repeat it only twice if you want. But do learn it. Later you'll get to tell people more about who and what you are.)

Adjectives: The Good, the Bad, and the Ugly

You might be able to live without adjectives, but then you'd be living without color, size, quantity, quality, and lots of other extras. Sounds pretty dull to me. If you prefer your life big, colorful, and exciting, read on.

UNPACK YOUR ADJECTIVES (BUT MAKE SURE THEY AGREE)

Adjectives modify or describe nouns: *tall* tree, *big* mistake, *heavy* load, *red* brick, *angry* bear, *annoying* insect, and so on. Yes, you knew this already. But perhaps you didn't know that Spanish adjectives work a little differently than English adjectives do.

In Spanish, adjectives *must* agree in number and gender with the nouns they modify. This means that if the noun is masculine, the adjective modifying it must also take a masculine ending. And if the noun is plural, the adjective must be pluralized.

For gender-conforming adjectives, the dictionary usually gives you the masculine form only. Unless the feminine form is unexpected, it probably won't be listed. But that's OK, because you'll know how to make the adjectives feminine all by yourself.

Let's look at four very basic adjectives:

bueno y malo	good and bad
alto o bajo	high or low

Note that these adjectives all end in –o. This means that they currently appear in their masculine form (or "O" class if you prefer). To write these adjectives in their feminine form ("A" class), just change –o to -a:

buena y mala	good and bad (fem.)
alta o baja	high or low (fem.)

Lazy Practice

Here are some more useful adjectives. In this list, they appear in either their feminine or masculine form. After reading through the list, change each adjective into the form for the opposite gender. For example, if the word is *alto* (which you would use to describe a tall masculine noun) change it to *alta* (which you would use to describe a tall feminine noun):

bonito	pretty
divertida	fun
enfermo	sick
fea	ugly
nuevo	new
pequeña	small
viejo	old
loco	crazy

So Where Do I Put That &*%^&@! Adjective

In Spanish, descriptive adjectives (as opposed to demonstrative adjectives—more on those in Chapter 14) are usually placed *after* the noun they modify. This is the opposite of what you are used to in English:

gato bueno	"cat good" = good cat
perro malo	"dog bad" = bad dog

Again, if the noun to be modified is feminine, the adjective takes the feminine ending *–a:*

comida buena	"food good" = good food
servico malo	"service bad" = bad service

Don't be thrown off if the noun ends in a letter other than *–o* or *–a;* the adjective must match only the *gender* of the noun. Use the article as your guide. The ending letters of the noun and adjective may be different:

un balcón alto	a high balcony
la canción linda	the pretty song
un bebé pequeño	a small baby
un pañal sucio	a dirty diaper

When adjectives modify plural nouns they add *–s:*

unos hombres buenos	a few good men
las palabras largas	the long words
las noches tranquilas	the quiet nights
los camiones pesados	the heavy trucks

QUICK ☞ PAINLESS

Yes, descriptive adjectives are generally placed after the nouns they modify. There are times, however, when the adjective in Spanish is placed *before* the noun. If you happen to see this in a text somewhere, don't panic! I'll discuss this phenomenon later. For now, breathe deeply and "become one" with the idea that adjectives are placed *after* the word or words they modify.

There are a few adjectives that never change at all—even when modifying a plural noun. And, to add insult to injury, some of these guys even have the audacity to end in –a or –o. Fortunately, there are relatively few of these, and they are generally not used in daily conversation. If you're dying to know about them, consult Appendix B.

Adjectives With Other Endings

Not all adjectives end in -o or –a (I'll bet you saw this coming). In fact, many adjectives end in -e or in a consonant such as -l, -r, -s, or -z. But the good news is that this actually makes things easier. Most adjectives that end in a letter other than -o or -a are said to be "invariable" (do not change) with respect to gender. So you can use the same form of the adjective with both masculine and feminine nouns:

un hombre *inteligente*	an intelligent man
una mujer *inteligente*	an intelligent woman
un vaso *grande*	a large glass
una fiesta *grande*	a big party
una reunión *urgente*	an urgent meeting
un caso *urgente*	an urgent case
el muchacho *feliz*	the happy boy
la muchacha *infeliz*	the unhappy girl
una pregunta *fácil*	an easy question
el problema *fácil*	the easy problem
un país *tropical*	a tropical country
un señor *cortés*	a polite gentleman
una persona *cortés*	a polite person

But be careful. Even though there may be no change for gender, such adjectives must still add -s (or –es when they end in a consonant) if they modify plural nouns:

ocho mujeres *inteligentes*	eight intelligent women
dos hombres *grandes*	two big men

tres turistas *felices*	three happy tourists
ochenta preguntas *fáciles*	eighty easy questions
doce señores *corteses*	twelve polite gentlemen

There is an exception to this: Adjectives referring to nationality or geographical division will take an *-a* if they end in a consonant (such as *-n, -s,* and *-l*):

un turista *alemán*	a male German tourist
una turista aleman**a**	a female German tourist
un señor *español*	a Spanish gentleman
una canción español**a**	a Spanish song
el pan *francés*	the French bread
la sopa frances**a**	the French soup
español	Spanish (masc. singular adjective)
*español***a**	Spanish (fem. singular adjective)
*español***es**	Spanish (masc. plural adjective)
*español***as**	Spanish (fem. plural adjective)

Lazy Practice

Now you've got a lot to work with. Create a list of about 15 NOUN + ADJECTIVE pairs by combining some of the nouns that you learned in the previous chapter with some of the adjectives that you're learning here. Feel free to find new words in your dictionary. Just follow the

YOU'LL THANK YOURSELF LATER

When adding suffixes to the end of words, áccent márks may appear or disappear. The added suffix may cause the stress to fall naturally on the expected syllable. Or the addition of suffixes may take the stress away from the expected syllable, thus requiring an áccent márk in order to preserve the correct stress.

models above: *el caballo pequeño, la ciudad nueva, los vecinos feos,* and so on. And don't forget to pluralize them, too.

Glue Word: *de*

De is a very important little word that basically means "of or belonging to." It shows possession, and can help you to say what something is made of, or it can describe a noun with another noun. It has numerous uses in Spanish, and you can't live without it. It also means "from," as in "We are from France" ("We belong to France," if you like). I call words like *de* "glue words" because your Spanish would pretty much fall to pieces without them.

In English, we can use nouns to modify other nouns: *lead* pencil, *house* paint, *arm* chair, *gold* watch, *computer* terminal, *garage door* opener, etc. But this doesn't work in Spanish. Though *reloj* means "watch" and *oro* means "gold," I can't say *"reloj oro"* or even *"oro reloj"* to mean "gold watch." Here's where *de* comes in. To say "gold watch," I say *reloj de oro* ("watch of gold"). Observe:

la camisa *de* algodón	the cotton shirt
el monitor *de* computadora	the computer monitor
la puerta *de* madera	the wooden door
el boleto *de* avión	the airplane ticket
el viaje *de* placer	the pleasure trip
el señor *de* Cuba	the gentleman from Cuba

Lazy Practice

Here are five nouns from your *cocina* (kitchen):

mesa	table
silla	chair
refrigerador	(shame on you if you can't guess)
estufa	stove
horno	oven

Here are three materials:

madera	wood
metal	(shame on you if you can't guess)
plástico	(shame on you if you can't guess)

Now, have some lazy fun with *de:*

el horno de plástico de mi amigo Juan.	my friend Juan's plastic oven.
el refrigerador de madera del vecino.	the neighbor's wooden refrigerator.

See what happens when I give you the words for these exercises? You'd better consult your dictionary and pick some better (and more useful) alternatives on your own. But do follow this model. You'll find that you can express a lot of ideas this way.

IF YOU'RE SO
INCLINED

Revisit the adjective list in the last *Lazy Practice* session and make all the adjectives plural. It's simple: just add *–s*.

QUICK PAINLESS

The word *de* also shows possession, much like our *-'s:*

el coche *de* Juan	Juan's car
la mamá *de* Oscar	Oscar's mom
la experiencia *de* mi tío	my uncle's experience
el reloj *de* oro *de* Felipe	Felipe's gold watch

Contraction: *del*

When *de* comes before the definite article *el,* the contraction *del* is formed. In sentences like the following, you must use *del.* It's not optional. In the following sentences you can't say "de el":

la bandera *del* país	the country's flag
el libro *del* estudiante	the student's book
los libros *del* estudiante	the student's books
la interna *del* presidente	the president's intern

However, you should use *"de el"* if the *el* is part of a proper name, or if the *él* refers to a masculine living thing:

la ciudad *de El* Paso, Texas	the city of El Paso, Texas
la gente *de El* Salvador	the people of El Salvador
el libro *de él*	his book ("of him")

De can link several nouns together:

el gato *de* mi amigo	my friend's cat
el gato *de* mi amigo *de* la escuela.	my friend from school's cat
el gato *de* mi amigo *de* la escuela *de* música.	the cat that my friend from music school

GOOD, GOODER, GOODEST: COMPARISONS AND SUPERLATIVES

We often use adjectives to compare things. This is known as (get ready for this one) a *comparative:* "I run *faster* than he does." And if we want to indicate which noun or nouns among several possesses or possess the most or least of a certain quality, we call that a *superlative:* "I'm the *fastest* runner in the world."

In English, many adjectives follow the "fast, faster, fastest" pattern. But we also use the "difficult, more difficult, most difficult" pattern, which is closer to the Spanish model. To express these concepts in Spanish, we usually need the help of the word *más,* which means "more," or the word *menos,* which means "less." *Más* and *menos* are placed before the adjective.

Let's start with basic comparisons:

un hombre alto	a tall man
un hombre *más* alto	a man more tall (taller)
un hombre *menos* alto	a man less tall (shorter)
una idea interestante	an interesting idea
una idea *más* interesante	a more interesting idea
una idea *menos* interesante	a less interesting idea

Lazy Practice

Practice your comparatives. Take some adjectives and nouns that you know (or look some up) and follow the pattern: *un/a* NOUN *más/menos* ADJECTIVE. Use the previous examples as your guide. Stay away from *bueno, malo,* and *grande* for the moment. They're special.

Glue Word: *que*

The word *que* is another glue word. You can't live without it. It has many uses in Spanish (and, of course, we'll talk about those later on). But when *que* hangs out with comparative adjectives, it means "than," as in "I'm smarter *than* you because I passed the test and you didn't."

To indicate what's being compared to what, the tiny glue word *que* will be needed:

hombre *más* alto *que* …	taller man than …
José es inteligente.	José is intelligent.
Marco es *más* inteligente *que* José.	Marco is more intelligent than José.
José es *menos* inteligente *que* Marco.	José is less intelligent than Marco.

Superlatives

Now, to say "the most," "least," "best," or "worst" of something (superlative), we need to bring the definite article *el* or *la* back into the picture:

un hombre rico	a rich man
un hombre *más* rico	a richer man

el hombre *más* rico	the richest (most rich) man
un turista *menos* inteligente	a less intelligent tourist
el turista *menos* inteligente del mundo	the dumbest tourist in the world

Watch this:

El edificio es alto.	The building is tall.
El edificio es más alto que mi casa.	The building is taller than my house.
Yo no soy rica.	I'm not a rich woman.
Yo no soy más rica que Roberta.	I'm not richer than Roberta.

Our little friend *de* works with superlatives to indicate the group from which the subject is the most/least of the quality indicated:

Yo soy *la menos* rica del pueblo.	I'm the least rich woman in town. (of the town)
El edificio es *el más* alto de la ciudad.	The building is the city's tallest. (tallest of the city)
Es *el* edificio *más* alto de la ciudad.	It's the tallest building of (in) the city.
Yo no soy *el* autor *más* famoso del mundo.	I'm not the most famous author in the (of the) world.

IF YOU'RE SO
INCLINED

Take a few minutes to practice your superlatives, following this model: *el/la* NOUN *es el/la más/menos* ADJECTIVE *de* NOUN. Use nouns that you've learned in other chapters, or look up some new ones. Again, stay away from the adjectives *bueno, malo,* and *grande* for now.

Adjectives That Don't Follow the Rules

There's a small group of common adjectives that does not use *más* when making a comparative or superlative. They are invariable for gender. When *grande* refers to age, it follows the pattern indicated here:

Adjective	Comparison	Superlative
bueno	*mejor* (never "*más bueno*") = better	el/la mejor = best
malo	*peor* (never "*más malo*") = worse	el/la peor = worst
grande	*mayor* = older (*más grande* OK for bigger things)	el/la mayor = oldest

The plurals of these are logical:

los/las mejores

los/las peores

los/las mayores

Here are a few examples:

La comida del restaurante es *la peor* del mundo.	The restaurant's food is the worst in the world.
Soy *el mayor* de la familia.	I'm the biggest (oldest) in the family.
Es *mejor* no comprar pan hoy.	It's better not to buy bread today.
Pedro es *el mejor* estudiante de la clase.	Pedro is the best student in the class.

LOS COLORES

Technically, colors are both nouns and adjectives: "The red of the sunset," "The green of the grass." Normally, though, we use colors as adjectives to describe things. Here's a list of the colors in Spanish. Most of them end in -o and therefore must agree in gender with the nouns they modify. Some colors end in –e or a consonant, and thus don't change except for adding –s in the plural:

negro	black
azul	blue (pl. *azules*)
gris	gray
verde	green
anaranjado	orange (*una naraja* is "an orange")
rosado	pink
morado	purple
blanco	white
rojo	red
"color de café"	brown (see sidebar)
amarillo	yellow

When used as nouns, colors usually take a masculine article:

el blanco de los ojos	the white of the eyes
el azul del cielo	the blue of the sky

QUICK  PAINLESS

For some reason, Spanish doesn't have one all-purpose word for the color brown. In fact, there are several: *castaño, pardo, moreno, marrón.* They all have different uses. *Marrón* usually refers to man-made things, while *castaño* refers to eyes and hair. *Pardo* is usually used for animals and natural things, while *moreno* is used for someone's skin tone. If all this seems too confusing, use *color de café* ("coffee-colored").

But, when used as adjectives, they must agree:

los ojos azules	the blue eyes
el cielo azul	the blue sky

THE LAST WORD ON THE PLACEMENT OF ADJECTIVES

By now you should have accepted the idea that adjectives are placed after the nouns they modify. Now that you're comfortable with that, get ready for something completely different.

Certain adjectives have a different meaning depending on whether they are placed in front of the noun or after it:

Adjective	Before Noun	After Noun
antigio	ancient	former
cierto	some	definite
diferente	not alike	various
nuevo	another	new
grande	great, "grande"	large
pobre	pitiable	not rich
varios	several	varied, different
viejo	long-standing	old

Here are a few examples:

una casa *nueva*	a new house (built recently)
una *nueva* casa	a new house (a different house from the one you now live in; could be old)

un amigo *viejo*	an old friend (in age)
un *viejo* amigo	an old friend (long-standing)
un hombre *grande*	a large man
un *gran* hombre	a great man (may have been skinny)
una *gran* idea	a great idea (not "big idea")
la *gran* ciudad de Buenos Aires	the great city of Buenos Aires (*grande* becomes *gran* before nouns)
el papá *pobre*	the destitute father (no money)
mi *pobre* papá	my poor dad (feel sorry for him)

IF YOU'RE SO INCLINED

Check out www.bahasa.com/BahasaSpanish013.html for some fun adjective practice. Or do a search for "Spanish Adjectives" and surf through the Web sites generated. There are several sites on the Web that can help you learn new adjectives.

Descriptive adjectives can also be placed in front of a noun to emphasize the quality of the characteristic being described:

los *malos* sueños de Juan	Juan's bad dreams
los *bellos* ojos de María	María's beautiful eyes
las *verdes* plantas de la selva	the green plants of the jungle

Bueno, Malo, Grande, and Friends

A small group of adjectives have a shorter form that must be used before any masculine *singular* noun. Some of these you have met before, while others are new:

Adjective	Becomes	
bueno (good)	*buen* hombre	good man
malo (bad)	*mal* hombre	bad man
alguno (some)	*algún* hombre	some man
ninguno (no, none)	*ningún* hombre	no man
primero (first)	*primer* hombre	first man
tercero (third)	*tercer* hombre	third man
uno (one)	*un* hombre	a man
santo (holy, saint)	*San* Juan	Saint John

ACTIVITY: SYNONYMS AND ANTONYMS

Create a word table in your notebook of adjectives paired with their opposites (don't use colors unless you're an art student). Here's a few to get you started:

English	Spanish
big/small	*grande/pequeño*
tall/short	*alto/bajo*
thin/fat	*delgado/gordo*
hard/soft	*duro/suave*

Now, use your dictionary, the Internet, or another resource to continue building up your list. This is a good way to group adjective pairs together. Happy adjective hunting!

Santo shortens to **San** before most names, except for *Santo Domingo, Santo Tomás,* and *el santo padre* (the Pope, "the Holy Father").

Verbs and Adverbs: He Said, She Said Very Well

You spend your days coming, going, reading, working, sleeping, eating, and who knows what else. Soon you'll be doing all these things and more in Spanish, too. Many people balk at the thought of having to conjugate verbs and navigate through the various verb tenses. But never fear: *The Lazy Way* is here!

THE SPANISH VERB

Spanish verbs are listed in the dictionary in what is known as the *infinitive* form. All verbs in this form end in either *-ar, -er,* or *–ir.* Though these endings come at the end of the verb (as most endings do), the *-ar, -er,* and *–ir* part roughly corresponds to the "to" part of an English verb: "*to* go," "*to* eat," "*to* love," "*to* sleep," "*to* be or not *to* be," and so on. Take a look at the following list:

hablar ("speak-to")	to speak
trabajar ("work-to")	to work

comer ("eat-to")	to eat
entender ("understand-to")	to understand
leer (etc.)	to read
querer	to want
ver	to see
tener	to have
saber	to know
salir	to go out; to exit
vivir	to live
ir	to go

IF YOU'RE SO
INCLINED

Grab a Spanish text and look for words that end in –ar, -er, or –ir. The vast majority of the words that you'll find are verbs in their infinitive form. After you find a few, try looking them up in your dictionary to see what they mean.

There's not much you can do with an infinitive all by itself. You'll either need to conjugate it (more on this in a minute) or use it in conjunction with other words.

There is, however, a very handy phrase that can quickly get you using lots of verbs without having to

Querer + INFINITIVE:

Yo quiero bailar.	I want to dance.
Yo quiero cantar.	I want to sing.
Yo quiero comer.	I want to eat.
Yo no quiero trabajar aquí.	I don't want to work here.
Yo no quiero ir.	I don't want to go.
Yo no quiero pagar.	I don't want to pay.
Yo quiero tener ocho hijos.	I want to have eight children.

worry about conjugation. To say "I want," say *Yo quiero* (yoh kyeh-roh). *Quiero* is the "I" form of the verb *querer.* If you follow this phrase with an infinitive, you are saying that you "want to (whatever)." Use "no" before *quiero* to make it negative.

The *Yo* part is actually optional, since the *–o* at the end of *quiero* signifies "I" by itself:

Quiero salir.	I want to leave.
Quiero morir.	I want to die.
No quiero saber más.	I don't want to know any more.

Lazy Practice

Use some of the verbs in the following list (and in the previous list) to make sentences following the *Quiero +* INFINITIVE model you just learned (*Yo quiero saber* = "I want to know"):

caminar	to walk
ayudar	to help
ver	to see
correr	to run
subir	to go up; to ascend
jugar	to play (a game)
tocar	to play (an instrument); to touch

Don't forget to practice the negative forms as well.

While Spanish verbs do follow logical patterns, they also constitute one of the most complex parts of the language. So I'm not going to overload you with too much information at once. That would be insensitive. This chapter will give you a solid idea as to how Spanish verbs work. Later we'll be looking at other aspects of Spanish verbs in small, easy-to-swallow pieces. *¡Buena suerte!*

The word "tense" comes from the Latin word *tempus,* which means "time." The tense of a verb tells you when something occurred, for how long, and whether the action has been completed or not.

Verb Cognates

Here's a list of some verbs that are cognate with English. These will get you started as you build your verb vocabulary. But this is only a short list. There are many more verbs out there. Don't be afraid to look in your dictionary:

acompañar	to accompany; to go with
celebrar	to celebrate
comenzar	to commence; to start
declarar	to declare
eliminar	to eliminate
entrar	to enter
explicar	to explain
aprender	to learn (think "apprentice")
invitar	to invite
modificar	to modify
observar	to observe
practicar	to practice
preparar	to prepare
reparar	to repair
reservar	to reserve
terminar	to terminate; to end
usar	to use
verificar	to verify

cubrir	to cover
decidir	to decide
escribir	to write (think "scribe")
omitir	to omit; to leave out

CONJUGATION 101

Conjugating a verb means that you're changing the verb's form to indicate when, how long, and who or what does, did, or will do the action. By conjugating the verb, you are committing it to actually doing something, where before you just had an infinitive suggesting some general action. For example, the English verb "to go" is not a conjugated verb, whereas "John *goes*" or "John *went* home" is.

To get you started conjugating Spanish verbs, you'll need to learn the Spanish subject pronouns first.

The Subject Pronouns

The first five pronouns listed are singular. Thus they are used when referring to one person or thing only:

yo	"I" (You learned this before.)
tú	"you" (Friends, family, equals. The accent is written to make sure it isn't confused with the *tu* that means "your.")
usted	"you" (This is the polite form. Use it most of the time for now. Also written as *Ud.* It is used with both men and women.)

One subject pronoun is not covered in this book: *vosotros.* It's used in Spain (and sometimes in church services elsewhere). *Vosotros* is the plural form of *tú,* and is used with groups of friends or family. Unless you're in Spain, you'll probably never see it. If you do go to Spain, you'll pick it up quickly. Use *ustedes* until you do. Visit www.studyspanish.com/tutorial.htm on the Web for more info about *vosotros.*

The Lazy Way

él	"he" (The áccent márk is written simply to make sure it isn't confused with the *el* = the.)
ella	"she"

The rest are plural. When using these, you must be talking about more than one person (or living thing):

nosotros	"we" (males and mixed groups)
nosotras	"we" (women only)
ustedes	"you all" (as in "Y'all come back now"; also written as *Uds.*)
ellos	"they" (men or both)
ellas	"they" (all women)

Men will always say *nosotros.* Woman will use *nosotras* in a group made up entirely of women. Women who are part of a mixed group (even though there may be only one man among many women), will use *nosotros* (men will say *ellas* when referring to women).

The word *ustedes* is the second person plural pronoun and is gender-neutral. This means that you'll use it to address any group of people of two or more. It doesn't matter if the group consists of men, women, or both.

Lazy Practice

First, look at these:

José = *él*

María = *ella*

José y María = *ellos*

María y Juanita = *ellas*

José, María y Juanita = *ellos*

You are male and you are with friends = *nosotros*

You are a woman and so are all your friends = *nosotras*

You are a woman and you are with a mixed group = *nosotros*

Your male cat = *él*

Your female cat = *ella*

Mr. Gonzalez = *usted*

You are talking to Mr. Gonzalez and his friends or to a large group = *ustedes*

Your close friend Juan or María = *tú*

Juan and María together = *ustedes*

Now, think of different combinations of people and figure out which pronoun you would use.

The Present Indicative Tense

The first tense that you're going to learn is called the *present indicative.* It's used to express the idea of "now-and-in-general-but-not-necessarily-at-this-very-minute." It can also be used colloquially to indicate what someone is willing to do in the near future.

Conjugations in Spanish usually have you removing the *-ar, -er,* or *–ir* part of the infinitive and adding some ending. The ending indicates who's doing the action of the verb. When you remove the infinitive ending, the part left behind is called the stem. So, the stem of *hablar* is "*habl-*" and the stem of *comer* is "*com-.*"

Whack off the endings of some of the infinitive verbs in the previous lists. What you'll have left will be the stem. Yes, there is a plant metaphor in there somewhere.

So far, so good. At the bottom of this page are the endings for the "regularly" conjugated -ar verbs:

Using these endings, the quintessential regular –ar verb *hablar* looks like this:

yo	*hablo*	I speak
tú	*hablas*	you speak
él/ella/usted	*habla*	he/she/it/you speaks
nosotros/nosotras	*hablamos*	we speak
ellos/ellas/ustedes	*hablan*	they/you all speak

Now look at the following sentences. They are all examples of regularly conjugated -ar verbs in the present indicative tense:

Yo hablo (el) inglés. (the article is optional)   I speak English.

-ar Verbs:

yo	-o	first person singular
tú	-as	second person singular
él/ella/usted	-a	third person singular
nosotros/nosotras	-amos	first person plural
ellos/ellas/ustedes	-an	second and third person plural

¿Habla usted (el) alemán?		Do you speak German?
Hablamos con Hector cada semana.		We speak with Hector every week.
Tú hablas un poco de (del) español.		You speak a little Spanish.
Ella canta, pero él no.	(cantar)	She sings, but he doesn't.
Nosotros caminamos cada día a la tienda.	(caminar)	Every day we walk to the store.
Ellos aman la música caribeña.	(amar)	They love Caribbean music.
Ustedes viajan en avión cada año.	(viajar)	You all travel by airplane every year.
Mañana compro una nueva bicicleta.	(comprar)	Tomorrow I'll buy a new bicycle.

-er Verbs

These act very much the same as –ar verbs, except that the -a is replaced by –e:

The regular –er verb comer (to eat) looks like this:

yo	como	I eat
tú	comes	you eat
él/ella/usted	come	he/she/it/you eats

QUICK ⊙ PAINLESS

Learn the word cada now. It will help you to understand the uses of the present indicative tense. The word cada means "each" or "every." Cada is invariable with respect to gender. It never changes to cado.

| nosotros | comemos | we eat |
| ellos/ellas/ustedes | comen | they/you all eat |

Here are some sentences using *comer:*

Yo no como fruta, como dulces.	I don't eat fruit, I eat candy.
Usted come demasiado.	You eat too much.
El niño come mucho pan.	The child eats a lot of bread.
Ella come dos naranjas cada día.	She eats two oranges each day.
Nosotros no comemos la carne de puerco.	We don't eat pork.
Ellos/Ustedes comen verduras cada día.	They/You all eat vegetables every day.

-er Verbs:

yo	-o	first person singular
tú	-es	second person singular
él/ella/usted	-e	third person singular
nosotros/nosotras	-emos	first person plural
ellos/ellas/ustedes	-en	second and third person plural

–*ir* Verbs

The only difference between –*er* verbs and –*ir* verbs is that the *nosotros* form for –*ir* verbs takes –*imos* instead of –*emos*. So, the regular –*ir* verb *vivir* (to live) looks like this (note that most –*ir* verbs are not regular):

yo	*vivo*	I live
tú	*vives*	you live
él/ella/usted	*vive*	he/she/it/you lives
nosotros	*vivimos*	we live
ellos/ellas/ustedes	*viven*	they/you all live

Lazy Practice

Try conjugating the following verbs. They are all "regular" and offer no surprises:

amar	to love
cantar	to sing
beber	to drink
tomar	to take; to drink (more common for drinking than *beber*)
escribir	to write
abrir	to open
pagar	to pay
apagar	to turn off
aprender	to learn

When asking a question, place the pronoun after the conjugated verb: *¿Habla usted el español?* But you'll find that some Spanish speakers don't always follow this pattern. Often a rising tone is all that's required to indicate a question. Thus you may hear *¿Usted habla el español?* There is virtually no difference in meaning between these two structures.

STEM-CHANGING VERBS

Now that you've examined some "regular" verbs, let's look at some "not-so-regular" verbs. Most of these are "stem-changing verbs," because in addition to the ending, there is actually a change within the stem during conjugation.

The Stem Just Can't Take the Pressure

Think of stem-changing verbs as weak verbs that can't handle the stress. As you know, infinitive verbs are all stressed on the last syllable ("hah-BLAHR," "coh-MEHR") because they end in a consonant other than "n" or "s." However, conjugation can shift the stress back to the penultimate syllable, and sometimes the vowel in that syllable turns into a diphthong because it's "too weak" to handle all that stress by itself.

Let's look at some stem-changing verbs and the various changes that can occur:

contar	to tell; to count	o—ue
poder	to be able	o—ue
jugar	to play (a game)	u—ue
querer	to want	e—ie
pensar	to think	e—ie
pedir	to ask for	e—i

Both *contar* and *poder* have an "o" in the stem. When they are conjugated in the present indicative tense, the stress falls naturally on that "o" because, as you remove the consonant ending, the stress falls back to

the penultimate syllable ("cOn-to" and "pO-do"). But this *"o"* is too weak to carry all that stress, so it turns into the diphthong *"ue."* For *jugar,* this would be "jugo" (which means "juice," by the way). The *"u"* in *jugar* does the same thing as the "o" in the other verbs. Watch this:

Pronoun:	contar:	poder:	jugar:
yo	cuento	puedo	juego
tú	cuentas	puedes	juegas
él/ella/usted	cuenta	puede	juega

In the *nosotros/as* form, however, the syllable with the "o" is no longer the penultimate syllable, and so is off the hook here. Now the "a" or "e" of the *-amos* or *-emos* ending is sitting in the penultimate spot (same for *–imos* ending in *-ir* verbs):

   nosotros/nosotras   contamos podemos jugamos

In the second/third person plural (*ellos/ellas/ustedes*), the stress falls back on the poor "o" because it has once again become penultimate:

   ellos/ellas/ustedes   c*ue*ntan p*ue*den j*ue*gan

The verbs *querer* and *pensar* work in a similar way. But the "e" in its stem changes to *"ie."* The verb *pedir* (to ask for) has an "e" in its stem that changes to *"i."* Check these out (you don't need to see subject pronouns anymore—you're an expert now):

QUICK  PAINLESS

querer:	pensar:	pedir:
qu*i*ero	p*i*enso	p*i*do
qu*i*eres	p*i*ensas	p*i*des
qu*i*ere	p*i*ensa	p*i*de
queremos	pensamos	pedimos (not here)
qu*i*eren	p*i*ensan	p*i*den

Lazy Practice

Here are some stem-changing verbs. Practice conjugating them. Just follow what you just learned:

mostrar	(o—ue)	"to show"
perder	(e—ie)	"to lose"
volver	(o—ue)	"to return"
repetir	(e—i)	"to repeat" (second "e")
dormir	(o—ue)	"to sleep"

"–go" Verbs

Some relatively common verbs end in "-go" in the first person singular form (the *yo* form). Some of these guys are also stem-changing verbs like those we just looked at. Others are regular in all other aspects except for the -*go* part:

tener (to have):	hacer (to do):	poner (to put):
tengo	hago	pongo
tienes	haces	pones
tiene	hace	pone
etc.	etc.	etc.

IF YOU'RE SO INCLINED

Most dictionaries tell you when a verb is stem-changing or has some other irregularity. Your dictionary should include something like *(o—ue)* or *(e—ie)* or *(e—i)* after the verb. Or it may refer to another common verb that is conjugated in the exact same way. If you have a minute, look through your dictionary to see how it indicates stem changing verbs. If it doesn't, you might consider buying a better dictionary.

Other such verbs are: *decir* (*digo, dices*) "to say," *salir* (*salgo, sales*) "to go out," *oír* (*oigo, oyes*) "to hear," *traer* (*traigo, traes*) "to bring," and *venir* (*vengo, vienes*) "to come."

THE VERB *HABER* AND THE PAST PARTICIPLE

The verb *haber* means "to have." But its role in Spanish is pretty much confined to that of a helping verb. It does the same thing as the "have" in the English sentence: "I have written this book and you haven't."

And just what is a participle? Well, participles are made from verbs. But they are not conjugated. In fact, they are mostly used like adjectives. For example, words like "opened," "closed," "finished," and "defeated," are all participles, because they are adjectives that have been formed from verbs.

When used with *haber,* the past participle is always left in the masculine form. The tense formed by *haber* + PAST PARTICIPLE is known as the present perfect tense.

Haber:

yo	he	I have (but not "I own")
tú	has	you have
él/ella	ha	etc.
nosotros/nosotras	hemos	
ellos/ellas/ustedes	han	

3 More Bad Things to Do With Your Spanish:

1. Use *haber* for "to own." That's where *tener* comes in.

2. Try to translate Spanish to English word for word. You'll have many headaches if you do.

3. Change words like *abierto* to "*abierta*" when they are used with *haber,* even if you or the person doing the action is a woman, or the object of the action is a feminine noun.

See the present indicative conjugation of *haber* in the box on the previous page. You won't be using these by themselves. You must use them with a past participle. Remember, the "h" is silent:

As I mentioned before, you won't find yourself using these by themselves. Familiarize yourself now with the conjugation of *haber*. Then keep reading to learn about the past participle.

How to Make the Past Participle

With most verbs, just drop the ending and add the past participle ending. For –*ar* verbs, add the ending –*ado.* It doesn't matter if the verb is stem-changing in the present indicative … it's the same deal. This ending is roughly equivalent to "–ed" or "-en" in English:

Verb:	Participle:	Definition:
amar	*amado*	loved
hablar	*hablado*	spoken
cantar	*cantado*	sung ("sing-ed")
mirar	*mirado*	watched
comprar	*comprado*	bought ("buy-ed")
jugar	*jugado*	played
mostrar	*mostrado*	shown

For *–er* and *–ir* verbs, the ending is *–ido:*

Verb:	Participle:	Definition:
salir	*salido*	left ("leave-ed")
aprender	*aprendido*	learned
saber	*sabido*	known ("know-ed")
sentir	*sentido*	felt ("feel-ed")
oír	*oído*	heard ("hear-ed")
comer	*comido*	eaten ("eat-ed")

Now, if you combine these with *haber,* you can make some great sentences. Although technically a present tense construction, this formula is a good way to express a "past" tense aspect for actions that you have completed. In fact, you should consider this as your "past" tense for the moment:

Yo he cantado la canción.	I have sung the song.
Hemos comprado los boletos.	We have bought the tickets.
Ustedes han aprendido muy bien el español.	You all have learned Spanish very well.
Quiero haber terminado el trabajo.	I want to have the work finished.
No hemos estado en Puerto Rico todavía.	We haven't been to (in) Puerto Rico yet.

YOU'LL THANK YOURSELF LATER

Many adjectives having to do with feelings of hunger, thirst, temperature, fear, etc. actually go with the verb *tener* even though we may use the verb "to be" in English: *Tengo hambre* ("I have hunger") = "I'm hungry"; *Juan tiene sed* ("Juan has thirst") = "Juan is thirsty"; *Tenemos calor* ("We have heat") = "We are/feel hot"; *Tienen miedo* ("They have fear") = "They are scared."

Irregular Past Participles

Most Spanish verbs follow the regular patterns I've just outlined. But there's a group of common verbs that form irregular past participles. There's no way to avoid these, and I can offer you no tricks to make them any easier. You'll just have to learn them as is:

abrir	*abierto*	open
absolver	*absuelto*	absolved (any *solver* verb)
cubrir	*cubierto*	covered (any *cubrir* verb)
decir	*dicho*	said
escribir	*escrito*	written (any *escribir* verb)
hacer	*hecho*	done; made
morir	*muerto*	died
poner	*puesto*	put (any *poner* verb)
romper	*roto*	broken (not "*rompido*")
ver	*visto*	seen (and compounds)
volver	*vuelto*	returned (and compounds)

QUICK ⬛ PAINLESS

You learned "*Quiero +* INFINITIVE" before to say "I want to (whatever)." Now, learn the verb *necesitar*. It means "to need" and is completely regular. Use it the same way as "*querer +* INFINITIVE" to say that you need to so something: *Necesito comprar pan* = "I need to buy bread"; *Necesitamos viajar a Colombia* = "We need to travel to Colombia." You can express most of your needs directly and simply using this form.

Some of these verbs can be found as part of other verbs. For example, the verb *volver* means "to come back." The verb *devolver* means "to give something back." It's a different verb, but as you can see, it has *volver* in it, so it acts like *volver*.

Lazy Practice

Follow the patterns in the examples and create some sentences to help you practice this *haber* + PAST PARTICIPLE construction. Use the word lists and the examples as your guide. Confirm any new verbs in your dictionary to make sure they form regular past participles. Unless the verb looks like one of the verbs in the irregular past participle list, it's most likely regular. *¡Buena suerte!*

ADVERBS

Adverbs modify verbs, adjectives, or other adverbs. English words that end in *–ly* such as "quickly," "happily," and "unfortunately" are adverbs. Other adverbs are shorter, such as "right" and "well." Spanish adverbs work in a similar way. Some are formed by adding an ending to an adjective, while many of the more common adjectives are simply short little words with no special ending. Unlike adjectives, Spanish adverbs do not take *-a* or *–o* as endings, and are NEVER affected by gender, even when they modify an adjective which is gender-specific.

The equivalent ending for "-ly" in Spanish is *-mente.* Spanish adverbs can be formed by adding *–mente* to the feminine form of the adjective. If the adjective is

YOU'LL THANK YOURSELF LATER

Although the present indicative is mainly for the here and now, it's also used as a future-like tense. It suggests what you are willing to do later. To use this correctly you should state a future time: *Hablo con él mañana* = "I'll talk with him tomorrow" (I'm willing to talk ...) and *Salgo más tarde* = "I'll leave later on." More on the future tenses in a future chapter.

IF YOU'RE SO
INCLINED

Check out these cool Web sites to work on your verbs and adverbs: ilisa.com/adverbs.htm and www.studyspanish. com/tutorial.htm.

invariable and ends in –e or with a consonant, –mente may be added:

rápido (fast)	*rápida*	*rápidamente* = quickly
honesto (honest)	*honesta*	*honestamente* = honestly
básico (basic)	*básica*	*básicamente* = basically
natural (natural)		*naturalmente* = naturally
urgente (urgent)		*urgentemente* = urgently

It's good to know about the –mente ending, but you'll find that most of the common adverbs you'll use on a daily basis won't need –mente. Some adjectives can't take –mente at all to make an adverb. Adjectives denoting physical appearance, origin, nationality, and religion do not take –mente.

Here are some common "non –mente" adverbs. A few are also adjectives:

bien	well	*hablar bien* = speak well
más	more	*más facil* = easier
menos	less	*menos facil* = less easy
mejor	better	*hablar mejor* = speak better

peor	worse	*cantar peor* = sing worse
mal	poorly	*hablar mal* = speak poorly
jamás	never ever	*hablar jamás* = never speak
nunca	never	*nunca cantar* = never sing
casi	almost	*casi hecho* = almost done
muy	very	*muy facil* = very easy
siempre	always	*siempre habla* = always talks
también	also	*también canta* = sings, too
tampoco	either	*no hay tampoco* = (see sidebar)
tan	so	*tan dificil* = so difficult
tanto	so much	*hablar tanto* = talk so much
todavía	still	*todavía está* = still here
ya	already, now	*ya está* = (see sidebar)

QUICK ⬤ PAINLESS

The adverb *tampoco* is the negative form of *también*. Since *también* means "also," *tampoco* means "not also" or "either": *No hablo el francés, y tampoco no hablo el alemán* = "I don't speak French, and I don't speak German, either." Don't say "también no." *Ya* means "already." It can also mean "now." When used with "no," it means "anymore": *Ya no toco el violín* = "I don't play the violin anymore."

Here are a few examples (you'll also see more adverbs in future chapters):

Es muy difícil leer el chino.	It is very difficult to read Chinese.
Tampoco no es fácil pronunciar el chino.	It's not easy to pronounce Chinese, either.
Mi suegra todavía está aquí con nosotros.	My mother-in-law is still here with us.
El bebé siempre llora.	The baby always cries.
El rey es tan rico.	The king is so rich.
Las montañas son tan grandes.	The mountains are so big.

The *con* + NOUN Construction

You can also use nouns adverbially using the word *con* ("with") plus a noun. I sometimes think of this as the "Night Before Xmas" construction, as in: "The stockings were hung by the chimney *with care*." Observe:

El profesor siempre lee el diario con cuidado.	The professor always reads the newspaper with care.
Vamos a esperar con paciencia.	We are going to wait patiently. (with patience)
Luis habla de su familia con mucho amor.	Luis speaks lovingly of his family. (with a lot of love)

ACTIVITY: YOUR FAVORITE

YOU'LL THANK YOURSELF LATER

Few *–mente* adverbs are false cognates: *Ultimamente* means "recently," not "ultimately"; *casualmente* means "by chance," not "casually"; and *eventualmente* means "possibly," not "eventually."

ACTIVITIES?

Make a list of your top ten favorite activites. Then look up the verbs in your dictionary and conjugate them. Don't worry if they aren't regular verbs, just do the best you can. See if your dictionary gives you any hints as to how these should be conjugated.

Making Sense of Sentences: Putting It All Together

Now that you've got a handle on the basics, you're ready to start building more complex sentences. In this chapter, you'll learn important and useful grammatical structures, and really begin to unlock the secrets of the Spanish language. You'll be linking complicated ideas together in no time. So hold on to your *sombrero,* 'cause here we go … *¡Adelante!*

THE VERB *IR*

To get you going, let's start with the verb *ir,* which means "to go." It's pronounced like those things on your head that you hear with. Take a look at its conjugation in the present indicative tense:

yo	*voy*	I go
tú	*vas*	you go

él/ella/usted	*va*	he/she/you/it goes
nosotros/nosotras	*vamos*	we go
ellos/ellas/ustedes	*van*	they/"you all" go

Take a look at the following examples. They'll demonstrate some of the principal uses of this versatile little verb. I recommend that you also consult your dictionary (or a larger Spanish/English dictionary at the library) under *ir* for even more examples:

Voy a las montañas.	I'm going to the mountains.
Vamos al centro.	We're going (Let's go) downtown.
El camino va por la costa.	The road goes along the coast.
La cerveza no va bien con el helado.	Beer and ice cream don't go well together.
Los turistas van en el autobus.	The tourists go on the bus.

You may already have heard of *¡Vamos!* It can mean both "we go" and "let's go," depending on the context.

Lazy Practice

Think of some places that you and/or your friends would like to go. Make your own sentences using *ir* + *a* + PLACE. Remember that you can also use *querer* + *ir* + *a* + PLACE (*Quiero ir a la tienda* = "I want to go to the store."); *necesitar* + *ir* + *a* + PLACE (*Necesitamos ir al aeropuerto* = "We need to go to the airport."); and *tener que* + *ir* +

a + PLACE (*Mi niño tiene que ir a la escuela* = "My son has to go to school.").

Have fun with this. Incorporate other things that you've learned: *Vamos con el vecino al restaurante más grande de la ciudad.* You have more tools to work with than you may realize.

The Future Tense with *ir* + *a* + INFINITIVE

If you put an infinitive verb after the *a*, you can express a future idea—very much like the English "I'm going to X." This form of the future tense is very common in daily speech, and should come somewhat naturally to you, since it follows the same pattern as English. Look at these:

Voy a viajar mañana.	I'm going to travel tomorrow.
Vamos a ver.	Let's see.
Vamos a ver una película.	We're going to see (Let's go see) a movie.
¿Vas a pagar la cuenta?	Are you going to pay the bill?
No va a poder ir.	He/she will not be able to go.
Vamos a querer salir temprano.	We are going to want to leave early.
Van a vivir en Bolivia por muchos años.	They are going to live in Bolivia for many years.
Vas a tener que comprar una nueva casa.	You're going to have to buy a new house.

YOU'LL THANK YOURSELF LATER

You met the other Spanish contraction *del* in the last chapter. The contraction *al* is used for *a* + *el*. You must use *al* for "to the + *masc. singular noun*" unless the *el* is part of a proper name or the third person singular *él* as in "he/him/it." So, for "Let's go to the park," you would say *"Vamos al parque,"* not *"Vamos a el parque."*

Jorge va a necesitar hablar con usted.	Jorge will need to talk to (with) you.
Van a construir un nuevo puente aquí.	They are going to build a new bridge here.

When *ir* + *a* + INFINITIVE itself is the object of a verb (more on objects later), it translates as "in order to":

Quiero ir a jugar al fútbol.(jugar a = "to play 'X' GAME")	I want to go and play soccer. ("in order to play")
Piensan ir a conocer el lugar.	They are thinking of going and getting to know the place.
No puedo ir a ver el show mañana.	I can't go and see the show tomorrow.

Lazy Practice

Take some of the infinitives that you already know (or look up new ones) and express them in the future by following the previous *ir* + *a* + INFINITIVE examples. Be sure to vary the person/s who will be doing these things.

SER VS. ESTAR

You'll find it difficult to make a lot of meaningful sentences without the verb "to be." In Spanish, there are two verbs which we translate as "to be" in English: *ser* and *estar*. Each has its own special uses. This phenomenon often causes confusion for English speakers. But you'll do fine if you follow these tips.

YOU'LL THANK YOURSELF LATER

The verbs *ser, estar, ir,* and *dar* (to give) have an *–oy* ending in the first person singular: *Yo soy, estoy, voy, doy.* Since these verbs are so short, it was probably a good idea to give them a slightly longer ending in the *yo* form. Otherwise they would have been *"so," "esto," "vo,"* and *"do."*

Conjugation of *Ser* and *Estar*

Ser and *estar* are both "irregular" verbs. In reality, *estar* is only irregular in the first person. *Ser*, however, is its own animal.

So far, so good!

Ser and *Estar* With Nouns

Ser is used to indicate where nouns come from, their relation to one another, and the groups to which they belong. *Ser* describes who owns a noun or what it's made

Ser:

yo	soy	I am
tú	eres	you are
él/ella/usted	es	he/she/it is
nosotros/nosotras	somos	we are
ellos/ellas/ustedes	son	they/"you all" are

Estar:

yo	estoy	I am
tú	estás	you are
él/ella/usted	está	he/she/you/it is
nosotros/nosotras	estamos	we are
ellos/ellas/ustedes	están	they/"you all" are

IF YOU'RE SO
INCLINED

To help you remember the uses of *ser*, learn "PONMORR" or *"People On Neptune Must Often Rent Robots"*: Profession, Origin, Nationality, Material, Ownership, Relationship, Religion.

of. *Ser* usually speaks to a quality that is unchanging, static, and at least semi-permanent:

Profession:	*Mi padre es ingeniero.*	My father is an engineer.
Origin:	*Soy de México.*	I am from Mexico.
Nationality:	*Mi mamá es colombiana.*	My mother is Colombian.
Material:	*La casa es de madera y ladrillo.*	The house is made from wood and brick.
Ownership:	*El libro es de Juan.*	The book is Juan's.
Relationship:	*Ellos son mis nietos.*	They are my grandchildren.
Religion:	*Jorge es católico.*	Jorge is Catholic.

When used with nouns, the verb *estar* is mostly used with location and position:

Location:	*Yo siempre estoy en casa.*	I am always at home.
	El libro todavía está en mi cuarto.	The book is still in my room.
	El Museo del Prado está en Madrid.	The Prado is (located in) Madrid.
Position:	*Está al lado de la puerta.*	It is next to the door.
	Ya estamos cerca del hotel.	We are already near the hotel.

Lazy Practice

Create a list of sentences that will help you to practice using *ser* and *estar* with nouns. For *ser,* follow the information you just read and use the examples as your guide. Avoid adjectives that do not fall into the categories of PONMORR.

For *estar,* practice saying where people, places, and things are located. Since we haven't really covered prepositions yet, you may find yourself somewhat limited here. Don't be afraid to use your dictionary. When in doubt, just say that things are *aquí* (here) or *ahí* (there).

Ser and *Estar* With Adjectives

Ser is used to express characteristics that are not expected to change any time soon. Use *ser* to be objective about the state or appearance of something. *Ser* is used to define things at their core.

Estar, on the other hand, is used to indicate more temporary characteristics or situations (how things are at the present time). Use *estar* when you want to express a more subjective opinion about something. *Estar* is used more for descriptions than for definitions. Read the following examples carefully:

Soy guapo.	I am good-looking.	(Always have been. Not just now. Handsome to the bone.)
Estoy guapo.	I am (looking) good.	I may have the face of a pit bull, but *today* I look faaaantastic!

YOU'LL THANK YOURSELF LATER

> Although you'll almost always use *estar* to indicate where someone or something is located, *ser* can be used for the location of an event: *Entonces, hombre. ¿Dónde es la fiesta?* ("So, dude. Where's the party?")

QUICK PAINLESS

You already know *es*. It comes from *ser* and means "is." And you have also seen *estar* in *está aquí*. Learn these again here.

María es loca.	Maria is crazy.	She suffers from a mental disorder or condition and may need to be institutionalized.
María está loca	María is (acting) crazy.	She's behaving strange at this moment, but usually she's got both feet on the ground.
Ellos son pobres.	They are (really) poor.	They are permanently without money and are expected to remain so.
Juan está pobre.	Juan's broke.	He may actually be wealthy, but last week in Vegas he lost a lot of *dinero* in the slot machines. Better luck next time.
Miguel es gordo.	Miguel is fat.	Miguel is a large man. He has always been that way, and is expected to remain so.

Miguel está gordo. Miguel is (looking) fat. He has been eating too much lately and has developed a paunch. He'll probably go back to normal after the holidays.

Take another look at the last two examples. Let's say that Miguel is tired of everyone saying *"Miguel es gordo."* So he goes on a diet. Once he is visibly thinner, people will start saying *"Miguel está delgado,"* "Miguel is (looking) thin." This means that although he usually isn't thin, he appears so now. He might gain the weight back in the near future. But if he remains thin for an extended period, sooner or later people will start saying *"Miguel es delgado"* ("Miguel is a thin man"). The change from *estar* to *ser* indicates that people no longer think of him as *gordo.*

Ser and *Estar* With the Past Participle

For *ser,* the same rules apply to past participles as for all other adjectives. You can use *ser* if the past participle describes some permanent characteristic. At this stage, you won't find yourself using *ser* with past participles very often (return to the previous chapter if you need to review what past participles are):

Julio es un hombre . Julio is a well-known
bien conocido man.
(from the verb conocer = "to know a person")

Now and then you'll come across an expression that doesn't quite follow the rules. For example, *Juan está muerto* means "Juan is dead," even though most people consider death to be rather permanent. Sometimes both *ser* and *estar* can be used to express the same concept. For example, the Spanish word for "married" is *casado/a.* You can say *Estoy casado/a* or *Soy casado/a.* It makes no difference.

Ser + PAST PARTICIPLE can also be used in a passive construction to describe an action or event: *Es comprado por los turistas* = "It is bought by tourists"; *Es sabido por todos* = "It is known by everyone." You'll eventually want to use this construction, but it's rarely used in conversation. You'll learn a more common way to form passives later on.

You'll be using *estar* with past participles all the time. In the last chapter you used *haber* to say "who" or "what" did an action, as in: *El dueño ha cerrado la tienda* = "The owner has closed the store." Now you can use *estar* to describe the condition of a noun (in this case, a store), without considering who made it that way: *La tienda está cerrada* = "The store is closed."

El mercado está abierto, pero las tiendas están cerradas.	The market is open, but the stores are closed.
Estoy perdido. (*perder* = "to lose")	I'm lost.
Estamos perdidos.	We're lost.
El agua está purificada. (*purificar* = "to purify")	The water is purified. (remember: agua is f. but takes *el*)
El teléfono está roto. (not *"rompido"*)	The telephone is broken.
Ellas están muy preocupadas. (preocupar = "to be worried")	They (women) are very worried.

Lazy Practice

Go back to Chapter 9 and review the section on past participles. Look at the irregular ones, too. Now practice using *estar* to describe various nouns. Use the previous examples as your guide.

OBJECTS AND OBJECT PRONOUNS

I know that "object pronoun" might sound a bit too much like high school grammar for your tastes, but I figured that I'd better tell what these things are called in case you need to look them up in a textbook some day. In order to speak Spanish effectively, you must dominate, control, manipulate, and otherwise have complete hegemony over the object pronouns. There's no way around it.

But don't get stressed out just yet. These guys really aren't that bad. You use all sorts of objects and object pronouns every day when you speak English. No need to lose sleep over them in Spanish. Here's the deal ....

Transitive and Intransitive Verbs

First we need to talk about verbs again. Basically, there are two kinds: those that pass on their action to something else and those that seem to just sit there. For example, in the sentence "I throw a stone," the verb "to throw" requires that I throw *something*. I can't just "throw." The "stone" is the object of my throwing. This kind of verb is called a transitive verb. So, the "stone," being the thing thrown, is the "direct object" of this verb.

Here are few more examples of *direct objects* with transitive verbs:

- I see *Hermann*.

- Diane is learning *Spanish*.

- Glenn answered *the telephone*.

Past participles used with *haber* are always left in the masculine form, even if the person doing the action is a woman, or the object noun is feminine: *Ella ha enviado la carta* = "She has sent the letter." But with *estar* we are focused on description, so the past participle must agree in gender and number with the noun being modified. Remember, past participles are merely adjectives derived from verbs.

- Lillian sent *an e-mail.*

- Karin got *the job.*

- Issac said *no.*

- Nicholas eats *paste.*

- The dog bit *the man.*

- The man bit *the dog.*

Verbs that don't or can't take a direct object are called "intransitive." They pretty much just "are":

- "I *think,* therefore I *am.*" (Descartes)

- Problems *exist.*

- The story *evolved.*

- The telephone *rang.*

- The dog *sat* near the door.

- He *waited* patiently.

Most verbs can be used both transitively and intransitively, depending on whether they are taking an object or not:

Intransitive	Transitive
Peggy eats every two hours.	Peggy eats *cake* every two hours.
Our baby weighs nine pounds.	The butcher weighs *meat* on a scale.
The bell rang.	Peter rang *the bell.*

Sometimes the direct object of a transitive verb is not actually in the sentence, but merely understood. For example, in the sentence "He threw from the infield," the object of his throwing is still a baseball, even though the baseball is not mentioned. The verb is still transitive. However, "He throws with his left arm" is intransitive, because there is no direct object.

The Direct Object Pronoun (DOP)

The Spanish object pronouns are not the same as the subject pronouns you learned when conjugating verbs (*yo, tú, él, ella,* etc.). But they do perform a similar function in that they also stand in for nouns so that you don't have to keep repeating the nouns ("them"—I could have said "them" here!). To use the direct object pronouns, or DOP for short, the noun for which the pronoun is substituting must be the direct object of a transitive verb. In other words, to avoid always having to re-state the object of the verb, we use the DOP.

In English the DOPs are "me," "you," "it," "him," "her," "us," and "them." Look at these examples:

- He hit *me.*
- I love *you.*
- We eat *it.*
- The dog bit *him* and *her.*
- They hate *us.*
- We saw *them.*

Naturally, you'll need to do the same thing in Spanish. Here are the words you'll need:

me	me	(sounds like "May")
te	you	
lo/la	him/her/you	(must match gender)
nos	us	
los/las	them/you all	(must match gender)

IF YOU'RE SO INCLINED

Grab a book or newspaper (in English) and practice looking for direct objects.

So Where Do I Put That &*%^&@! DOP?

The direct object (I mean the real noun, *not* the pronoun) of a transitive Spanish verb usually ends up in the same place that it does in an English sentence (*Yo compro pan* = "I buy bread").

However, when a Spanish direct object *pronoun* is used with a *conjugated* transitive verb, it must come **before** the verb, not after it. Let me say that again: When a Spanish direct object *pronoun* is used with a *conjugated* transitive verb, it must come **before** the verb, not after it.

This can be tricky for English speakers because this structure is vastly different from what we're accustomed to. In English, we say "I see you." In Spanish, it's "I *you* see." So, to substitute a pronoun for "bread," I need to put it before the conjugated verb: Yo *lo* compro ("I *it* buy") = "I buy it." The *lo* stands in for "bread." We need *lo* (and not *la*) because "bread" is masculine. If it had been *Yo compro harina* ("I buy flour"), then it would have been *Yo la compro.*

Remember that a third person noun must already have been stated or be understood. Otherwise, no one will know what the "it" stands for:

"Cristina, te amo."	"Cristina, I love you."
"¿Habla usted el español?"	"Do you speak Spanish?"
"Sí, lo hablo."	"Yes, I speak it."
"¿Quién tiene la pelota?"	"Who has the ball?"

"Yo la tengo."	*"I have it."*	
"¿Ves las montañas?"	"Do you see the mountains?"	
"No, no las veo."	"No, I don't see them."	
"¿Sabe usted la letra del himno nacional?" (saber = "to know")	"Do you know the words to the national anthem?"	
"No, en realidad, no la sé."	"No, actually, I don't."	

A DOP, when used as the object of an unconjugated *infinitive* (the only kind there is), may be placed at the end of the infinitive verb. It may also be placed before a conjugated verb, if the infinitive is the object of that verb. There's no change in meaning between these two forms. Only the placement of the DOP has changed. These examples will show you what I mean:

Puedo *verte.*	*Te puedo ver.*	I can see you.
¿Quieres *verme?*	*¿Me quieres ver?*	Do you want to see me?
Necesitamos *pagarlo* ahora.	*Lo necesitamos pagar ahora.*	We need to pay it now.
Ella quiere *llamarnos.*	*Ella nos quiere llamar.*	She wants to call us.
Vamos a *hacerlo* mañana.	*Lo vamos a hacer mañana.*	We'll do it tomorrow.
No puedo *entenderla.*	*No la puedo entender.*	I can't understand her.
Tienes que *decirlos* ahora.	*Los tienes que decir ahora.*	You must say them now.

Don't expect to understand everything the first time you read it. Some of these structures are quite alien to your English ear. My suggestion: Read through the entire chapter once, then take a break. Come back to it a little later and review the material section by section. Eventually, it *will* all make sense.

The Lazy Way

¿No vas a besarme?	*¿No me vas a besar?*	Aren't you going to kiss me?
Vamos a querer *leerlo* hoy.	*Lo vamos a querer leer hoy.*	We're going to want to read it today.
No van a poder *oírnos.*	*No nos van a poder oír.*	They aren't going to be able to hear us.

Lazy Practice

Create sentences that will help you practice your DOP, using the examples as your guide. Start with the same words that you find in the examples, changing the person of the verb, and the gender and number of the nouns. Go between Spanish and English. Add new words if you want. If you create a sentence that you can't translate, write it down and come back to it after re-reading the chapter.

Indirect Objects and the Indirect Object Pronoun (INDOP)

The indirect object is the final destination of a transitive verb's direct object. It isn't *what* is given, but *who* gets it: "to whom." For example, in the sentence "Jane gave John her phone number," the object is "her phone number" and "John" is the indirect object because he was the recipient of her giving. In the sentence "I throw stones at my neighbor's house," the object is "stones," and the indirect object is "my neighbor's house."

The best way to explain indirect objects is by example. The indirect objects in the following sentences are *italicized:*

- I gave the ball to *Frank.*
- I gave *Frank* the ball.
- He told *Craig* the story.
- We sold *Thomas* a boat.
- We sold a boat to *Thomas.*
- Congress will send *the president* a bill.
- The police gave *Richard* a hard time.

Notice that the placement of the indirect object in English can vary from sentence to sentence. If it's at the end, you'll need to put a "to" there to indicate that what follows is the indirect object: "to Walter."

The Spanish indirect object pronoun (INDOP for short) looks practically the same as the DOP. In fact, the only difference between them is in the third person. The good news is that these guys are not gender-specific—only *person*-specific:

me	to me
te	to you
le	to him/her/you
nos	to us
les	to them/to you all

QUICK ⬤ PAINLESS

When the direct object of a verb is a defined person or pet, "a" must come before it: *Veo a Juan* ("I see Juan"); *Amo a mi perro Fido* ("I love my dog Fido"); but *Veo el avión* ("I see the airplane"). Remembering to use the personal "a" can be hard at first, but it will come naturally with time. Just remember, "a" goes with the people and animals you know when they are objects.

Note that the INDOP can also indicate "for someone," not just "to someone." In the last example, (*¿Me puedes hacer un favor?*), the idea is "Can you do a favor for me" rather that "Can you do a favor *to* me."

Study the following examples:

María nunca le dice la verdad.	Maria never tells him the truth.
Les doy mi número de teléfono.	I'll give them my phone number. (could also be to "you all")
¿Me vas a dar un beso o no? (also: *¿Vas a darme … ?*)	Are you going to give me a kiss or not?
Ellos no pueden darnos mucha información. (*nos puedan dar*)	They can't give us a lot of information.
¿Quiere usted venderme el coche?	Do you want to sell me the car?
Te compro una nueva mochila.	I'll buy you a new backpack.
¿Me puedes hacer un favor? (*puedes hacerme … *)	Can you do me a favor?

Getting the DOP and the INDOP Together

Except for third person combinations, putting the DOP and INDOP together is easy. The INDOP always comes first. And, as before, you have some choices as to where they go. If there's an infinitive, you may stick the two together at the end. If there is a conjugated verb only, the INDOP and DOP must go first.

When placed before a conjugated verb, the INDOP and DOP are written separately: *te lo, me los,* etc. But if they are placed at the end of an infinitive, they are written together.

Remember, it's the verb that indicates *who* is doing the action. You must pay close attention to the verb, because the *yo, tú, él* part may not be there. In other words, the verb indicates "who" is doing, "what" they're doing, and "when" they are doing it. The DOP indicates the "object" of their doing, and the INDOP indicates "who" or "what" is receiving that object.

Me lo dan.	They give it to me.
Te lo digo.	I'll tell it to you.
Nos la compran.	They buy it for us.
Te las mando. (*mandar* = "to send"; "to order")	I'll send them to you.
Me los van a dar mañana.	They're going to give them to me tomorrow.
Puede decírtelos. (áccent márks will appear when an INDOP and DOP are attached to an infinitive)	He/She can tell you them.
Te lo voy a comprar un día. (also: *Voy a comprártelo…*)	I'm going to buy it for you one day.

Third Person DOP Meets Third Person INDOP

You're probably thinking that if you put the third person DOP and the third person INDOP together you'd get *"lelo," "lela," "leslo," "lesla,"* and *"leslos."* And you're also no doubt thinking that the following examples should be entirely correct: *"dárlelo"; "decírlela"; "comprárlesla"; "comprarlelos"; "le los compro"* ("I buy them

As you can see from the examples, the INDOP comes first, then the DOP. When attached to an infinitive, the INDOP and DOP are stuck together, and áccent márks will appear to maintain accurate stress.

Make up some sentences. Choose a subject, a transitive verb, an object, and an indirect object to receive the object of the verb: "**SOMEBODY + Verb + INDIRECT OBJECT + DIRECT OBJECT**" or "**SOMEBODY + Verb + DIRECT OBJECT + "to" + INDIRECT OBJECT**": "I give Walter the money" or "I give the money to Walter."

for him/her/you"); *"les las doy"* ("I give them to them"), etc. Seems logical to me, too. Unfortunately, all of these examples are WRONG.

Whenever a third person DOP and a third person INDOP are put together in an sentence, whether the objects are singular or plural, the INDOP always turns into *"se,"* not *"le"* or *"les."* For example, when you want to say "give it to him" = *dar + le* (or *les*) + *lo* (or *la, los, las*), the *le* or *les* needs to be replaced by *se*.

So, in the sentence *Se lo doy,* the little word *se* is standing in for *le,* which is standing in for "to a person we know." The *lo* indicates that the thing given is a singular masculine noun, and the *doy* indicates "I give."

Here are more examples:

Se las mando.	I'll send them to him/her/*usted.*
Se los van a dar mañana.	They're going to give them to him/her/*usted* tomorrow.
Puede decírselos.	He/She can tell him/her/*usted* them.
Se lo voy a comprar un día. (also: *Voy a comprárselo ...*)	I'm going to buy it for him/her/*usted* one day.

But Can't This Get a Bit Confusing?

Yes, sometimes it can. Usually the context makes things clear what noun the INDOP is referring to. Gender won't be a problem with the DOP, but it can be with the INDOP, since *le* can mean to "him," "her," "it," or *"usted."* Same thing with the plurals. Also, since *se* stands in for *le* and *les,* ambiguity may result, since it may not be clear whether the *se* is singular or plural, or if it refers to a man or a woman or both.

Whenever the possibility for confusion exists, or when you wish to emphasize just who is actually involved, you can clarify the object by adding *"a"* plus the person, persons, or things:

a él	to him
a ella	to her
a usted	to you sir/madam
a ellos	to them
a ellas	to them (women)
a ustedes	to "you all"
al señor	to the gentleman
a la organización	to the organization

and so on ...

This *"a"* is similar to the personal *"a"* I mentioned earlier. It's called the dative *"a."* But don't worry about its name. Just use it.

Se lo voy a decir a él.	I'm going to tell it to him.
Ya se lo he dado a Juan.	I've already given it to Juan.
Le doy a María un peso.	I give Maria a peso.
María nunca le dice la verdad a Hector.	Maria never tells Hector the truth.

A COMPLETE WASTE OF TIME

The 3 Worst Things to Do When Making Sentences:

1. Say *"lelo,"* *"leslos,"* etc. Just saying it feels funny. Always remember to use *se* for the INDOP when you mean "to a third person."

2. Use forms of *ser* to say where things are. It's hard to remember, but location (except for events) always needs *estar.*

3. Think of *ir* as an ending without a verb. *Ir* is its own animal. You'll use it all the time, so it's best just to learn it as a special case.

| *Te lo he escrito mil veces.* | I have written it to you a thousand times. |
| *¿Nos lo va a decir a nosotros?* | Is he/she going to say that **to us**? (emphasis) |

Lazy Practice

Create sentences that will help you to practice the third person INDOP + the third person DOP. Remember to use *se*. Use the examples as your guide. You have the vocabulary (and the dictionary) to do this for hours if you want. But 15 minutes will suffice the first time.

ACTIVITY: MAGAZINE OR NEWSPAPER

I know that you already have a few texts in Spanish. Now, see if you can find a Spanish magazine or newspaper. If you live in a city with a large Hispanic population, this should be relatively easy. If not, check an out-of-town newsstand or your local or college library.

The Internet is one of the best sources for Spanish. Visit **www.el-castellano.com** or do a search for "Spanish" or "Español" and you'll have more than you need. Start reading these texts and see how much you can understand. Keep your dictionary handy. And don't worry if you see things that you don't recognize. There's much more Spanish to come.

Chapter eleven

La Buena Cultura: Poise and Politeness for All Occasions

Spanish speakers use many more formal expressions in their daily conversations than you're probably used to. While these phrases may seem overly ceremonious to you at first, you'll eventually find yourself using them all the time. It's hard to be too formal in Spanish, at least when meeting people for the first time. Even if your Spanish is far from perfect, you'll quickly see that by using a few well-placed courteous phrases, you will almost always be able to break the ice.

THE ART OF *CORTESÍA*

Spanish speakers will always appreciate your efforts to be courteous and respectful when you talk to them. Far too many English-speaking tourists and business people have stuck their foot deep in their mouth by inadvertently saying something inappropriate, or by omitting a much-needed courtesy. This

There's actually a verb that means "to use *tú* with someone." The verb is *tutear.* If someone says "*Me puede tutear,*" it means that you can call him or her *tú* if you wish. No, there's no verb "*ustedear,*" except perhaps as a joke.

section has been included here to help you avoid such foot-swallowing.

Usted vs. *Tú*

As you've already noticed, you have a choice between two pronouns and verb forms when addressing people: *usted* and *tú.*

In very general terms, *usted* is used with strangers, superiors, and with people for whom you wish to show added respect. *Tú* is used for friends, family members, young children, and for one's peers. While *tú* is not in itself disrespectful, it must be used appropriately.

¿Cómo está usted?	How are you? (polite)
¿Cómo estás tú?	How are you? (familiar)

Usted is almost always appropriate when meeting someone for the first time. However, it may also be used with people whom you have known for years. For example, my dentist lives in Mexico. I've been hopping across the border for dental appointments with him for nearly ten years. He calls me Steven and I call him Raúl. Nonetheless, we always use *usted* with each other. Why? Because even though our interaction is relatively friendly and relaxed, ours is still a professional relationship. I'm his client, and he's my healthcare practitioner. He respects me as his patient by using *usted* and I respect him as a professional by using *usted* back. If we were to start using *tú,* there would be a palpable change in the nature of our relationship from that of a professional one to one of equal friends. If someday he is no longer my dentist, then perhaps we might consider using *tú*. But maybe not.

Tú is used when:

- Speaking to a child
- When you are a child and you're talking to friends
- Speaking to a family member (most of the time)
- Praying (supreme beings are addressed as *tú*)
- Speaking to a fellow student
- You and the other person have openly agreed to use *tú*
- Someone insists that you use *tú* with them

Except when addressing children and fellow students (if you happen to be a student yourself), you should begin your conversations with *usted* and the third person singular verb form that goes with *usted*. Unless you have a clear reason for not addressing someone as *usted*, you may risk unintentionally insulting people with *tú*.

If you inadvertently start off with *usted* when the situation would have allowed for *tú*, you'll be kindly instructed to use *tú*. As a non-native speaker, it's unlikely that any offense will be taken. However, it's a lot harder to backpedal once you've used *tú* with someone to whom you should have said *usted* from the very beginning.

Now that I've covered the "textbook" uses of *usted* and *tú*, I must tell you that the ways in which *usted* and *tú* are used in practice can vary considerably from place to place. In parts of Central America, you may hear people using *tú* (or *vos*—see sidebar) and *usted* in the same

QUICK ⬤ PAINLESS

In parts of Latin America, there's another word for *tú*. In Argentina, Uruguay, most of Central America, highland Ecuador, and a few other places, people say "vos." *Vos* is an old form for "you" that disappeared from most Spanish, just as "thou" faded away in English. The *vos* form of the verb is slightly different from the *tú* form. If you're in a country where folks say *vos*, you'll pick it up quickly. Just use *tú* until you do and you'll be fine.

sentence with the very same person (*usted* can sometimes be used simply to emphasize a point). You may hear Colombians using *usted* with their close friends and dogs, and Chileans using *usted* verb forms with their young children. On the other hand, in the Caribbean, *usted* is rarely used at all. Cubans and Puerto Ricans can be heard using *tú* with just about everybody all the time.

Nevertheless, in spite of the subtleties and regional preferences involved, it's still best to follow the general rules I've outlined until you're comfortable with the way the locals are using these forms of address. Stick with *usted* until you're sure that *tú* is appropriate.

Lazy Practice

Think about the people you know and whether you would use *tú* or *usted* with them. Then, go to the mall or some other public place and spend some time watching people pass by. Try to decide whether you would use *tú* or *usted* with them were you to be introduced.

Polite Phrases and Expressions

This section contains numerous courteous expressions that you should learn by heart. You'll do well by having these phrases ready to go whenever you meet someone. Though some may seem like an unnecessary formality, I promise that these expressions won't affect the spontaneity of your conversations. On the contrary, they'll actually help you to break through any barriers so that you can truly start communicating with people.

Things to Say When Being Introduced

Here's a list of phrases you'll need to start your conversations:

Mucho gusto	Nice to meet you
Un placer	A pleasure
Encantado	Charmed (said by men)
Encantada	Charmed (said by women)
me da mucho gusto conocerlo/la (DOP matches gender of the person you meet)	Nice to meet you
El gusto es mío	The pleasure is mine
(Your name), a sus ordenes	"At your service"
(Your name), para servirle/la	"At your service"

The last two phrases are usually used by men only. *Encantado* (said if you're a man) and *encantada* (if a woman) are also quite popular. *El gusto es mío* is a good response if someone says *mucho gusto* to you first. Be careful not to respond with *"Sí"* to *el gusto es mío* (I've heard this!), which would mean "Yes, the pleasure *is* all yours, I'm sure."

Remember that the gender-specific ending of encantado/a must match your gender, not the person whom you are addressing (encantar = "to enchant"). If a man says "encantada" to a woman, he would be saying "You must be very enchanted to meet me, handsome devil

QUICK ⬤ PAINLESS

that I am … " (probably not the best way to make a good first impression, guys).

Polite Forms for Questions

When traveling, you'll often find that the reason you're approaching people is to ask them about something. Here's a list of courteous phrases you can use to ensure that you get the answers you need (see the next chapter for *podría* and *sería*). You can add these to the "hello" phrases that you learned in Part 2:

Polite Forms of Questions

Poder hacer el favor de + INFINITIVE
¿Me podría hacer el favor de decir la hora?

"To be able to do the favor of X"
Could you do me a favor and tell me what time it is?

Poder ayudar con ...
¿Me puede ayudar con esto, por favor?

"To be able to help with ... "
Can you help me with this, please?

***¿No le importa si+*
CONJUGATED VERB**

¿No le importa si cierro la ventana?

"Do you mind if I ... "

Would you mind if I close the window?

Poder decir una cosa ... ?
Disculpe, señora. ¿Me podría decir
una cosa? ¿A qué hora sale el tren?

"To be able to tell someone something"
Excuse me, madam. Could you tell me
something? At what time does the train leave?

No ser posible + INFINITIVE
Señor, ¿no sería posible
abrir la ventana un poco?

"Is it (not) possible to X"
Sir, would it be possible to open the window
just a bit?

Permitir hacer una pregunta
Señorita, ¿me permite hacerle

"To be allowed to ask a question"
Miss, may I ask you a question please?

Thank You and You're Welcome

You already know how to say "Thank you" and "No, thank you." Here are some more phrases to add right after you say *gracias:*

Gracias …

muy amable	(you are) very kind
por su ayuda	for your help
por su atención	for helping me
estoy muy agradecido/ a por su tiempo (*agradecer* = "to thank")	I'm very grateful for your time
espero que no haya sido molestia	I hope that it hasn't been too much trouble

When someone says *gracias* to you, you should respond with one of the following:

De nada	You're welcome
Por nada	You're welcome
A usted	Thank YOU
No hay de qué	Don't mention it
No faltaba más	"No need to thank me"
No se preocupe	Don't worry about it
A la orden	At your command (Carib.)
Para servirle	At your sevice
A usted por su cortesía	Thank YOU for your courtesy

The first two are rather common and not too formal, but they're fine for general use. Try using the more formal expressions now and then. Don't forget that you

YOU'LL THANK YOURSELF LATER

The verb *molestar* doesn't mean "to molest" in the way that this verb is usually used in English. It simply means "to bother" or "to cause inconvenience." Thus the expression *"No se moleste"* does not mean "Don't molest yourself," but rather, "Don't trouble yourself or create any unnecessary inconvenience in your life on my behalf."

Atender (*atiendo, atiendes*) doesn't mean to "attend" as in "to go to school." *Atender* means "to serve or help." If you enter a store and can't find anyone to help you, ask: *"¿Quién atiende aquí?"* for "Who's here to help the customers?" The noun *"atención"* can mean "attention" in the English sense, but it can also mean "help." The verb *asistir* is used for "to attend some event or institution."

can always add *"señor"* or *"señora"* to the end of such phrases to increase the level of courtesy: *No se preocupe, señora.*

When someone wishes something good for you (such as *buena suerte* = "good luck"), respond with:

Gracias, igualmente	Thanks, same to you
Que le vaya bien (also *les*)	Good luck (may it go well for you)
Gracias, muy amable	Thanks, (you're) very kind

The expression *Que le vaya bien* is especially popular in Mexico. It's said mostly to people who are going away. Don't say *Que les vaya bien* to people you're leaving behind, even if you do want to wish them well. (I've done this, and it has caused much laughter among the locals.)

Lazy Practice

Create more sentences following the previous examples and translate them into Spanish. Remember that these are "mix and match," not written in stone. By combining these phrases with the Spanish you've learned so far, you should be able to come up with some pretty good sentences. Underline anything that you can't figure out and come back to it after you've read the entire book.

Do whatever you need to do to learn these polite expressions before leaving on a trip. I guarantee you that they will be very useful to you during your travels.

IMPORTANT VERBS: *SABER* AND *GUSTAR*

Saber means "to know." Therefore, *you* should know *it.* It's regular in the present indicative tense except for the first person singular: *Yo sé* = "I know"; *Yo no sé* = "I don't know." The rest follows the regular pattern: *sabes, sabe, sabemos, saben.* Make sure that the áccent márk appears on *sé* to distinguish it from other *"se"* words.

The verb *saber* is **not** used for knowing people. If you say *"lo sé"* it will never mean "I know him," no matter how much you want it to. The verb *conocer* is used for knowing people (more on *conocer* later). *Saber* can be followed with an infinitive: *Yo no se jugar al golf* = "I don't know how to play golf." It is often followed by *que:*

Yo sé que es muy dificil.	I know that it's very hard.
Juan no sabe que la ópera puede ser tan bella.	Juan doesn't know that the opera can be so beautiful.
Ya sabemos que los turistas tienen mucho dinero.	We already know that tourists have a lot of money.
No saben nada de eso.	They don't know anything about that.

Now that you've learned the indirect object pronouns in Chapter 10, you're ready for *gustar.* Saying that you like something in Spanish works differently than it does in English. There is no verb "to like," as such. Rather, things give you pleasure or they don't. And the person doing the "liking" is actually the indirect object of *gustar*.

Gustar belongs to a small class of verbs that only takes the third person form when conjugated. Forms other than the third person are "not officially recognized." You can only say *gusta* and *gustan* (not *"yo gusto," "tú gustas," "nosotros gustamos,"* etc.). To make *gustar* work for you, you must pay close attention to who is receiving the pleasure from the thing giving it:

me gusta	I like (it)	It gives me pleasure
me gustan	I like (them)	They (those things) give me pleasure
te gusta	you like	It gives you pleasure
le gusta	he/she likes	It gives him/her …
nos gustan	we like (them)	They (those things) give us …
nos gusta	we like it	It gives us …
les gusta	they like	It gives them …
no me gusta	I don't like	It doesn't give me …
no les gustan	they don't like them	(etc.)

In addition to *gustar*, you can use the verb *encantar* ("to enchant") to say the same thing. *Encantar* is a bit stronger than *gustar*.

Me gusta el baile.	I like dancing.
Le gusta comprar cosas.	He/She likes to buy things.
Nos gustan las playas.	We like beaches.
¿Qué te pasa?	What's wrong with you?

You've heard "gusto" in English: "Bungie jumping takes a lot of gusto." In Spanish, it means "pleasure." Say *Me da (mucho) gusto* + INFINITIVE to say that you like something abstract, such as being somewhere, or knowing something: *Me da mucho gusto estar en su país* = "It gives me much pleasure to be in your country"; *Le da gusto a mi mamá saber que estamos bien* = "It makes my mother happy to know that we're OK."

¿No te gusta el helado?	Don't you like ice cream?
A mi tío le encanta viajar.	My uncle loves to travel.

HAY—IT AIN'T JUST FOR HORSES

The word *hay* (rhymes with "pie" and "sky") means "there is" or "there are." Technically it's a verb-form derived from *haber,* but unlike all other verbs, it doesn't change with respect to singular or plural. Use *hay* when you want to state that (or ask if) some thing or things exists. Once you know *hay,* you'll be all set:

Hay un problema aquí.	There is a problem here.
No, no hay problemas.	No, there are no problems.
Hay mucha gente en el mundo.	There are a lot of people in the world.
Señor, disculpe. ¿Hay agua? ¿Hay comida?	Excuse me, sir. Is there (do you have) any water? Food?
¡Hay un incendio en mi casa!	There is a fire in my house! (My house is on fire!)
Hay tres autobuses que van a la ciudad cada día.	There are three buses that go to the city every day.
Hay muchos hoteles y restaurantes en el pueblo.	There are many hotels and restaurants in the town.
Sí, no hay bananas.	Yes, we have no bananas.

Hay also works with *que* + INFINITIVE to say "we need to" or "one must" or "ya gotta." *Hay que* is more

A COMPLETE WASTE OF TIME

The 3 Worst Things to Do When Using *tú, saber,* and *gustar:*

1. Use *tú* unless you have a clear reason to do so.

2. Use *saber* for knowing people. Use the verb *conocer.*

3. Try conjugating *gustar* except in the third person. *"Yo gusto," "tú gustas,"* and so on are wrong.

general and less specific to a single person or persons than *tener que:*

¿Hay que pagar antes o después?	Do I/we have to pay before or after? (in general)
Hay que comer para vivir.	One must eat to live. ("Ya gotta eat to live")
Hay que tener paciencia.	We need to be patient. ("Ya gotta have patience")
Hay que trabajar para ganar dinero.	People need to work to earn money. ("Ya gotta work … ")
Bueno, si no hay que ir en autobús, vamos a pie.	Well, if it's not necessary to go by bus, let's go on foot.

Lazy Practice

Using the previous examples as your guide, practice using *hay.* Use it any time you want to say or ask if something exists. *Hay* even works with abstract nouns: *Hay consecuencias* = "There are consequences." While you practice asking questions with *hay,* don't forget to use your courteous question phrases.

DIALOGUE: JAMES AND JOSÉ

Here's a conversation that might take place in an airport, bus station, or on the street. Yes, the dialogue is a bit contrived, but it does illustrate several important points.

QUICK ☜☞ PAINLESS

Remember that *hay* means both "there is" and "there are." It may take you awhile to get used to using *hay* with plurals. In general, when *hay* is used with a singular noun the indefinite article is often required: *Hay un hombre aquí* "There is a man here." For plural nouns, the indefinite article may be left out: *¿Hay manzanas?* "Are there any apples?" However, you will find exceptions to these rules.

Notice how James and José pepper their conversation with courteous phrases (no, I couldn't fit all of the phrases in the previous lists into one dialogue). Notice the *le*, indicating the *usted* form of address.

Here are three ways to say "of course." They're good responses to a question when the answer is obviously going to be "yes": *Sí, cómo no; Sí, por supuesto; Sí, desde luego.* **The last one is used mostly in Spain.**

James:	Señor, buenos días.
José:	Buenos días. ¿En qué le puedo ayudar?
James:	Me llamo James Johnson. Soy de los Estados Unidos.
José:	Mucho gusto. Mi nombre es José Nuñez. Bienvenido a México.
James:	Gracias, el gusto es mío. Estoy muy feliz de estar en su país. Disculpe, ¿me permite hacerle una pregunta?
José:	Sí, cómo no …
James:	¿Me puede decir cuántos habitantes hay en México?
José:	Pues, no sé exactamente, pero somos muchos. Hay aproximadamente unos cien millones de habitantes en el país.
James:	¡Caramba! Hay mucha gente aquí. Gracias por la información. Usted es muy amable.
José:	No hay de qué. Oiga, ¿le gusta la comida mexicana?
James:	Sí, me encanta.
José:	¿Así? Eso está bien. A mí me gustan las hamburguesas. ¿Y adónde va ahora?
James:	Voy al hotel. Está en el centro. Hay que ir en taxi, ¿verdad?
José:	Sí, en taxi. Por aquí pasan cada tres minutos. Bueno, que le vaya bien.
James:	Gracias, igualmente.

You'll notice a different format for Chapters 11 to 18. In addition to the main topics discussed, each chapter will contain one or two dialogues, or a Spanish text. These texts are intended to give you a sense of how the language flows in "real-life" scenarios. Study them carefully, and don't be afraid to come up with similar scenarios for *lazy* practicing on your own.

The Lazy Way

Translation:

James: Good day, sir.

José: Hello. How can I help you?

James: My name is ("I call myself ... ") James Johnson. I'm from the United States.

José: Nice to meet you ("A lot of pleasure"). My name is José Nuñez. Welcome to Mexico.

James: Thanks. The pleasure is mine. I'm very happy ("It gives me a lot of pleasure") to be here in your country. Pardon me, may I ask you ("do you permit me to make to you ... ") a question?

José: Yes, of course ...

James: How many people ("inhabitants are there") are there in Mexico?

José: Well, I don't know exactly, but there are a lot of us (we are many). There are approximately 100 million people in our country.

James: Wow! There's a lot of people here. Thank you for the information. You are very kind.

José: Don't mention it. So, ("hey"; "listen") do you like Mexican food?

James: Yes, I like it very much ("it enchants me").

José: Is that right? That's good. I really like hamburgers. So, where are you going now?

James: I'm going to my (the) hotel. It's downtown. I need ("one needs") to go by taxi, right?

José: Yes, by taxi. They pass by every three minutes. Well, good luck.

James Thanks, same to you ("equally").

ACTIVITY: IT HAPPENED ONE DAY ...

A few years ago, during an overland trip through Central America, I found myself in a less-than-savory part of a downtown market. I had just approached a fruit stand when a burly young man appeared from behind me and tapped my shoulder. He looked to be about two years my junior. But since I wasn't exactly sure what he wanted from me, I figured it would be best to err on the side of caution and address him by *usted.*

"*Buenos días señor. ¿Cómo está usted?*" I said, figuring that the conversation would probably not go beyond the requisite "*Muy bien, gracias.*" To my surprise, he responded in English.

"OK. You are tourist?" He gazed at me steadily, trying to determine if I could understand what he had said.

"*Sí,*" I replied.

"OK," he responded. As I looked around, I could see that the attention of the people nearby had shifted toward the two of us, and I could sense the approach of several other youths. "Mister," he continued, "Did you come here to die?"

My heart leaped to my throat. As the other young men continued to move in, my fight-or-flight response (I'm rather partial to flight) began to kick in. The only words I could muster were a dry "*Oh no señor, disculpe, por favor ... *"

As I was struggling to talk my way out of the situation, the young man reached down to his belt, pulled a knife from its holder and deftly exposed the blade. Surrounded by a circle of onlookers, I thought I was done

IF YOU'RE SO INCLINED

You may wish to read the dialogues aloud for practice. Read them several times. If you feel up to it, you may want to record your voice on a tape recorder. If you know any native Spanish speakers, ask them to read the dialogues aloud for you. You could even record them and listen to the tape later.

QUICK ⊕ PAINLESS

for. But then, just as I was preparing to flee, he reached forward to the fruit cart, grabbed a mango, and calmly began to slice it open.

"Oh, you did not come here to die. Did you come here yester-die?"

In this activity, use your imagination to think up some scenarios where you would need to be polite. Be creative. If you have a friend who is willing to be your guinea pig, act out some of these scenes with him or her and practice as many of the formal expressions as you can.

¡Buen Viaje!: Traveling

No doubt about it. You'll get much more out of your adventures in Latin America and Spain if you can *conversar* with the locals. Whether you're in Argentina on business, in Madrid visiting the Prado, in the Yucatan assisting at an archeological dig, or in northeastern Peru exploring the rainforests, you'll need to communicate effectively in order to get around and be safe.

DIALOGUE: EN EL AEROPUERTO INTERNACIONAL DE EZEIZA, BUENOS AIRES, ARGENTINA

Let's start right off with a dialogue. Read it through a few times (aloud if you like) and then study the translation that follows.

William:	Buenas tardes, *señor.*
El agente:	Buenas tardes. ¿De dónde es?
William:	Soy de Inglaterra.
El agente:	Su pasaporte, por favor.
William:	Sí, cómo no. Aquí lo tiene.

El agente:	Muy bien. ¿Cuál es el motivo de su viaje a la Argentina?
William:	Ser un viaje de placer. Tengo amigos aquí en Buenos Aires, y he venido a vistarlos. También me gustaría hacer un viaje al sur. Me encantaría ver los pingüinos.
El agente:	Claro, el sur es muy lindo. ¿Por cuantos días permanecerá usted en la república?
William:	Hasta el 18 de febrero. O sea, son 30 días en total, más o menos.
El agente:	Bien. Su visa vencer en 60 días. Espero que su estadía sea agradable.
William:	Gracias. ¿Disculpe, me puede decir una cosa?
El agente:	A ver …
William:	¿Qué hora es aquí? Quiero ajustar mi reloj.
El agente:	Ya son las 11:45.
William:	Gracias, *señor.* Usted es muy amable.
El agente:	No hay de qué.

Translation:

William:	Good afternoon, sir.
Agent:	Good afternoon. Where are you from?
William:	I'm from England.
Agent:	Your passport, please.
William:	Yes, of course. Here you go. ("here you have it")
Agent:	Very good. What is the reason for your trip to Argentina?

William:	It will be a pleasure trip. I have friends here in Buenos Aires, and I've come to visit them. I'd also like to take a trip down south. I'd love to see the penguins.
Agent:	Sure, the south is very pretty. How many days will you be staying in the country? (republic)
William:	Until February 18th. So, it'll be 30 all together, more or less.
Agent:	All right. Your visa will expire in 60 days. I hope that you have a pleasant stay.
William:	Thank you. Pardon me, can you tell me something?
Agent:	All right … ("let's see what it is … ")
William:	What time is it here? I want to adjust my watch.
Agent:	It's 11:45 now.
William:	Thank you, sir. You are very kind.
Agent:	Don't mention it. ("there is no need to thank me")

¿CUÁNDO ES? WHEN IS IT?

When you're traveling, time is of the essence. If you're unable to understand when your flight (bus, train, boat, burro) leaves, you could be left in the dust—or jungle. Your Spanish will be incomplete if you can't tell people what time it is, or explain to someone the day or date when an event will occur.

¿Qué Hora Es? What Time Is It?

Telling time in Spanish is actually easier than most people think. The hours of the day all take the feminine

IF YOU'RE SO INCLINED

Many people like to carry a pocket phrasebook while traveling. Though these books can indeed be useful, it's practically impossible to learn a language from a phrasebook alone. That's where *Learn Spanish The Lazy Way* comes in. Still, a good phrasebook would make an excellent companion to this book. Buy one if you like. Just remember that phrasebooks won't actually teach you the structure of the language.

article. And except for 1:00, they're all plural. Just use *las* (or *la* for 1:00) and the number of the hour. Use *ser* as your verb:

la una	1:00	*Es la una.*	It's 1:00.
las dos	2:00	*Son las dos.*	It's 2:00.
las tres	3:00	*Son las tres.*	It's 3:00.
las cuatro	4:00	*Son las cuatro.*	It's 4:00.
las cinco	5:00	*Son las cinco.*	It's 5:00.
etc.			
las once	11:00	*Son las once.*	It's 11:00.
las doce	12:00	*Son las doce.*	It's 12:00.

At the half hour, add: *y media* ("and a half"), or simply read the number and say 30 (*treinta*):

la una y media	1:30	*Es la una y media.*
las dos y media	2:30	*Son las dos y media.*
las nueve y media	9:30	*Son las nueve y media.*
las once treinta	11:30	*Son las once treinta.*

For the quarter hour, the phrase *y cuarto* ("and a quarter") is used. You may also just say 15 (*quince*):

Son las tres y cuarto.	It's a quarter past three.
Es la una quince.	It's 1:15 (one fifteen).

When it's fifteen minutes before the hour, as in 10:45, you can say either *las once menos cuatro* ("11 minus a quarter") or *un cuarto para las once* ("a quarter to 11"). You can also simply say *las diez cuarenta y cinco.*

Perhaps the simplest way to express the time of day is to state the hour, then say *con* ("with") and the number of minutes (radio announcers love this one):

3:10	*Son las tres con diez minutos.*
9:50	*Son las nueve con cincuenta minutos.*
1:38	*Es la una con treinta y ocho minutos.*

To say "at a certain time," use the preposition *"a."* When you want to say "until," use *hasta*:

Tengo que estar en el aeropuerto a las tres.	I need to be at (in) the airport at 3:00.
El vuelo ha llegado a las once cuarenta y cinco.	The flight has arrived at 11:45.
Van a abrir la puerta a las siete y cuarto.	They're going to open the door at 7:15.
El autobús no va a salir hasta las seis y media.	The bus isn't going to leave until 6:30.
La visa de William vence al medio día.	William's visa expires at noon.
El banco cierra a las cinco y media.	The bank closes at 5:30.
Mis amigos van a estar en mi casa hasta las nueve menos diez.	My friends are going to be in my house until 8:50.

At this point, you're probably wondering how to differentiate between 9:00 in the morning and 9:00 at night. Well, most of the time the context will make it clear. If you say: "We eat dinner at 6:00," people will assume you mean 6:00 in the evening. But there are

times when you should indicate which 6:00 you're talking about. To avoid any confusion, just add one of the following phrases to the hour:

de la mañana	in the morning
de la tarde	in the afternoon
de la noche	at night
de la madrugada	the "wee hours" of the night

The hours 1:00 a.m. to 5:00 a.m. are collectively known as *la madrugada*. Technically, the word *madrugada* means "dawn," but it's also used to distinguish the hours 1:00 to 5:00 a.m. from those same hours in the afternoon:

Son las tres de la madrugada.	It's 3:00 in the morning.
Son las cinco de la madrugada.	It's 5:00 in the morning.

After 6:00 a.m., you should say *de la mañana*:

El tren sale a las nueve de la mañana.	The train leaves at 9:00 in the morning.
Los agentes han salido del trabajo a las once de la mañana.	The agents have left work at 11:00 a.m.
El autobús no llega hasta las siete de la mañana.	The bus doesn't arrive until 7:00 a.m.

From 1:00 p.m. to 8:00 p.m., say *de la tarde*. From 8:00 to midnight, say *de la noche*.

QUICK ⬤ PAINLESS

The Days of the Week

Here are the names of the days of the week. Remember that unless they appear at the beginning of a sentence, the days and months are not capitalized.

Monday	*el lunes*
Tuesday	*el martes*
Wednesday	*el miércoles*
Thursday	*el jueves*
Friday	*el viernes*
Saturday	*el sábado* (think "Sabbath")
Sunday	*el domingo (los domingos)*

Examples:

Hoy es lunes, mañana es martes.	Today is Monday, tomorrow is Tuesday.
Vamos a viajar al sur el vienes.	We are going to travel to the south on Friday.
La aduana estar cerrada el próximo lunes.	The customs office will be closed next Monday.
El agente no trabaja los miércoles.	The agent doesn't work on Wednesdays.
Ya no hay vuelos a Miami los jueves.	There aren't any flights to Miami on Thursdays anymore.

The expression *hoy en ocho días* means a "week from today." So, if today is Sunday, and you want to say next Sunday, you can say *el próximo domingo* ("next Sunday") or *hoy en ocho días.*

The Months of the Year

These don't take the article as often as the days of the week. Use *"en"* or *"para"* when you want to say "in a specific month." Use *"durante"* to mean "during":

January	*enero*
February	*febrero*
March	*marzo*
April	*abril*
May	*mayo*
June	*junio*
July	*julio*
August	*agosto*
September	*septiembre*
October	*octubre*
November	*noviembre*
December	*diciembre*

Examples:

Vamos a hacer un viaje a la selva en noviembre.	We're going to take a trip to the jungle in November.
El evento está programado para abril.	The event is scheduled for April.
No hay servicio de tren al sur durante el mes de mayo.	There's no train service to the south during the month of May.

Other Time Words You'll Need

Here's a list of some additional time-related words. You'll be using them all the time (pun intended):

now	*ahora*
not now	*ahora no*
right now	*ahora mismo* ("the same now")
not anymore	*ya no*
second	*segundo*
minute	*minuto*
hour	*hora*
today	*hoy*
tomorrow	*mañana*
yesterday	*ayer*
the day before yesterday	*anteayer*
the other day	*el otro día*
the day after tomorrow	*pasado mañana*
week	*semana*
month	*(el) mes*
year	*año*
next week	*la próxima semana*
next month/year	*el próximo mes/año*
last month/year	*el mes/año pasado*
last week	*la semana pasada*
century	*siglo*

A COMPLETE WASTE OF TIME

The 3 Worst Things to Do With Years and Ages:

1. Ask *"¿Qué viejo es usted?"* for "How old are you?" This might mean "Which old guy are you?"

2. Use *ser* when referring to someone's age: *"Yo soy 18 años"* makes no sense. Use *tener*.

3. Forget to put the tilde (~) over the *"n"* when writing the word *año*. Look up *ano* in your dictionary to see why *"mi niño tiene cuatro anos"* is extremely bizarre.

By the way, when saying how old a person is, use the verb *tener: Yo tengo 33 años* = "I am 33 years old." Don't say *Yo soy 33 años.* Years in Spanish are "had": *Mi pap tiene 65 años* = "My dad has (is) 65 years old." For babies: *El bebé tiene dos meces* = "The baby is two months old."

millennium	*milenio*
What time is it?	*¿Qué hora es?*
What time is it?	*¿Qué horas son?*
at what time?	*¿A qué hora?*
at "X" time	*a la(s) …*
in a while	*al rato* (no, not a rat)
after "X" time/month	*a partir de …*

The Date

To express the date in Spanish, simply follow this pattern: *el # de* MONTH.

Hoy es el 14 de noviembre	Today is November 14th.
Mañana es el 12 de diciembre	Tomorrow is December 12th.

For the 1st of the month, use *primero* instead of "one":

el primero de abril	April 1st

Lazy Practice

On a sheet of paper, write down a list of different times during the day. Then say them in Spanish. Do this exercise several times a week. Refer to this book if you get stuck. Eventually, saying the time in Spanish will come naturally.

Do the similar activities for the days, months, and dates. Write the Spanish months and days of the week on all your calendars. Take advantage of every opportunity to think, write, or say the day, month, time, or date in Spanish.

THE FUTURE AND CONDITIONAL TENSES

You are now officially ready to meet some new verb tenses. Since the future and conditional tenses are very similar in form (though not in function), it's a good idea to learn them together.

The Future Tense: You Will Do It

The future tense in Spanish is similar to the "shall" future tense in English: "I shall return." It isn't as common in daily conversation as the *ir + a +* INFINITIVE model that you learned a few chapters ago. However, when you do use it, it's as clear as a bell. Use it to indicate what you will or will not do.

Forming the future tense is easy. For most verbs, just add the future ending to the end of the infinitive. Notice how these endings, with the exception of the *nosotros* form, are all accented on the last syllable.

The Future Tense Endings

yo	-é	hablaré	I shall speak
tú	-s	bailarás	you shall dance
el/ella/usted	-	comer	he/she/you shall eat
nosotros/nosotras	-emos	veremos	we shall see
ellos/ellas/ustedes	-n	pagarán	they/you shall pay

Here are some examples of the future tense:

¿Bailaremos?	Shall we dance?
Hablaré con el agente de viajes mañana.	I will speak with the travel agent tomorrow.
Estaremos en Madrid por un mes.	We will be in Madrid for a month.
No irás jamás al cine con ese tipo.	You will never ever go to the movies with that guy.
¿Cuántas personas serán?	How many people will you all be? (in your group/party)
Veremos qué pasar.	We'll see what happens.
Servirán comida durante el vuelo.	They will serve food during the flight.
¿De veras servirán comida durante el vuelo?	Will they really serve food during the flight?
Perderás tu mochila si la dejas en el autobús.	You will lose your back-pack if you leave it on the bus.
Qué será, será.	Whatever will be, will be.

The Conditional Tense

In daily speech, the Spanish conditional tense is more common than the future tense you just learned. I like to think of it as the *Mr. Roger's Neighborhood* tense: "Would you be mine, could you be mine, won't you be my neighbor?" The conditional tense is used where we use the helping verbs "would" and "could" in English.

The conditional can be used to soften a request. You've already seen some of these. For example, *¿Me puede ayudar con mi equipaje?* ("Can you help me with my luggage?") is a fine sentence. But you can make the request even more courteous by using the conditional: *¿Me podría decir usted si el tren llegar a las seis y media, por favor?* ("Could you please tell me if the train will arrive at 6:30?")

The endings are slapped on to the end of the infinitive. Pay attention to the áccent márks as seen in the table below.

Here are some examples:

Yo hablaría con el guía, pero ahora no tengo tiempo.	I'd talk with the tour guide, but I don't have time now.
Hoy me gustaría ir a las ruinas.	I would like to travel to the ruins today.
Les gustaría viajar a las once de la noche.	They would like to go at 11:00 p.m.
Compraríamos dos boletos de avión, pero no tenemos dinero.	We would buy two plane tickets, but we don't have any money.
¿No sería posible llegar a la ciudad a las dos?	Wouldn't it be possible to arrive at the city at 2:00?
¿Serías? ¿Podrías ser? ¿No serías mi vecino?	(guess!)

QUICK ● PAINLESS

You'll notice that the *yo* form and *él/ella/usted* form are the same in the conditional tense. Usually, the context makes it clear who the subject of the sentence is. But you can always add the subject pronoun to your sentence to avoid any ambiguities: *yo hablaría, él hablaría.*

Conditional Tense Endings

-ía	*hablaría*	I would talk
-ías	*entenderías*	you would understand
-ía	*escribiría*	he/she/it/you would write
-íamos	*comeríamos*	we would eat
-ían	*pagarían*	they/you all would pay

Verbs With Stem Changes in the Future and Conditional

Many verbs that have stem changes in the present indicative (such as *pensar* becomes *pienso*), are quite regular in the future and conditional (*pensará, pensaría*). However, there are several common verbs which do change their stem when forming the conditional and future tenses. The change is exactly the same for both.

Here is a list of the main verbs in this category. You'll just have to learn them "as is." There are no tricks. But at least they seem to follow a similar pattern:

VERB:	STEM:	EXAMPLE:	MEANING:
poner	pondr-	*pondría*	would put
poder	podr-	*podrían*	could; would be able
tener	tendr-	*tendr*	shall have
saber	sabr-	*sabrías*	would know
venir	vendr-	*vendríamos*	would come
valer	valdr-	*valdrían*	would be worth
haber	habr-	*habría*	would have
hacer	har-	*har*	shall do
decir	dir-	*diría*	would say
salir	saldr-	*saldré*	shall leave
querer	querr-	*querría*	would want

DIALOGUE: EL HOTEL *"LA ESTRELLA DE ORO"* (GOLD STAR HOTEL)

This conversation uses several future and conditional verb forms. Read the Spanish dialogue a few times, then study the translation carefully.

Kathy:	Disculpe, señora. Buenas tardes. ¿Trabaja usted aquí?
La recepcionista:	¿Eh? ¿Si trabajo aquí? Sí, claro.
Kathy:	Muy bien. ¿Podría ser tan amable de decirme si hay habitaciones para dos personas?
La recepcionista:	Sí, hay. ¿Sería para dos mujeres?
Kathy:	Sí. Querríamos con dos camas. ¿Sería posible con baño privado?
La recepcionista:	No, no hay baños privados. El baño está en el pasillo. Pero ahora no hay mucha gente, y el baño estará disponible todo el día.
Kathy:	¿Y habría agua caliente?
La recepcionista:	Sí, a veces.
Kathy:	Bueno. ¿Cuánto nos costaría por noche?
La recepcionista:	Serían 200 pesos cada noche.
Kathy:	¿Así? ¿Por qué tan cara?
La recepcionista:	Porque la habitación es muy grande.
Kathy:	Grande sí, pero sin baño privado. Yo no diría que valdría tanto.
La recepcionista:	¿Que no? Pues, ¿le gustaría ver la habitación?
Kathy:	No, muchas gracias. Tendremos que encontrar algo más económico.

QUICK PAINLESS

As you know, the word *sí* means "yes." There is also another *si* (written without the áccent márk) which means "if." *Si mi amigo no puede venir ...* means "If my friend can't come ...." *Está bien si ...* means "It's all right if ...." *Si Juan no sabe, ¿entonces qué haremos?* means "If Juan doesn't know, then what shall we do?" *No sé si Juan podría venir* means "I don't know if Juan would be able to come."

La recepcionista:	Bueno, está bien. Buena suerte.
Kathy:	Gracias, señora. Y discuple la molestia.
La recepcionista:	No se preocupe.

Translation:

Kathy:	Excuse me, madam. Good afternoon. Do you work here?
Receptionist:	¿Huh? If I work here? Yes, of course I do.
Kathy:	Great. Would you be so kind as to tell me if there are rooms available for two people?
Receptionist:	Yes, there are. Would it be for two women?
Kathy:	Yes. We want two beds. Would it be possible to have (with) a private bathroom?
Receptionist:	No, there aren't any rooms with a private bath. The bathroom is in the hall. But there aren't many people now, and the bathroom will be available all day.
Kathy:	And, would there be hot water? (*habría* = conditional form of *hay*)
Receptionist:	Yes, sometimes.
Kathy:	OK. How much would it cost us per night?
Receptionist:	It would be 200 pesos per night.
Kathy:	Really? Why so expensive?
Receptionist:	Because it's a very big room.

Kathy:	Big, yes, but without a private bathroom. I wouldn't say that it would be worth that much.
Receptionist:	You wouldn't? Well, would you like to see the room?
Kathy:	No, thank you. We will need to find something more inexpensive.
Receptionist:	OK, that's fine. Good luck.
Kathy:	Thank you, madam. I'm sorry to trouble you.
Receptionist:	Don't worry about it.

IF YOU'RE SO INCLINED

Every time you look at a watch or clock, say the time to yourself in Spanish.

Lazy Practice

Create as many sentences as you can where you need the future and/or conditional tense. Use your dictionary for vocabulary. Think of things that you "will do," "would do," and "could do" (*poder* becomes *podr-*). Learn and practice the verbs that change their stem in the future and conditional tenses. In addition, review your Spanish texts and locate any verbs in the future or conditional tenses. Look them up if you don't know them already.

ACTIVITY: A TRIP TO MEXICO

Create a fantasy trip to Mexico. Pretend you'll be arriving by air and traveling overland for 14 days. Imagine the situations you'll encounter in airports, bus stations, hotels, and travel agencies. Visit **www.go2mexico.com** for ideas, or check out what's available at your local library. Practice some of what you've learned in this chapter (and previous chapters, of course).

A la Mesa: Food and Drink

Both Latin America and Spain boast some of the best foods on the planet! We've all heard of tortillas, tacos, and tostadas. But that's just a small fraction of the many delectable dishes you'll be tasting during your travels. In this chapter, you'll learn how to order some of the many gastronomic delights that await you (with a large side-order of grammar, *naturalmente*).

DIALOGUE: EN EL RESTAURANTE "LA FONDA"

Let's see what happens to José and María when they stop for lunch at a small restaurant:

El mesero:	Bienvenidos a La Fonda.
María:	Gracias, joven. Una mesa para dos personas, por favor.
El mesero:	Cómo no, señora. Síganme por favor. Su mesa está cerca de la ventana.

José:	¿Así? Excelente. Tenemos mucha hambre. (They sit down.)
El mesero:	Muy bien. Díganme, ¿qué desean tomar?
María:	Para mí, una limonada. Ya sé que mi esposo va a querer un jugo de naranja.
José:	No, querida, no quiero nada de eso. Joven, tráigame una cerveza bien fría.
María:	Pero, mi amor, no te olvides de tu salud, y del problema que tienes con el hígado y todo, tú sabes …
José:	Pues, tienes razón. Entonces, déme un vaso de leche, por favor. (Waiter leaves and returns with drinks.)
El mesero:	Aquí tienen las bebidas. Ahora, ¿qué van a querer? [also: *pedir, ordenar, comer*]
José:	Es que no estamos listos todavía, joven. Dénos la oportunidad para estudiar [*leer*] el menú, y vuela en dos minutos, si no sería gran molestia.
El mesero:	Está bien. (Waiter leaves and returns 15 minutes later.) Bueno, ¿ya están listos?
María:	Sí, joven, ya. Yo voy a probar el filete de pescado.
José:	Y yo el caldo de res, y el pollo rostizado. Pero dígame una cosa, joven. ¿Es picante el caldo?
El mesero:	No, señor. No tiene nada de picante.
José:	Está bien, entonces. Usted sabe … por lo del estomago … hay que tener cuidado.
El mesero:	Sí. El pollo va acompañado de papas fritas y de una ensalada de verduras.
José:	Eso está muy bien. Ahora, lleve los vasos vacíos a la cocina y dígale al cocinero que prepare la comida de una vez. Es que tenemos mucha prisa.

IF YOU'RE SO INCLINED

Learn Spanish The Lazy Way is not a cookbook. There are so many different foods in Latin America and Spain that it would be impossible to list them all here. Check your local library or the Internet for cookbooks and Web sites about Spanish and Latin American cuisine. I'll include some food-related Web sites at the end of the chapter.

El mesero:	Sí, señor. Como usted diga.
José:	Espere, tengo una pregunta más. ¿Qué pasa con los cubiertos?
El mesero:	Ya se los traigo. (Waiter leaves and goes to the kitchen.)
El mesero: (to the cook)	¡Oye, Manuel! Hay un tipo en la cinco que quiere que le hagas la comida de una vez.
El cocinero:	¿Así? ¡Qué lástima! Es que estoy muy cansado. Ya no quiero cocinar. Que espere hasta que me dé la gana.

When referring to something abstract, *lo* serves as a neuter pronoun. In the dialogue, José says *"lo del estomago."* This translates literally as "the thing about the stomach." Other examples: *lo de Juan* = "the issue (problem, idea) about Juan"; *lo único que no sé hacer* = "the only thing that I don't know how to do"; *lo que me dices* = "the thing (subject, issue) you are telling me." *"Vamos a lo de Julio"* might mean "Let's go over to Julio's place."

Translation:

The waiter:	Welcome to La Fonda.
María:	Thanks. You're very kind. A table for two, please.
The waiter:	Very good. Please follow me. Your table is near the window.
José:	Excellent. We're very hungry.
The waiter:	Great. What would you like to drink?
María:	For me, a lemonade. I already know that my husband is going to want orange juice.
José:	No, dear, I don't want that. Young man, bring me a very cold beer, please.
María:	But honey, don't forget about your health, and the problem with your liver, you know …
José:	Well, you're right. In that case, I'm going to order a glass of milk.
The waiter:	Here are your drinks. Now, what will you have?

José:	Well, we're not ready yet. Give us a chance to study the menu and come back in two minutes, if it wouldn't be too much trouble.
The waiter:	All right. (Waiter leaves and returns 15 minutes later.) So, are you ready now?
María:	Yes, young man, we are. I'm going to try the fish fillet.
José:	And I'm going to try the beef stew and the rotisserie chicken. But tell me something, young man. Is the stew spicy?
The waiter:	No, sir. There's nothing spicy in it.
José:	Well, that's fine then. You know … my stomach problems … you have to be careful.
The waiter:	The chicken comes with French fries and a vegetable salad.
José:	That's fine. Now, take these empty glasses to the kitchen and tell the cook to prepare the food at once. We're in a hurry. ["We have a lot of hurry."]
The waiter:	Yes, sir. As you wish ("Whatever you say").
José:	Wait, one more thing. What about the silverware?
The waiter:	I'll bring it to you right away.
The waiter: (to the cook)	¡Hey, Manuel! There's a guy [*tipo* = *"type"*] at table five ["la" refers to *mesa*] who wants you to make his food right away [at once].
The cook:	Oh yeah? What a shame! You see, I'm very tired. I don't want to cook anymore. Let him wait until I feel up to it.

YOU'LL THANK YOURSELF LATER

Literally, *Es que* means "It's that … " But a better translation might be "You see … " "What's happening is that … " "The thing is that … " etc. By starting with *Es que,* the cook is explaining his actions or situation. In the right context, the statement *Es que Roberto no tiene dinero* could mean "You see, the problem is that Roberto doesn't have any money, so that's why he can't buy/do the thing we're talking about."

AT THE RESTAURANT

You'll find a glossary of food terms included in Appendix C. Now, in order to actually eat some of this tasty food, you'll need the items discussed in the following sections.

Los Cubiertos

Silverware and eating accouterments are known collectively as *cubiertos.* If you don't have any silverware at your table, you can say: *"Los cubiertos, por favor."* If you want to be more specific, ask for them by name:

un tenedor	a fork
una cuchara	a spoon
un cuchillo	a knife

Other things that you might need:

plato	plate
servilleta	napkin
vaso	drinking glass
taza	cup (for tea or coffee)
tazón	bowl
mesa	table
copa	wine glass
la sal	salt
pimienta	pepper
salsa	sauce; salsa
silla	chair
la cuenta	the bill

QUICK ☎ PAINLESS

Learn ¡*Buen provecho!* This is the Spanish version of *"Bon appetite."* Before people begin to eat, or if you enter a room where people are already eating, say *Buen provecho.* The response is a simple *gracias.*

una propina	a tip
el desayuno	breakfast
el almuerzo	lunch
la cena	dinner

Intentar, tratar de, and ***probar*** all mean "to try," but *intentar* and *tratar de* + INFINITIVE are more common for actually trying to do something: ***Voy a tratar de hacerlo bien*** = "I'm going to try to do it well." Though *probar* can sometimes be used this way, it works best in the context of "to taste something": ***¿Quiere probar la comida?*** = "Do you want to try the food?"

Useful Restaurant Verbs

Here's a list of some verbs you'll need at a restaurant:

cocinar	to cook
guisar	to cook (Mex.)
preparar	to prepare
servir	to serve
probar	to try; taste (*yo pruebo*)
saber a	to taste like
ordenar	to order
llevar	to take away
tomar	to drink
beber	to drink (always understood, but not used as often as *tomar*)
pedir	to ask for (*yo pido*)
querer	to want
desear	to desire; to want
pagar	to pay
dejar	to leave behind (on the table)

WELCOME TO THE SPANISH SUBJUNCTIVE

I've done my best to spare you from this as long as possible. But just like death and taxes, sooner or later you'll have to face it. Many people who study Spanish head for *las montañas* when the topic turns to the subjunctive. But the good news is that with careful explanation, it really isn't that bad. Meet the "kinder, gentler subjunctive … "

So, What Is the Subjunctive?

The subjunctive is not a tense. Rather, it's a "mood." The subjunctive mood is the "alter-ego" of the indicative. It's an alternate form of a verb that serves an entirely different grammatical function.

A verb in the subjunctive removes the subject a few steps away from the certainty of the action or state of the verb: "I did it" (indicative) versus "It is possible that I might have done it but nobody can really be sure at this moment in time" (subjunctive). While the indicative mood is certain, quantifiable, and solid, the subjunctive is "possible," "doubtful," "indirect," "emotional," "pliable," "opinionated," and "contrary-to-fact." There are both present and past forms of the subjunctive (there's also a future subjunctive, but it's only used in legal documents). We'll focus on the present subjunctive here.

How to Form the Present Subjunctive

Making the present subjunctive is sort of like putting the "wrong ending" on the verb. With its "shoes on

QUICK **PAINLESS**

Perhaps you didn't know that English also has a subjunctive. We use it most often in "contrary-to-fact" sentences, such as "I wish I were in the land of cotton" (but I'm not). Nowadays, many people incorrectly say "I wish I was in Dixie," which technically should be "I wish I were in Dixie." The verbs "may" and "might" also help to form the English subjunctive: "May he rest in peace"; "Be that as it may … "

backwards," so to speak, you can imagine how the poor verb feels: unsure, vulnerable, and plagued by self-doubt. In the subjunctive, -ar verbs take the endings that you worked so hard to learn for -er and -ir verbs, and the -er and -ir verbs take the endings used by -ar verbs. The only real deviation is in the first person singular yo form. The yo form in the subjunctive is the same as the third person (él, ella, usted).

The key to forming the present subjunctive correctly is to start with the yo form of the verb in the indicative, then build your subjunctive from there. I'll show you why in a minute. In most cases, the whole thing is pretty straightforward.

Let's say that we're dealing with our regular old friend hablar. Follow these three steps to form the present subjunctive:

Present subjunctive endings for -ar verbs:

Ending:	Example:	Subjunctive:	Definition:
-e	hablar	hable	I may speak
-es	cantar	cantes	you may sing
-e	dudar	dude	he/she/it/you may doubt
-emos	pensar	pensemos	we may think
-en	tomar	tomen	they/you all may take

1. Recall the endings for -er verbs (remembering the change in the yo form).

2. Make the yo form of the verb in the indicative (*hablo*).

3. Remove the -o, and put the subjunctive ending in its place (*hable*).

The steps you'll follow for –er and –ir verbs are the same. Only the endings have changed:

1. Recall the endings for your -ar verbs (remembering the change in the yo form).

2. Make the yo form of (*comer = como; vivir = vivo*).

3. Remove the -o, and put the subjunctive ending in its place (*coma; viva*).

Present subjunctive endings for -*er* and -*ir* verbs:

Ending:	Verb:	Subjunctive:	Definition:
-*a*	creer	*crea*	I may believe
-*as*	vivir	*vivas*	you may live
-*a*	correr	*corra*	he/she/it/you may run
-*amos*	vender	*vendamos*	we may sell
-*an*	comer	*coman*	they/you all may eat

Verbs that end in *-cer*—such as *conocer* (to know/meet a person), *establecer* (to establish), *parecer* (to seem/to appear), and *crecer* (to grow)—change to *conozco, establezco, parezco,* and *crezco* in the first person *yo* form. When forming the subjunctive of such verbs, you must maintain this ending throughout: *conozca, establezcas, parezcan, conozcamos,* etc. This is why you should start with the *yo* indicative form and work from there.

You see, forming the subjunctive isn't really that difficult. The only hard part is to remember that you must start with the indicative *yo* form (until you have memorized the subjunctive forms, at which time they will come naturally to you) as your template for the subjunctive. Any changes in the stem that occur there will be reflected *throughout* the subjunctive form. Here are some examples:

Verb:	Yo Form:	Subjunctive:	Definition:
tener	tengo	*tenga, tengas, etc.*	may have
decir	digo	*diga, digas, etc.*	may say
poner	pongo	*ponga*	may put
pensar	pienso	*piensa*	may think
morir	muero	*muera*	may die
pedir	pido	*pida*	may ask for

There are also some common verbs that have irregular forms in the subjunctive:

Verb:	Subjunctive Form:	Definition:
ver	vea, veas, vea, veamos, vean	may see
saber	sepa, sepas, sepa, sepamos, sepan	may know
dar	dé, des, dé, demos, den	may give
estar	esté, estés, esté, estemos, estén	may be

Verb:	Subjunctive Form:	Definition:
ir	vaya, vayas, vaya, vayamos, vayan	may go
ser	sea, seas, sea, seamos, sean	may be
haber	haya, hayas, haya, hayamos, hayan	may have
estar	esté, estés, esté, estemos, estén	may be

The Subjunctive and Those Spelling Rules

Adding this "wrong" ending can necessitate some spelling changes. At first, these may look odd, but they actually make perfect sense if you recall the spelling rules we discussed in Chapter 2.

Take, for example, the verb *pagar.* If we follow the steps for forming the present subjunctive, we start with *pago.* Now, since this is an *–ar* verb, we remove the *–o* and add *–e,* which gives us *page.* But this would be pronounced as *pah hay,* because the "g" goes soft before "e" and "i." We must add "u" after the "g" to protect it from the softening effects of the *–e.* Thus, the present subjunctive of *pagar* is *pague.*

Verb:	1st Person Ind.	Wrong!	Right!
sacar	*saco*	sace	saque
arrancar	*arranco*	arrance	arranque
jugar	*juego*	juege	juegue

By the way, such changes in spelling are sometimes known as "orthographic conveniences." While these rules may seem rather inconvenient at first, they really do serve to maintain the logic of Spanish spelling.

YOU'LL THANK YOURSELF LATER

Tipping in restaurants is not as common in Spain and Latin America as it is in the United States. You may wish to leave some extra change on the table for a job well done. But generally, no tip will be expected. This may not be the case, however, at tourist resorts, where the staff may have become used to getting tips from uninformed *turistas.* In upscale restaurants, there may be a service charge (*servicio*). Check your bill.

WHEN TO USE THE SUBJUNCTIVE

Now that you've learned how to make it, it's time to
learn how to use it.

USTED COMMANDS

Directly telling someone to do or not to do something is
known as a command or imperative. When using *usted*
(or *ustedes* for more than one person), you must use the
subjunctive form of the verb for all commands:

Hable con el cocinero, por favor.	Please speak to the cook.
Paguen la cuenta en la caja, señores.	Pay the bill at the cashier, gentlemen.
Dígame por favor si la comida está lista o no.	Please tell me if the food is ready or not.
No vayan al restaurante que está detrás del hotel.	Don't go to the restaurant behind the hotel.
Hágame el favor de darme el menú.	Please give me (Do me the favor of giving me) the menu.
Tráigame un nuevo. tenedor, por favor.	Bring me a new fork, please.

Even though you may be using *usted* or *ustedes* out
of respect, you'll still need to request that these people
do things for you now and then. So, using the subjunctive third person forms create sentences in which you are
telling people what to do (or not to do). Remember that
a well-placed *por favor* goes a long way to soften such
commands.

INDIRECT COMMANDS

When someone's will is directed at or imposed upon something or someone else, the subjunctive form of the verb must be used. If I say "I want John to eat the bread," I'm expressing my will that John do something. It doesn't matter if John and I use *tú* with each other. I am imposing my will or desire (no matter how subtle or well-meant) upon something other than myself. If John replies that he's not hungry and wants me to leave him alone about the bread, he'll have to use the subjunctive when he imposes his will on me:

No quiero que John coma todo el pan.	I don't want John to eat all the bread.
El cocinero quiere que el mesero sirva la comida.	The cook wants the waiter to serve the food.
Quiero que la comida esté rica.	I want the food to taste good ("be rich").
María no permite que su esposo tome cerveza.	María doesn't allow her husband to drink beer.
Juan desea que el mesero vuelva en unos minutos.	Juan wants (desires) the waiter to return in a few minutes.
Nosotros insistimos en que tú nos pagues el dinero ahora.	We insist that you pay us the money now.
Mis padres quieren que yo haga los quehaceres.	My parents want me to do my chores.
Su novia quiere que yo conozca a su hermana.	His girlfriend wants me to meet her (or his) sister.

IF YOU'RE SO INCLINED

The word for "waiter" changes from place to place: *mesero* (most of Latin America), *mesonero* (Venezuela), *garzón* or *mozo* (Argentina), *camarero* (Spain, Caribbean). You may want to ask the locals: *"¿Cómo se dice 'mesero/camarero' aquí?"* (How do you say "waiter" here?").

It doesn't always have to be a person who does the wanting. The subjunctive must also be used in "impersonal" expressions showing opinion or emotion, such as "It's wonderful that ... " or "It's too bad that ... ":

Es fantástico que Antonio haya preparado la comida.	It's great that Antonio has prepared the food.
Es una lástima que María no conozca mejor a su esposo.	It's a shame that Maria doesn't know her husband better.

NEGATIVE *TÚ* COMMANDS

When you tell a child, friend, or family member *not* to do something, the *tú* form of the subjunctive is required:

No me digas que tú vas a comer tres tostadas.	Don't tell me you're going to eat three tostadas.
Juanito, no juegues con tu comida.	Juanito, don't play with your food.
No me dejes solo, . mi amor	Don't leave me alone, my love.

IMPERSONAL WISHES, HOPES, AND LETTING SOMEONE ELSE DO IT

You'll see what I mean by the examples. These are usually preceded by *que.* In sentences expressing hope, the verb *esperar* ("to wait"; "to hope") is optional:

Que la pague David.	Let David pay it. (la cuenta)

When one noun places its will on another, there is a change in subject. When there is no change in subject, there is no need for the subjunctive. So *Quiero ir* = "I want to go," but *Quiero que tú vayas* = "I want you to go."

Que lo repare el gobierno.	Let the government fix it.
(Espero) Que sirvan la comida ahora mismo.	I hope they serve the food right now.
(Espero) Que gane mi equipo.	I hope my team wins.
¡Que coman pastel!	Let 'em eat cake!
Que descanse en paz. (descansar)	May he rest in peace.
¡Viva el Rey! (the que is understood)	Long live the King!

UNSPECIFIED FUTURE TIME

Use the subjunctive when the exact time an event will (or may) occur is uncertain or unimportant. These sentences often translate as "whenever" in English:

Pagaremos la cuenta cuando venga el mesero	We'll pay the bill whenever the waiter gets here (could take awhile).
Te llamo cuando yo . pueda	I'll call you whenever I can.
Nadie sabe cuando vaya a acabar el mundo.	Nobody knows when the world will end.
Felipe dice que lo hará en cuanto termine la cena.	Felipe says that he'll do it as soon as he finishes dinner.
María, cuando crezcas serás famosa. (crecer)	María, when you grow up you'll be famous.

The 3 Worst Things to Do With the Subjunctive:

1. Using stand-alone phrases such as *Yo haga, Él no sepa,* or *Ellos vayan.* You'll need to start these sentences with phrases such as *Es posible que* or *Es importante que* to make them work.

2. Don't forget to start with the *yo* form of the indicative to allow for any stem changes in the subjunctive.

3. Agonizing too much about using the subjunctive in complex sentences. People will still understand you if you accidentally use the indicative.

AFTER CERTAIN STOCK PHRASES

By their very nature, some phrases take the subjunctive. Most end in *que:*

aunque	although
es posible que	it's possible that
hasta que	until
después de que	after
es importante que	it's important that
puede ser que	it may be that
tan pronto que	as soon as
en cuanto	as soon as
a pesar de que	in spite of the fact that

Here are some other situations when you should use the subjunctive. Use it when a statement is:

▪ potentially true (but not really true)

Es posible que mi equipo gane mañana.	It's possible that my team may win tomorrow. (but it's unlikely)

▪ colored by emotion

Estoy tan feliz de que el restaurante esté abierto ahora.	I'm so happy that the restaurant is open now.
Estoy tan triste de que tú me hayas abandonado.	I'm so sad that you have abandoned me.

doubtful or not true

No creo que María tenga el dinero para pagarlo.	I don't think that María has the money to pay it.
Es posible que Juan lo sepa.	It's possible that Juan knows. (but I doubt it)
No puede ser que Humberto sea rico.	Humberto can't be rich. (no matter what people say, I know he's dirt poor)
Tenemos miedo de que lo hayan robado.	We're afraid that they may have stolen it. (but we have no proof)

Sometimes both the indicative and subjunctive are possible in a particular sentence. The decision to use the subjunctive or the indicative depends on how certain, opinionated, or emotional the speaker feels. For example:

*Aunque Julio **es** inteligente, no puede solucionar el problema.*	Although Julio is intelligent, he can't solve the problem. (There is no doubt that Julio is an intelligent man.)
*Aunque Julio **sea** inteligente, no puede solucionar el problema.*	Although Julio may be intelligent, he can't solve the problem. (The speaker is casting some doubt as to Julio's intelligence.)
No es cierto que existe Santa Claus. (existir)	Santa Claus does not exist. (Science has proved it.)

No es cierto que exista Santa Claus.

There is no Santa Claus. (But some people still believe in him and I can't prove that he doesn't exist.)

Remember the sentence from Chapter 5: *¿Hay alguien aquí que hable el inglés?* The reason *hablar* is in the subjunctive (*hable*) in this sentence is because we're not sure if such a person exists or not. Even if there is an English speaker in the house, we can't know (and don't particularly care) who he might be. Another translation of this sentence might be: "Is there anyone here who might be able to speak English?" If we replace *hable* with *habla* (*¿Hay alguien aquí que habla el español?*), the sentence would mean: "So, there's someone here who speaks English?" The response to this might be: "Well, good! I look forward to meeting this person."

Lazy Practice

I know there's a lot in this chapter. But don't allow yourself to become overwhelmed. Simply review the different conditions under which the subjunctive is used and create a few English sentences that follow the examples. Then translate your sentences into Spanish. Take your time. You *can* do this.

ACTIVITY: CREATE A MENU

Design an authentic Latin American or Spanish menu. Visit your library and check out any cookbooks that feature recipes from the Spanish-speaking world. Or, visit

IF YOU'RE SO INCLINED

No matter how you slice it, using the Spanish subjunctive isn't always easy. For more practice, visit the Spanish subjunctive tutorial at www.unc.edu/courses/span003/gram.html.

some of the excellent Web sites on the Internet about Spanish and Latin American food, such as:

www.geocities.com/NapaValley/6430/food.html

www.caribead.com/latina.html

www.goodcooking.com/caricen.html

For more Web sites, search for "Spanish food" or "Latin American food," or use the name of a country or region, such as "Caribbean" or "South American" food.

You're making great progress! It's time to eat. Have lunch or dinner at a good Mexican restaurant (and I don't mean that fast-food place with the 69¢ tacos). Enjoy yourself and try not to think about Spanish for awhile.

The Lazy Way

Shopping

It's only natural to want to come home with a few souvenirs in your bag. Though the markets and stores may be intimidating at first, shopping in Spain and Latin America can be a snap when you're linguistically prepared. After this chapter, you'll be haggling in Spanish like a pro!

DIALOGUE: EL MERCADO "GRINGOTENANGO"

Guillermo and Marga are Spanish tourists in Guatemala. They've stopped at an artisan's shop in a market to purchase some Guatemalan souvenirs. Read the following dialogue in Spanish a few times, then read the translation.

Guillermo:	Buenas tardes, señor.
El artesano:	Buenas tardes. ¿Cómo están ustedes?
Marga:	Muy bien. ¿Usted?
El artesano:	Bien, gracias.
Marga:	Somos de España y queremos comprar unos recuerdos de Guatemala. Nos interesan mucho las artesanías guatemaltecas.

There are several ways to ask how much something costs in Spanish in addition to *¿Cuánto cuesta?* Here are three:

> *¿Cuál es el precio?* = "What is the price?"

> *¿A cómo (cuánto) se da?* = "At how much is it given?"

> *¿A cúanto (cómo) sale?* = "At how much does it leave?"

It's good to know a few of these. Shopping may get a little boring if you have to keep saying *¿Cuánto cuesta?* all the time.

El artesano: Sí, todas estas cosas son de aquí, hechas a mano en Guatemala. Déjenme enseñarles algunas de las más finas. Por ejemplo, estas camisas son muy típicas de Guatemala.

Marga: Son muy lindas. (She tries one on.) No, ésta no me queda. ¿Me permite la otra camisa por favor?

El artesano: ¿Cuál? ¿ésta?

Marga: No, ésa. La que está al lado. Sí, ésa. Gracias. Ahora, ésta sí me queda mejor. Guillermo, quiero comprar esta camisa.

Guillermo: Sí, está bien. Ahora, ese retrato que está en la mesa es muy interesante.

El artesano: Gracias, pero ése no se vende. Pertenece a mi familia.

Guillermo: Bueno, estos zapatos también son muy lindos.

El artesano: Sí, son típicos de este pueblo. Son muy cómodos también.

Guillermo: A ver si tiene en mi talle. (He tries on shoes.) No, éstos me quedan grandes. Y ésos no me quedarían tampoco. Ahora sí, éstos me quedan bien.

Marga: Bien. Entonces, vamos a comprar la camisa y los zapatos. ¿Nos podría decir cuánto costarán?

El artesano: Normalmente, todo esto costaría dos cientos Quetzales. Pero para ustedes, que son muy simpáticos, les voy a dar un precio especial de ciento cincuenta Quetzales.

Marga: Bueno, no sé. Es mucho dinero. Le damos cien Quetzales.

El artesano:	No, eso no es posible. Miren, estas cosas son de la mejor calidad. Ciento cincuenta Quetzales sería el mejor precio.
Magra:	El mejor para usted, pero no para nosotros. Está seguro de que no saldría en cien?
El artesano:	Sí, estoy seguro. Desafortunadamente, ese precio no sería posible.
Guillermo:	Bueno, lástima. Nos vamos entonces. Adios. (They start to leave.)
El artesano:	¡Oigan! Esperen un momento, por favor. Está bien, se los vendo en ciento veinte y cinco.
Guillermo:	Está bien. ¿Se aceptan cheques de viajero?
El artesano:	¿Cómo? Esteeeee, no. Lo siento. Yo no puedo aceptarlos. Pero si necesitan cambiar dinero, hay una casa de cambio.
Marga:	¿Dónde?
El artesano:	¿Ven aquel edificio? La casa de cambio está ahí.
Guillermo:	Perfecto. Vamos a cambiar dinero entonces. Volveremos en diez minutos.
El artesano:	Aquí los espero.

Translation:

Guillermo:	Good afternoon, sir.
The artisan:	Good afternoon. How are you?
Marga:	Very well. And you?
The artisan:	Fine, thanks.
Marga:	We're from Spain and we want to buy some souvenirs from Guatemala. We're interested in Guatemalan handicrafts.

IF YOU'RE SO INCLINED

Bargaining and haggling over prices is quite common, especially in Latin America. Generally, the vendor offers you a price, you counter with a substantially lower amount, and the two of you go back and forth until an agreement is reached.

The artisan:	Yes, all of these things are from here, handmade in Guatemala. Allow me to show you some of the finest (things). For example, these are very typical Guatemalan shirts.
Marga:	They're very nice. (She tries one on.) No, this one doesn't fit me. May I see the other shirt please?
The artisan:	Which one? This one?
Marga:	No, that one. The one next to it ["la" refers to "camisa"]. Yes, that one. Thanks. Now, this one really does fit me better. Guillermo, I want to buy this shirt.
Guillermo:	Yes, that's fine. Now, that picture that's on the table is very interesting.
The artisan:	Thanks, but it's not for sale [is not sold]. It belongs to my family. [*pertenecer* = *pertenezco, perteneces,* etc. "to belong to"]
Guillermo:	Well, these shoes are also very nice.
The artisan:	Yes, they're typical shoes from this town. They're also very comfortable.
Guillermo:	Let's see if you have (any) in my size. (He tries on shoes.) No, these are too big. And those wouldn't fit me either. Now, these fit me very well.
Marga:	OK. So, we're going to buy the shirt and the shoes. Could you tell us how much they will cost?
The artisan:	Normally, all of this would cost 200 Quetzals. But for you, who are very nice (people), I'm going to give you a special price of 150 Quetzals.
Marga:	Well, I don't know. It's a lot of money. We'll give you 100 Quetzals.

QUICK  PAINLESS

Vendors in Spain and Latin America may quote you different prices for their currency, U.S. dollars, or credit cards. If you have cash to spare, U.S. dollars may get you the lowest price.

The artisan:	No, that's not possible. Look, these things are of the best quality. 150 Quetzals would be the best price.
Marga:	The best price for you, but not for us. Are you sure it wouldn't go for 100?
The artisan:	Yes, I'm sure. Unfortunately, that price wouldn't be possible.
Guillermo:	Well, that's a shame. We're leaving then. Good-bye. (They start to leave.)
The artisan:	Listen! Wait a moment, please. All right, I'll sell them for 125.
Guillermo:	OK. Do you take travelers' checks?
The artisan:	Huh? Uhhhh, no. I'm sorry. I can't accept them. But if you need to change money, there's a change house.
Marga:	Where?
The artisan:	See that building over there? The change house is over there.
Guillermo:	Great. We'll change money then. We'll be back in ten minutes.
The artisan:	I'll wait for you all here.

SOME SHOPPING VERBS

Here are some verbs you'll need while you're out shopping around:

comprar	to buy
llevar	to take away; "to buy"
vender	to sell
pagar	to pay
enseñar	to show

YOU'LL THANK YOURSELF LATER

What we know as "browsing" isn't quite as common in Latin America and Spain as it is in English-speaking countries. Vendors in stores usually assume that you are there to actually buy something, not just to look around for fun, and may become frustrated with you if you walk away without buying anything. However, vendors in open-air markets know that you're out hunting for the best deals, and so are much more accustomed to people leaving empty-handed.

You should be firm when bargaining, but not unrealistic. While you shouldn't let them guilt-trip you into paying too much, if your price really is too low, the vendor won't (and shouldn't) sell.

tocar	to touch; to hold in your hand
costar	to cost (*cuesta*)
cobrar	to charge; to take money
buscar	to look for; to search for
encontrar	to find (*encuentra*)
regatear	to bargain, to haggle
volver	to come back (*vuelve*)
andar viendo	to look around ("window-shop")
cambiar dinero	to exchange money

DEMONSTRATIVES: THIS, THAT, THESE, THOSE

Demonstratives are used to indicate which noun or nouns you're talking about. You use demonstratives all the time: "this table"; "that person"; "these words"; "those buildings over there." We can also think of these as "pointing words."

Spanish recognizes three levels of proximity. First, there are the things that are really close by. Then there are the things that are not so close, but are not necessarily out of reach. Finally, we have those things that are quite distant. Depending on the context, these could be anything from a building across the street to a faraway galaxy.

There are two classes of demonstratives in Spanish: adjectives and pronouns. Both must match the gender and number of the noun or nouns being modified. While this may take you awhile to get used to, the good news is that the words for the adjectives and pronouns are the same. The only difference is that the pronouns are written with áccent márks and the adjectives aren't. Take a look at this:

DEMONSTRATIVE ADJECTIVES

Let's start with the demonstrative adjectives. Notice that there are no written áccent márks.

For Masculine Singular Nouns:

este	*este sombrero*	this hat
ese	*ese reloj*	that watch
aquel	*aquel edificio*	that building far away

For Feminine Singular Nouns:

esta	*esta flor*	this flower
esa	*esa alfombra*	that carpet
aquella	*aquella mujer*	that woman far away

For Masculine Plural Nouns:

estos	*estos platos*	these plates
esos	*esos zapatos*	those shoes
aquellos	*aquellos hombres*	those men far away

For Feminine Plural Nouns:

estas	*estas muñecas*	these dolls
esas	*esas camisas*	those shirts
aquellas	*aquellas playas*	those faraway beaches

Now, study these examples. The demonstrative adjectives will always appear together with the nouns they modify:

The Spanish word for "people" is *gente*. It's always feminine, even if you have a group of men in mind: *la gente de aquí* = "people from here." Be careful not to say "*gentes*." *Gente* is by nature plural and thus doesn't need the *-s* at the end. The only time you might see *gentes* would be when talking about "the different peoples of the world." But even then, *gente* works just fine as is, and causes far less confusion in conversation.

Queremos comprar estas cosas. ¿Cuánto nos costarán?	We want to buy these things. How much will they cost us?
¿Cuánto cuestan estos juguetes cada uno?	How much do these toys cost each? ("each one")
Aquellos tres turistas ya no tienen dinero.	Those three tourists over there don't have any money left.
¿A cuánto salen esas camisas?	How much do those shirts go for?
¿Hay un descuento si compramos estos tres sombreros?	Is there a discount if we buy these three hats?
Aquel hombre es vendedor de recuerdos típicos.	That man over there is a seller of typical souvenirs.
¿Cuánto te han cobrado por esos zapatos?	How much have they charged you for those shoes?
Se puede comprar esas cosas en aquella tienda.	You (one) can buy those things in that store over there.
Este regalo será para mi abuelo. Ese regalo será para Juan.	This present is (will be) for my grandfather. That present is for Juan.

Lazy Practice

Create some basic sentences in English using "this," "that," "these," and "those." Use the previous examples as your guide. Include the name of the noun or nouns you are referring to. Now, translate these sentences into Spanish. Consult your dictionary as needed.

DEMONSTRATIVE PRONOUNS

These are the same words that you just learned—only with áccent márks. But while the adjectives modify

Masculine Singular:

éste	this one
ése	that one
aquél	that one far away

Feminine Singular:

ésta	this one
ésa	that one
aquélla	that one far away

Plurals:

éstos	these (masc.)
éstas	these (fem.)
ésos	those (masc.)
ésas	those (fem.)
aquéllos	those far away (masc.)
aquéllas	those far away (fem.)

The 3 Things Worst Things to Do With Demonstratives:

1. Worrying about the áccent márks when speaking. Don't worry about them, except when writing. The pronunciation is the same for adjectives and pronouns.

2. Stressing too much over the "ese vs. aquel" issue. Many people use ese, esa, and eso for "that," when technically aquel, aquella, or aquello should be used. Nonetheless, don't let this be an excuse for not trying to use aquel, etc. correctly.

3. Forgetting that the neuter demonstratives can save you a lot of grief about gender. Use them.

nouns, pronouns actually stand in for nouns. The gender and number of the demonstrative pronoun will link it to the nouns in question, so there is no need to mention them. You can often translate these as "this one," "that one," and even "these ones" in English.

Study these examples to see how they differ in usage from the demonstrative adjectives. Again, the noun or nouns being referenced won't actually be mentioned. The pronouns are here to give the real nouns a break:

Queremos comprar éstas.	We want to buy these. (feminine things)
Éste cuesta dos mil pesos, y ése cuesta mil quinientos.	This one costs 2,000 pesos, and that one costs 1,500.
Aquéllos no son baratos.	Those over there aren't cheap.
¿A cuánto salen ésas tres?	How much do those three cost? (three feminine things)
¿Cuál es el precio de éste?	What is the price of this one?
Éstos no me interesan. Son muy caros.	These don't interest me. They're very expensive.
En este mercado no hay, pero en áquel sí.	There aren't any in this market, but there are in that one (in that one yes).
Éste será para mi abuelo, y ése será para Juan.	This one is for my grandfather, and that one is for Juan.

Lazy Practice

Same deal as before. Create some basic sentences in English using "this," "that," "these," and "those." Use the previous examples as your guide. But now, don't include the name of the noun or nouns you are referring to. Give the nouns a rest by using the demonstrative pronouns. Translate these sentences into Spanish. Consult your dictionary as needed.

NEUTER DEMONSTRATIVE PRONOUNS: *ESTO, ESO, AQUELLO*

Both the demonstrative adjectives and pronouns must match the gender and number of the nouns being modified. But there are times when the "this" or "that" you are referring to isn't a specific or quantifiable noun, but rather an idea, a series of things or concepts, or something you don't know the name of yet. When you say "This is great" or "That's a shame," you're referring to concept or situation in general. And if you ask "What is that?," you won't know the gender of the noun because you don't know what the thing is yet—that's why you asked!

Neuter Demonstrative Pronouns:

esto	this
eso	that
aquello	that over there (this one isn't used very often)

Meet the neuter demonstrative pronouns: *eso, esto,* and *aquello.* These guys are great! If you don't know the name (much less the gender) of the noun (or item you want to buy), these are the pronouns for you. No need to worry about gender. If the thing you're referring to ends up being feminine, it won't matter until later.

Now, read the following examples to see the neuter demonstratives in action:

¿Qué es esto?	What is this? (could be an unknown noun or a situation)
¿Cómo se llama esto?	What do you call this?
No queremos comprar esto, queremos comprar eso.	We don't want to buy this, we want to buy that.
Eso es una buena idea.	That's a good idea.
Esto no es justo.	This isn't fair.
Eso es una ganga.	That's a great deal (a bargain).
Aquello es otro tema.	That's another issue.
Eso sí que es.	"That's the way to do it" (also spells "S.O.C.K.S")

As I've mentioned, these are very useful pronouns. You can use them to make statements or to ask questions about anything, without having to focus on the gender of the thing you're talking about. Of course, once you do know the gender of the noun, you'll need to start using the gendered demonstratives. Here's what I mean:

¿Qué es eso?	What is that?
Es un cenicero.	It's an ashtray.
Ese cenicero es muy lindo.	That ashtry is very nice.
¿Y esto?	And this?
Una lampa.	A lamp.
Esta lampa es fea.	This lamp is ugly.

PASSIVE CONSTRUCTIONS WITH *SE*

The most common way in Spanish to form a passive construction (something "is done," "is said," "is known," etc.) is to use our little friend *se* in combination with the third person conjugation of a verb. The subject of these constructions may be a non-specific "it," as in "It's raining" and "It's getting hot in here."

This construction is not entirely new to you. You learned it long ago in *¿Se puede?,* which literally means "Can something be done?" The trick to recognizing these passive constructions is to look for a verb in the third person singular or plural conjugation next to *se.* You'll never see phrases such as *se hablas* or *se sabemos.* Study the following examples:

Se habla español.	Spanish is spoken.
Se venden joyas de plata.	Silver jewelry for sale.
El turco no se entiende en el Paraguay.	Turkish is not understood in Paraguay.
¿Cómo se dice eso en el inglés?	How do you say that in English? (How is that said?)
No se sabe si lo van a	It isn't known whether

YOU'LL THANK YOURSELF LATER

By the way, the word for "dollars" is *dólares.* People will assume that you mean U.S. dollars. For Canadian money, it's *dólares canadienses.* Be sure to pronounce the accent on the first "o." Otherwise, it might sound like "doLORes" which, oddly, is both a woman's name and a word meaning "pains."

cambiar o no.	they will change it or not.
¿Aquí se compran libros usados?	Do you buy used books here?
Sí, se compran.	Yes, we do. (They are bought.)

THE HIGHER NUMBERS

You learned 1 to 99 way back in Chapter 2. Now, it's time for the rest:

100	*cien*
101	*ciento uno*
102	*ciento dos*
185	*ciento ochento y cinco*
200	*doscientos*
300	*trescientos*
400	*cuatrocientos*
500	*quinientos* (keen-y-ehn-tohs)— **not** *cincocientos*
600	*siescientos*
700	*sietecientos*
800	*ochocientos*
900	*novecientos*— **not** *nuevecientos*
1000	*mil*
2000	*dos mil*
3000	*tres mil*

100,000	*cien mil*
200,000	*doscientos mil*
1,000,000	*un millón*
2,000,000	*dos millones*
1,000,000,000,000	*un billón (larger than the U.S. billion)*

Most of these are fairly straightforward. Just remember that the word used for 100 is *cien.* But as part of the numbers 101 to 199, you must use *ciento:*

| *Cien mujeres del Perú.* | One hundred women from Peru |
| *Cien Años de Soledad* | One Hundred Years of Solitude |

But ...

| *Ciento cincuenta y dos años de soledad* | 152 years of solitude |

The numbers for the hundreds (100, 200, 300, etc.) must match the gender of the noun if they are being used as adjectives. They will, naturally, also be pluralized:

| *El plato vale dos cientas lempiras.* | The plate is worth 200 lempiras. (Honduran currency) |
| *Hay ocho cientas personas en el mercado.* | There are 800 people in the market. |

But ...

| *Este sombrero no vale dos cientos pesos.* | This hat isn't worth 200 pesos. |

IF YOU'RE SO
INCLINED

Not all Spanish-speaking countries use the *peso* as their monetary unit: in Spain it's the *peseta;* in Guatemala, the *Quetzal;* in Honduras, the *Lempira;* in Venezuela, the *Bolivar;* and in El Salvador, the *Colón*—just to name a few.

In most of the Spanish-speaking world, numbers over 1,000 use periods where Americans and Canadians are used to using commas. Thus, one million looks like 1.000.000 rather than 1,000,000. Don't let this confuse you.

Lazy Practice

Using the names of the various Latin currencies, start discussing large numbers of money. Pick the numbers at random: *287 pesos, 10.945 pesetas, 2.532 colones.* Remember, numbers are hard to learn in a new language. You may need to practice them often. Be creative and design some of your own exercises to help you practice your Spanish numbers.

ACTIVITY: CURRENCY EXCHANGE

Make a list of some things that you might like to buy on your next trip to Mexico (or some other Spanish-speaking country). Don't limit your shopping list to souvenirs. Include things that you'll need to survive, like food and personal items.

Now, determine the current exchange rate between the U.S. dollar (or your home currency) and the Mexican peso—currently about 10.5 pesos to the U.S. dollar. If you're headed to a country other than Mexico, find out the exchange rate there. Or you can visit **www.customhouse. com/rates.html** or similar Web sites for exchange rate information. You may also contact a travel agency, bank, or the embassy or consulate of the country you plan to visit.

YOU'LL THANK YOURSELF LATER

Though you may eventually get into the mindset of having to bargain for everything, not all prices are negotiable. If you're at a modern supermarket, don't show up at the checkout counter and expect to start bargaining down the price of your groceries. Reserve your bargaining skills for markets and private shops where you're actually dealing with the owner or the owner's family.

Estimate what you expect to pay for some of the items on your list (don't worry if you're way off) and convert your prices into the local currency. Use a pocket calculator if you need to, and learn the conversion formula by heart before you go.

QUICK PAINLESS

You may see the $ sign in Mexico meaning *peso*. Don't let this confuse you. In Puerto Rico, they use the U.S. dollar, but most people call it a *peso*. If you like, investigate the name of the currency of your favorite Latin country and see how much it's worth to you.

¡Vamos al Museo!

When you're not eating the delicious food or cramming your luggage full of souvenirs, you might consider filling your soul with some culture. There are many fine art museums in Latin America and Spain. Some are small and feature regional artists. Others, like el Museo del Prado in Madrid, boast some of the finest art collections in the world. Since many of the works you'll see are legacies from the past, it seems only fitting that this chapter should cover the Spanish past tenses.

SPANISH TEXT #1: *LA ESCULTURA*

Rather than dialogues, this chapter includes two "real live" Spanish texts. Text #1 discusses the development of modern sculpture.

This is a very difficult passage, so don't worry about understanding everything. Your mission here, should you choose to accept it, is to simply search for and underline all the conjugated verbs in the paragraph. Sounds easy enough, right? Well, not always. Written Spanish at this level tends to be long, rambling, and difficult to follow. This entire paragraph

The Spanish texts in this chapter have not been included for the purposes of developing your vocabulary, but rather as a way to familiarize you with the kinds of texts you'll be confronted with in places like museums. Still, it certainly couldn't hurt to look up some of these words. Note the large number of cognates. The grammatical forms in these texts should, in large part, seem familiar to you.

contains only five sentences. There are seven conjugated verbs. Notice that the verbs are conjugated in the present indicative tense, even though the events discussed occurred in the past. This style is known as the "historical present."

Don't let this difficult text discourage you. I have included it here simply to show you the kind of language you'll be forced to deal with in museums and encyclopedias. Even native speakers can get lost reading this stuff. One trick to understanding a passage such as this is to locate the verb of the sentence first. Then you can work back and forth from there and try to understand who's doing what to whom. Good luck!

A lo largo de casi nueve siglos de arte, la escultura occidental, sin renuciar enteramente a la representación de imagenes de la naturaleza se aleja de ella cada vez más, bajo la influencia del impresionismo y de la abstracción. En el proceso impresionista de análisis y de recomposición de las formas se incoropra la técnica nueva del hierro soldado de maestros como Gonzáles, Picasso, Calder, y D. Smith. La depuración casi formal de Brancusi influye a varios escultores, como a Henry Moore. Además, los partidarios del constructivismo, después de Gabo y Pevsener, son menos numerosos, y están inspirados por una estricta disciplina del arte minimal. Sin embargo, el expresionismo, contenido en ciertos artistas por la referecia figurativa (Giacometti, G. Richier, etc.) se convierte en proyección impetuosa y lírica para centenares de escultores que realizan esta técnica.

THE PAST TENSES: PRETERITE AND IMPERFECT

There are two past tenses in Spanish: the *preterite* past and the *imperfect* past. This section will cover them both. But first, let's take a moment to talk about that other "past tense" you learned several chapters ago.

The Present Perfect Tense: I Have Done It

Earlier in this book, you learned how to express a past idea with *haber* + PAST PARTICIPLE: *Hemos visitado el museo de arte moderno* = "We have visited the modern art museum." While this is a fine way to express a completed past action, this construction is technically not a true past tense, since *he, has, ha, hemos,* and *han* are actually present indicative forms of *haber*.

When you use *haber* + PAST PARTICIPLE in this way, it's called the "present perfect" tense. It tells of an action that occurred at an indefinite time in the past, but which may still be ongoing or having an influence on the present. Observe:

¿Has visto las obras de Goya?	Have you seen the works by Goya? (People have seen, and are still seeing, Goya's works)
He visitado el Museo de Arte Impresionista de Santiago.	I have visited the Santiago Museum of Impressionist Art. (The exact time I visited it is not important)

QUICK ✦ PAINLESS

No han aprendido a pintar todavía.	They still haven't learned to paint. (They might someday)
Hasta hoy, no he podido ir a la exposición.	Up until today, I haven't been able to go to the show. (But I may do so soon)
¿Ha probado usted la paella?	Have you tried the paella? (If you have, you still know what it tastes like)

Given that most English speakers find this tense relatively straightforward, I encourage you to use it often, especially once you feel comfortable with the irregular past participles.

Still, in spite of its name, this tense is not perfect for all occasions. It should not be used when a precise time in the past is indicated: *Lo he hecho ayer* = "I have done it yesterday" sounds odd in both Spanish and English. When the perfect tense doesn't fit, you'll need to use one of the following two tenses:

The Preterite: I Did It and It's Over

The preterite past tense is used to indicate a past action or occurrence that both began and finished in the past. Concepts expressed with the preterite are not thought of as having a strong influence on the present—they are over and done with. Usually, the preterite tells of something that occurred only once. It may also express a past action or series of actions that occurred several times if they are considered to be related.

First, let's look at how the preterite tense is formed. The preterite endings are added to the verb stem. Notice that some of these have an áccent márk on the last syllable:

When forming the preterite, don't forget the Spanish spelling rules. As with the subjunctive, the addition of some endings may require that an orthographic

Preterite Endings for Regular –ar Verbs:

Ending:	Inf.	Example:	Definition:
-é	hablar	hablé	I spoke
-aste	pagar	pagaste	you paid
-ó	cantar	cantó	he/she/it/you sang
-amos	contar	contamos	we counted; we told
-aron	comprar	compraron	they/you all bought

Preterite Endings for Regular –er and –ir Verbs:

Ending:	Inf.	Example:	Definition:
-í	comer	comí	I ate
-iste	salir	saliste	you went out, left
-ió	vivir	vivió	he/she/it/you lived
-imos	entender	entendimos	we understood
-ieron	decidir	decidieron	they/you all decided

QUICK ✿ PAINLESS

For regular –ar verbs, the nosotros form of the preterite is the same as the nosotros form in the present indicative. Thus, hablamos can mean "we talk" or "we talked." The context usually indicates whether the statement is in the past or present. If necessary, the speaker may indicate "when" with words like ahora, ayer, el jueves, etc. to avoid misunderstandings: Hablamos cada día = "We talk every day"; Hablamos ayer = "We talked yesterday."

convenience be used to match the spelling to the pronunciation. For example, *pagar* becomes *pagué* in the *yo* form of the preterite, because the *"g"* would be soft next to that *"e."* We prevent that by inserting a *"u."* You should still consider these verbs as regular.

If the verb stem ends in a vowel, the *"i"* in *-ieron* becomes *"y."* So, *leer* becomes *leyeron* in the third person plural preterite tense, since its stem is *le-*.

Irregular Preterite Verbs

While most verbs are regular in the preterite, many common verbs have irregular forms. I can offer you no real tricks for memorizing these—you'll just have to bite the *bala* (bullet) and learn them. Most of these verbs are fairly common, so you'll get to practice them often when you speak Spanish. Here's a list of most of the irregular preterite verbs that you're likely to use. You can't avoid them, so I recommend that you take all the time you need to learn them now:

andar	anduve, anduviste, anduvo, anduvimos, anduvieron
caber	cupe, cupiste, cupo, cupimos, cupieron
dar	di, diste, dio, dimos, dieron
decir	dije, dijiste, dijo, dijimos, dijeron
dormir	dormí, dormiste, durmió, dormimos, durmieron
estar	estuve, estuviste, estuvo, estuvimos, estuvieron
haber	hube, hubiste, hubo, hubimos, hubieron

hacer	hice, hiciste, hizo, hicimos, hicieron
ir	fui, fuiste, fue, fuimos, fueron
morir	morí, moriste, murió, morimos, murieron
poder	pude, pudiste, pudo, pudimos, pudieron
poner	puse, pusiste, puso, pusimos, pusieron
querer	quise, quisiste, quiso, quisimos, quisieron
saber	supe, supiste, supo, supimos, supieron
sentir	sentí, sentiste, sintió, sentioms, sintieron
ser	fui, fuiste, fue, fuimos, fueron
tener	tuve, tuviste, tuvo, tuvimos, tuvieron
traducir	traduje, tradujiste, tradujo, etc.
traer	traje, trajiste, trajo, trajimos, trajeron
venir	vine, viniste, vino, vinimos, vinieron

YOU'LL THANK YOURSELF LATER

The preterite forms of *haber* are rarely used except for *hubo,* the past form of *hay: Ayer hubo un problema en el museo* = "There was a problem in the museum yesterday." Use *hubo* whenever you wish to say *hay* in the past. You can ignore the other preterite forms of *haber.*

Lazy Practice

Design an exercise to help you memorize the irregular preterite verbs and their forms. Flash cards? Lists? Games? Whatever suits your personal learning style. I know these irregular forms can be irritating. However, your Spanish will remain weak until you've learned these irregular preterite verb forms and are ready to use them at the drop of a *sombrero.*

Now, here are some examples to help you better understand the uses of the preterite tense:

Mario fue al Museo de Arte Moderno de Barcelona.	Mario went to the Modern Art Museum in Barcelona.

In the sentence *Compré diez coches el año pasado* ("I bought ten cars last year"), the preterite must be used—even though the transactions may have taken place at different times during the course of the year. The purchase of the vehicles is over and done with. The number of cars bought, and the time period in which this all occurred, are both fixed.

Ese retrato fue comprado recientemente por el Museo Nacional.	That painting was recently bought by the National Museum.
Goya evolucionó desde el barroco al rococó.	Goya evolved from the baroque to the rococo.
Velázquez pintó la Venus del espejo.	Velazquez painted "Venus of (in) the Mirror."
Me gustaron todas las obras de Orozco y Rivera.	I liked all of the works by Orozco and Rivera.
Todos los pintores de aquella época abandonaron el uso de esa técnica.	All of the painters of that period abandoned the use of that technique.
Rodin mezcló el realismo y el romanticismo en sus figuras y monumentos.	Rodin mixed realism and romanticism in his figures and monuments.

Here are some examples not related to art:

María tuvo que comprar una tarjeta postal.	Maria had to buy a postcard.
Cristóbal Colón descubrió las Américas.	Christopher Columbus discovered the Americas.
¿Pudiste conocer a mi primo?	Were you able to meet my cousin?
Pero mi amor, solo salí con ella una vez.	But honey, I only went out with her once.
Ayer estuve bien, pero hoy estoy mal.	Yesterday I was fine, but today I'm not well.

Anoche no pude dormir.	I couldn't sleep last night.
Ya pasó.	It's over.
El jueves pasado a las nueve, encontré un peso en la calle.	Last Thursday at nine o'clock, I found a peso on the street.
"¿Fuiste a la escuela?"	"Did you go to school?"
"Sí, fui."	"Yes, I did."
"¿E hiciste tu tarea?"	"And did you do your homework?"
"Sí, la hice."	"Yes, I did it."

Lazy Practice

Create sentences in the past tense and practice forming and using the Spanish preterite. Refer to the previous examples and explanations if you need guidance.

THE IMPERFECT TENSE: I USED TO DO IT OFTEN

The other past tense is called the imperfect tense. But there's absolutely nothing wrong with it. The imperfect tense is used to express past actions or events that occurred over an extended period of time. Use the imperfect to describe conditions in the past or to tell of actions done often or habitually.

Did I lose you? Well, I know that this can be confusing. But it will all make sense in a minute. Let's begin by learning how the tense is formed. As with the preterite, the imperfect endings are added to the verb stem:

IF YOU'RE SO INCLINED

You can express a recent past action by using the verb phrase *acabar + de + INFINITIVE*: *Acabo de salir del museo* = "I just left the museum"; *Acaban de ver las esculturas de Julio González* = "They just saw the sculptures by Julio González." *Acabar* can also be used in the imperfect tense: *Juan acababa de estudiar el retrato de Velázquez cuando cerraron el museo* = "Juan had just studied the painting by Velázquez when they closed the museum."

And below are the –*er* and –*ir* endings.

You may have noticed that the first person and third person singular forms look the same. The context usually makes it clear what's going on, but pronouns and names can also be added for clarity.

Imperfect Past Endings for -*ar* Verbs:

Ending:	Example:	Definition:
-aba	*hablaba*	I used to speak
-abas	*cantaba*	you used to sing
-aba	*pagaba*	he/she/you used to pay
-ábamos	*contábamos*	we used to tell (or "count")
-aban	*compraban*	they used to buy

Imperfect Past Endings for –*er* and -*ir* Verbs:

Ending:	Example:	Definition:
-ía	*vivía*	I used to live
-ías	*comías*	you used to eat
-ía	*sentía*	he/she used to feel
-íamos	*pedíamos*	we used to ask for
-ían	*sabían*	they used to know

Luckily, there are only three common verbs that take an irregular imperfect form: *ser, ir,* and *ver* ("to see"). You'll need these right away, though, so you should learn them now:

ser	*era, eras, era, éramos, eran*
ir	*iba, ibas, iba, íbamos, iban*
ver	*veía, veías, veía, veíamos, veían*

Lazy Practice

Make a list of 15 or so of your favorite verbs and practice forming the imperfect tense. Go through all the forms (first person, second person, etc.).

Here are some examples to help you understand the uses of the imperfect tense:

Description:

Era la mañana y llovía mucho.	It was morning, and it was raining a lot.
La casa estaba pintada de un color gris.	The house was painted a gray color.
Desde el techo se veía el mar.	From the roof one could see the sea.
Los pintores del siglo veinte eran todos muy extraños.	The painters of the twentieth century were all very strange.

Habitual action:

El pintor asistía a la escuela de arte cuando era niño.	The painter attended art school when he was a child.

YOU'LL THANK YOURSELF LATER

The verb *querer* in the past has two different meanings in the negative: *él no quiso* means "He refused," while *él no quería* means "He didn't want to."

IF YOU'RE SO
INCLINED

You already know most of the verbs in the list of irregular preterites. You may not know these: *andar* = "to walk; to go"; *caber* = "to fit" (the present indicative is the *yo* form is *quepo*); *morir* = "to die"; *sentir* = "to feel"; *traducir* = "to translate." Learn them now if you like.

Íbamos al museo de Dalí cada año cuando vivíamos en Florida.	We used to go the Dali Museum every year when we lived in Florida.
Mi papá compraba muchos coches.	My dad used to buy a lot of cars. (When and how many are not important)

Sometimes the imperfect and preterite can be used in the same sentence. This is a good way to tell of an action that was occurring when something else interrupted it. The imperfect tells what was going on when something "preterite" happened:

Yo estaba leyendo Don Quixote cuando sonó el teléfono.	I was reading *Don Quixote* when the phone rang.
Juan estudiaba el retrato de Picasso cuando se le cayó encima la escultura de Giacometti.	Juan was studying the painting by Picasso when the Giacometti sculpture fell on top of him.
	(*caerse* = "to fall down." See Chapter 17 for reflexive verbs)

Remember that perfect tense from before? Well, *haber* can also be used in the imperfect (yes, an "imperfect perfect tense"). This tense corresponds to the English "had done, had been, had seen, etc." It tells of a condition that existed prior to a later past occurrence or action. Observe:

No fue la primera vez. *Lo había visto en el '89.*	It wasn't the first time. I had seen it in '89.

Se había casado tres veces ya cuando conoció a su cuarta esposa.	He had already been married three times when he met his fourth wife.
Ya se había construido el edificio cuando se convertío en museo.	The building had already been constructed when it was converted into a museum.

SPANISH TEXT #2: *El MUSEO DEL PRADO*

This text discusses the construction of the Prado in Madrid. As with the previous text, you shouldn't worry about understanding it all right now. These long, convoluted texts are tough. In this exercise, simply read the text and underline any verbs you see in either the preterite or the imperfect tenses.

El actual Museo del Prado es uno de los edificios con los que se adornó, en el reinado de Carlos III, el que se llamó primero Salón del Prado y luego Paseo. Con ese Salón del Prado, concebido como una operación urbanística de gran escala, pretendió el rey, "el mejor alcalde de Madrid," también llamado "el rey albañil," dotar a la capital de sus reinos de un espacio de categoría urbana y monumental al modo de los que sí abundaban en las capitales de otros reinos europeos. El Madrid en el que él había nacido, poco había mejorado cuando a él regresó para ser rey luego de serlo de Nápoles. Madrid era todavía aquel pueblo pequeño que, convertido

IF YOU'RE SO INCLINED

As with the previous text, you don't need to look up these words, but it couldn't hurt. Note the cognates, and write down any words that interest you in your notebook.

repentinamente en capital de España por obra y gracia de Felipe II, había crecido precipitadamente y de un modo desordenado y poco consistente.

ORDINAL NUMBERS: FIRST, SECOND, ETC.

You learned the cardinal numbers (1, 2, 3, etc.) back in Chapter 2. Now, meet the ordinal numbers. These are adjectives, and thus must match the gender and number of the noun or nouns being modified. *Primero* and *tercero* become *primer* and *tercer* before singular masculine nouns. They are usually (but not always) placed before the noun:

primero (primer)	first
segundo	second
tercero (tercer)	third
cuarto	fourth
quinto	fifth
sexto	sixth
séptimo	seventh
octavo	eight
noveno	ninth
décimo	tenth

IF YOU'RE SO INCLINED

If you can't travel to Madrid any time soon, don't worry. *El Museo del Prado* has its own Web site: museoprado.mcu.es.

Now, here are some examples of how the ordinals can be used:

El primer pintor español de la etapa	The first Spanish painter of the period
La primera exhibición del año	The first exhibition of the year
Ésta es la segunda vez que estoy en Madrid.	This is the second time I have been in Madrid.
Los cubistas fueron los terceros en utilizar esta técnica.	The cubists were the third (group) to utilize this technique.
El Papa Juan Pablo Segundo	Pope John Paul the Second
Es el segundo Juan Pablo que he visto hoy.	He's the second guy named John Paul I've seen today.

There are additional ordinals beyond these, but you probably won't need to use them. If you must express an ordinal beyond ten, just use the cardinal number (11, 23, 45, 67, etc.) and you'll be understood.

Lazy Practice

Create sentences that include cardinal numbers. Use the word *vez* (time, occurrence) if you get stuck: *la primera vez* = "the first time."

A COMPLETE WASTE OF TIME

The 3 Worst Things to Do With the Past Tense:

1. Forget that many common verbs have irregular preterits. You can't avoid these. Learn them now.

2. Use the preterite tense for things you used to do habitually or during an extended period of time.

3. Use the imperfect tense for things that you did once at a specific time.

QUICK ⏿ PAINLESS

ACTIVITY: HISTORY

If you're interested in art, you might benefit from some additional study. Visit your local library and research the art of Spain and Latin America. Depending on your level of interest, you could spend anywhere from a few minutes to a lifetime on this subject.

Pick a genre that interests you (sculpture, painting) and see what you can find on the subject. Use some of the names mentioned in this chapter as leads. If you're not happy with the selection in your library, the Internet is an excellent resource. You get extra points for anything you read in Spanish.

Entre Amigos: Pleasant Conversation

If some of the best things in life are free, *la amistad* (friendship) must be one of the highest on the list. Spanish speakers delight in good conversation and making new friends. After this chapter, you'll be ready to "make friends and influence people" *en español.*

DIALOGUE: *NUEVOS AMIGOS:* TIM, YOLANDA, Y MARTÍN

After reading *Learn Spanish The Lazy Way,* Tim was inspired to travel to Latin America in order to practice his Spanish. Today he's in Cuzco, Perú, backpacking his way through the Andes. While sitting at a café paging through his travel guide (perhaps *Backpacking Through the Andes The Lazy Way?*), Yolanda and Martín, two young Peruvian tourists, approach his table and introduce themselves:

Yolanda:	Hola. ¿Qué tal? ¿De dónde eres?
Tim:	Hola. Soy de los Estados Unidos.
Martín:	¿Así? ¿De cuál estado?

Tim:	De Ohio. Soy de Cleveland. Me llamo Tim.
Yolanda:	Me llamo Yolanda, y mi amigo se llama Martín. ¿Podemos tomar asiento aquí contigo?
Tim:	Sí, cómo no. Ustedes son de aquí, ¿verdad?
Martín:	Pues, sí, somos de acá. Pero no de aquí de Cuzco. Yo soy de Lima y Yolanda es de Arequipa. De hecho, somos turistas aquí también. ¿Qué te parece el Perú?
Tim:	Me encanta. Llegué apenas anteayer. No me he acostumbrado todavía a la altura. Anoche no pude dormir bien y me dio un dolor de cabeza horrible. Ahora, parece que ya me ha pasado todo. Y ustedes, ¿Qué están haciendo en Cuzco?
Yolanda:	Pues, tú sabes, estamos haciendo el camino Inca. No es solamente para los turistas extranjeros, ¿verdad?
Tim:	Claro que no. Es una maravilla.
Martín:	Dime una cosa. ¿Cuánto gana un trabajador por día en los Estados Unidos? Tú sabes, acá la cosa es bien difícil. Uno trabajo muy duro, pero los sueldos son muy bajos. O sea, creo que ustedes están ganando mucho más que nosotros.
Tim:	Bueno, eso depende de la clase de trabajo que uno haga. Yo, siendo estudiante, vivo en parte de una beca y de lo poco que me están pagando de mi trabajo temporal en la cafetería universitaria.
Martín:	Pero, por hora, ¿cuanto te pagan?

YOU'LL THANK YOURSELF LATER

Conversations in Latin countries, especially among friends and family, can be fast-paced and loud. People may raise their voices, gesture enthusiastically, talk at the same time, and interrupt one another. Usually this behavior is simply their way of showing interest in the topic at hand. It's not considered disrespectful or rude. In fact, if someone decides not carry on this way, it may be interpreted as a lack of interest in what the other person has to say.

Tim:	Pues, se trata del sueldo mínimo permitido por ley. Son unos cinco dólares por hora, más o menos.
Martín:	¡Caray! En comparación con lo que se gana aquí, es mucho dinero.
Tim:	Tal vez. Pero hay que tener en cuenta que allá todo cuesta mucho más. Aunque parezca mucho dinero, en realidad no lo es.
Yolanda:	Oye, Martín. Basta con las preguntas acerca del dinero. ¿No ves que le estás molestando a Tim?
Tim:	No te preocupes, Yolanda. Todo el mundo me hace las mismas preguntas.
Yolanda:	¿Tienes hermanos?
Tim:	Sí, dos. Un hermano y una hermana. He aquí una foto de mi familia. (Takes picture from wallet.) Mira, él es mi padre, y ella mi madre. La que está a la derecha es mi hermana, Nancy, y el que está a la izquierda es mi hermano, Bob. Atrás están mis primos, mis tíos, y mis abuelos. Soy yo ahí, sentado en el piso.
Yolanda:	Y yo pensaba que las familias de ustedes eran muy pequeñas. La tuya es muy grande. La mía también es grande. Tengo cinco hermanos.
Martín:	Yo tengo seis. Mira, vamos a ir a una peña esta noche a las 9:00. ¿Quieres ir con nosotros? Sería más divertido si podríamos ir contigo.
Tim:	¿Conmigo? Bueno, sí, por supuesto. A mí me gustaría ir con ustedes.

QUICK ⬤ PAINLESS

The expression *Está bien* means "It's fine," and is used in conversations to mean "OK," "I understand," "All right," or "I follow what you're saying." The tone of voice and placement in the conversation indicates how the phrase is being used. Generally, you can say *Está bien* any time you would have said "OK" in English. *Muy bien* can be used the same way. Of course, *Está bien* may also refer to a person who is simply feeling well.

Yolanda:	Muy bien. Entonces, vete a la plaza central a las ocho y media. Podemos encontrarnos frente a la catedral y de ahí, podemos ir juntos a la peña.
Tim:	Perfecto. Nos vemos entonces a las 8:30.
Martín:	¡Sensacional!
Tim:	Bueno, hasta entonces. Oye, Martín, antes de que te vayas, hazme un favor. Me puedes sacar una foto? Aquí tenes mi máquina de fotos. Es muy fácil de usar. Oprimiendo este botón, se saca la foto.
Martín:	¿Listo? (Takes picture) Bueno, ya la saqué.
Tim:	Gracias. Ah, una última pregunta. ¿Qué es exactamente una peña?
Yolanda:	Es una fiesta andina con musica tradicional.
Tim:	¡Qué bueno! Nos vemos entonces.
Martín:	OK. Hasta luego.

Translation:

Yolanda:	Hi. How are you? Where are you from?
Tim:	Hi. I'm from the United States.
Martín:	Really? From which state?
Tim:	From Ohio. I'm from Cleveland. My name is Tim (I call myself).
Yolanda:	My name is Yolanda, and my friend's name is Martín. Can we take a seat here with you?
Tim:	Yes, of course. You're from here, right?
Martín:	Well, yes we're from here. But not from here in Cuzco. I'm from Lima and Yolanda is from Arequipa. In fact, we're tourists here too. What do you think of Peru?

Tim:	It's great. I just arrived the day before yesterday. I haven't gotten used to the altitude yet. Last night I couldn't sleep well, and I got a horrible headache. Now it seems that it has all passed over. And you? What are you doing in Cuzco?
Yolanda:	Well, you know, we're doing the Inca trail. It's not just for the foreign tourists, you know.
Tim:	Of course not. It's wonderful (a wonder).
Martín:	Tell me something. How much does a worker earn each day in the United States? You know, things are pretty tough here (the thing is …). You work very hard (one works), but the wages are very low. I mean, I think (believe) that you all are making a lot more that we are.
Tim:	Well, that depends on the kind of work you do (one does). Being a student, I live partly from a scholarship and partly from the little (I earn) from my part-time job at the school cafeteria.
Martín:	But, per hour, how much do they pay you?
Tim:	Well, it's the minimum wage allowed by law. It's about five dollars per hour, more or less.
Martín:	Wow! In comparison with what (that which) people earn (is earned) here, that's a lot of money.
Tim:	Perhaps. But you have to keep in mind that everything costs a lot more there. Although it might look like a lot of money, in reality it isn't.

YOU'LL THANK YOURSELF LATER

While *adios* does mean "goodbye," it can be a bit too final for some occasions. If you plan to see someone again reasonably soon, you should use one of these instead: *hasta mañana* ("until tomorrow"); *hasta luego* ("see you later"); *hasta la próxima* ("until next time"); *hasta la vista* ("until I see you again"). By the way, Arnold Schwarzenegger aside, this last one is not as popular as you might think.

QUICK PAINLESS

The quintessential Americanism "okay" has become practically universal. In Spanish, "okay" (*"oh que"*) is certainly a bit slangy, but most people seem to understand it. There's no reason why you shouldn't be able to use it now and then when talking to your Spanish-speaking friends. But "okay" should never entirely replace *Está bien* or *Muy bien*.

Yolanda:	Hey, Martín. Enough with the questions about money. Can't you see that you're bothering Tim?
Tim:	Don't worry, Yolanda. Everybody asks me the same questions.
Yolanda:	Do you have siblings?
Tim:	Yes, two. A sister and a brother. Here's a picture of my family. (Takes picture from wallet) Look (to Yolanda), he is my father, and she is my mother. The person (or woman) on the right is my sister, Nancy, and the one (male person = *el*) on the left is my brother, Bob. In back are my cousins, uncles (and possibly aunts) and my grandparents. That's me, sitting on the floor.
Yolanda:	And I thought that your families were very small. Yours is very big. Mine is also large. I have five siblings.
Martín:	And I've got six. Look, we're going to go to a *peña* tonight at 9:00. Do you want to come with us? It would be more fun if we could go with you.
Tim:	With me? Well, yes, of course. I'd love to go with you.
Yolanda:	Great. So, go to the central plaza at 8:30. We can meet in front of the cathedral and then, we can go together to the *peña*.
Tim:	Perfect. We'll see each other then at 8:30.
Martín:	Cool!
Tim:	Well, see you then. Hey, Martín, before you go, do me a favor. Can you take a

picture of me? Here's my camera. It's really easy to use. Just push this button to take the picture.

Martín: Ready? (Tim nods) OK, I just took it.

Tim: Thanks. Uhhh, one last question. What exactly is a *peña?*

Yolanda: It's an Andean party with traditional music.

Tim: That's great! We'll see each other later then.

Martín: See you later (until later).

THE TÚ COMMANDS: DO IT! SAY IT!

Now that you're making new friends, you'll have lots of people to boss around. The commands in the *tú* form (also known as the "second person imperative") are relatively simple. They are formed by removing the *–s* from the second person singular of the present indicative.

Tú Command Forms:

Verb:	Command:	Definition:
comer	*Come.*	Eat.
vivir	*Vive.*	Live.
cantar	*Cántala.*	Sing it.
escribir	*Escríbeme.*	Write me.
dar	*Dámelos.*	Give them to me.
contar	*Cuéntaselo.*	Tell him it.

Usually, this ends up being the same thing as the third person (*él/ella/usted*) form of the verb. Any stem changes in the present indicative will also show up in the imperative (see the table on the previous page).

So, to tell your friend to "speak," simply say *habla* (don't forget to be nice and add *"por favor"*). Any DOPs (direct object pronouns) and INDOPs (indirect object pronouns) are glued right on to the imperative verb—which may necessitate the addition of an áccent márk to maintain the correct stress: *habla, háblame.*

Generally, the *tú* imperatives aren't too difficult. But, as you have come to expect by now, there's a catch. Several common verbs have a short irregular form for the *tú* commands:

Verb:	Tú Command:	Example:	Definition:
hacer	*haz*	*Hazlo.*	Do it.
ir	*ve*	*Vete.*	Go away.
decir	*di*	*Dímelo.*	Tell me it.
tener	*ten*	*Ten cuidado.*	Be careful.
salir	*sal*	*¡Sal de ahí!*	Get out of there!
poner	*pon*	*Ponlos aquí.*	Put them (down) here.
venir	*ven*	*Vente.*	Come here.
ser	*sé*	*Sé fuerte.*	Be strong.

Here are a few more examples:

Háblame en español.	Talk to me in Spanish.
Hazme un favor. Cierra la ventana.	Do me a favor. Close the window.
Siéntate aquí y dime qué pasó. (sentarse = "to sit down")	Sit here and tell me what happened.

Remember, when you tell someone *not* to do something, you must use the subjunctive:

¡No me causes más problemas! (causar)	Don't cause me any more problems!
No la pagues, Juan. Yo te invité. La pagaré yo.	Don't pay it, Juan. I invited you. I'll pay it.
No se lo digas a mi esposa, por favor.	Please don't tell my wife.
No te preocupes. ¡Sé feliz! (preocuparse)	Don't worry. Be happy!

Lazy Practice

Create sentences in which you are directly telling a friend or family member to do something. Follow the previous examples and explanations for guidance. Consult your dictionary for new verbs. Make sure that you allow for any stem changes when forming the *tú* commands.

IF YOU'RE SO INCLINED

In countries where *vos* is used instead of *tú,* a different imperative form is required. The *vos* command is formed by removing the *–r* from the infinitive and áccenting the final vowel: *comé, viví, salí, poné, hacé, vení,* etc. You can learn this form if you want, but you needn't worry about it right now. Since it's pretty easy, you'll pick it up quickly if you need it. Use the *tú* commands until then, and everyone will understand you.

THE PRESENT PROGRESSIVE: DOING, TALKING, GOING

When something or someone is involved in an activity in the present moment, Spanish often uses what is known as the "present progressive" tense. This tense roughly corresponds to the –ing tenses we use all the time in English:

"Honey, what are you *doing?*"

"I am *leaving* you for another man."

"Oh no! And you're even *taking* the dog with you?"

"No, I'm *sending* him to my mother. Goodbye forever!"

"But, sweetheart. Why are you *being* so cruel?"

"Because I don't love you anymore."

"No, I was *talking* about giving our dog to your mother."

Remember the past participle? Well, as you might have expected, there's a present participle, too. It can also be called a "gerund," but for our purposes, present participle will do. Whatever you call it, you'll need one to form the Spanish present progressive tense. As you just saw, the English present participle ends in –ing: "doing, talking, giving, etc." The Spanish present participles are formed by adding the endings –ando to –ar verb stems and –iendo (or -yendo) to –er and –ir stems. Observe:

Verb:	Ending:	Present Participle:	Definition:
hablar	*-ando*	hablando	talking
cantar	*-ando*	cantando	singing
comer	*-iendo*	comiendo	eating
vivir	*-iendo*	viviendo	living
oír	*-yendo*	oyendo	hearing

The present progressive in Spanish is basically the same as the English construction "someone or something *is* doing": *estar* (to be) + PRESENT PARTICIPLE. Although *ser* also means "to be," it isn't used with the present participle. Most verbs form regular present participles. But, of course, a few common *-er* and *-ir* verbs have slightly irregular forms. Stem-changing *-ir* verbs such as *pedir* (pido) and *dormir* (duermo) change the "e" to "i" and the "o" to "u" in the present participle:

venir	viniendo
decir	diciendo
sentir	sintiendo
pedir	pidiendo
dormir	durmiendo
morir	muriendo

Also:

poder	pudiendo

If the verb stem ends in a vowel (*creer, caer, oír, leer*), then the "i" in *-iendo* becomes "y": *creyendo, cayendo, oyendo, leyendo*. Verbs ending in *–eír*, such as *reír* ("to

QUICK PAINLESS

The participle is always invariable. No matter who you are or what you're doing, the "o" at the end never becomes "a." It is also never pluralized with an "s." And when you have DOPs and INDOPs to deal with, you can put them before the conjugated verb ("*lo está diciendo*") or you can stick them right on to the participle (*está diciéndolo*). Just remember that áccent márks will appear if you add them to the participle to preserve stress.

laugh") and *sonreir* ("to smile"), lose both the "e" and the áccent márk: *riendo, sonriendo.*

Here are some basic sentences using the present progressive tense:

Estoy escribiendo una carta a mi viejo amigo.	I'm writing a letter to my old friend.
Antonio está viajando por España.	Antonio is traveling through Spain.
Estamos construyendo una casa nueva.	We are building a new house.
Están charlando juntos.	They are talking together.
Se me está terminando el dinero.	My money is starting to run out. (the money is running out on me)

The present participle can also be used after verbs like *seguir* and *continuar* (both mean "to continue") and the verb *ir* ("to go").

Siguen charlando.	They're still talking.
Voy entendiendo un poco mejor el español.	I'm getting to understand Spanish a bit better.
Continuarán reparando el camindo durante toda la semana.	They will be continuing to repair the road during the entire week.

The present participle also has some uses on its own. Use the present participle to say "By doing (whatever ...)" as in the following examples:

Hablando el español, aprenderás mucho.	By speaking Spanish, you'll learn a lot.

YOU'LL THANK YOURSELF LATER

The present participle of *ser* is *siendo*. It's not used often, but it's handy for saying "Being (whatever ...)" as in: *Siendo hombre, no pudo entender los dolores de parto de su esposa* ("Being a man, he couldn't understand his wife's labor pains").

Leyendo un poco cada día, aprenderás muchas nuevas palabras.	By reading a little every day, you will learn many new words.
Trabajando se gana la vida.	You live (one lives) by working.
Preguntando se llega a Roma.	"All roads lead to Rome." (By asking you can get anywhere.)

Note that the tense of *estar* can vary. You can use it in the imperfect, conditional, or future. While the present progressive is used for the here and now, it can also be used in the past and future:

Estaba hablando con mi amigo cuando sonó el teléfono.	I was talking with my friend when the phone rang.
Estaré viajando durante el próximo mes.	I will be traveling during the coming month.
Había estado mirando la televisión durante una hora cuando se le cortó la luz.	He had been watching television for an hour when the power went out.
Estaríamos charlando el español, pero él solo habla inglés.	We would be speaking Spanish, but he only speaks English.
¿Quién ha estado comiendo la avena mía?	Who has been eating my porridge?

Lazy Practice

Create sentences using the present progressive tense. Start with a few "somebody-is-doing-something" sentences in English. Then try to translate them into Spanish.

Use *hacer* with TIME EXPRESSION + *que* to say that something has been going on for a specific time period and is still continuing: *Hace tres días que leo esta novela* = "I've been reading this novel for three days (and I still am)." *Hace tres años que no fumo* = "I haven't smoked in three years (and I still haven't)." With a preterite verb, *hacer* means "ago": *Ocurrió hace dos semanas* = "It occurred two weeks ago."

Use the previous examples and explanations as your guide.

POSSESSIVES: I GOT MINE, YOU GOT YOURS

You've already learned a few of these in previous chapters. Now it's time to fill in the gaps. The possessives are pretty easy. Just remember that when more than one thing is being "possessed," an "-s" must be added for the plural. Note also that these do not have áccent márks on them. This is important, since *tú* means "you," while *tu* means "your." In the *nosotros* form, you must match the gender and number to the noun.

Singular:	Plural:	Definition:
mi	*mis*	my
tu	*tus*	your
su	*sus*	his/her/your/its
nuestro	*nuestros*	our (masculine nouns)
nuestra	*nuestras*	our (feminine nouns)
su	*sus*	their (plural)

Here are some examples that illustrate the use of the possessives:

Él es mi papá, y ella es mi mamá.	He is my dad, and she is my mom.
Nuestro perro es grande, pero nuestro coche es pequeño.	Our dog is large, but our car is small.
Mi casa es su casa.	My house is your house.

Sus amigos son muy simpáticos.	Their friends are very nice.
Tus hermanos son más altos que tu primo.	Your siblings are taller than your cousin.
Tus hermanos son más altos que los de tu primo.	Your siblings are taller than your cousins.

In addition to these possessives, there is a second set of possessives called "possessive adjectives." In English, we also make this distinction when we say "my car" and "the car is mine." These work the same as other adjectives:

Singular:	Plural:	Definition:
mío/mía	*míos/mías*	mine
tuyo/tuya	*tuyos/tuyas*	your
suyo/suya	*suyos/suyas*	his, hers, your
nuestro/nuestra	*nuestros/nuestras*	our
suyo/suya	*suyos/suyas*	their (plural)

Here are a few examples:

Esta mochila es mía, pero la otra es de Oscar.	This backpack is mine, but the other one is Oscar's.
Ese perro es más grande que el nuestro.	That dog is bigger than ours.
"Oye, ¿son tuyas estas cosas?"	"Hey, are these things yours?"
"No, son suyas. Son de aquel señor allí."	"No they are his. They belong to that gentleman over there."

QUICK 🔲 *PAINLESS*

Some English speakers, especially men, have trouble remembering that the possessive adjectives match the gender of the object owned, not the gender of the person speaking. So there's no need to feel awkward saying *la casa es mía* if you're a man, or *el coche is mío* if you're a woman. Possessive adjectives have nothing to do with *your* gender, just the gender of your possessions.

Lazy Practice

Talk about all the things that you own. Then talk about other people's stuff. Practice using the possessives with these sentences. Refer to the previous examples and explanations for guidance.

WITH ME, WITH YOU: *CONMIGO, CONTIGO*

You've already learned that *con* means "with" (*chile con carne* = "chile with meat"). There's nothing really special about *con*, except that when it's used with "me" and "you," it takes a special form:

con + yo	*conmigo*	with me
con + tú	*contigo*	with you

Here are some examples to show you what I mean:

¿Quieres ir conmigo al cine?	Do you want to come with me to the movies?
Me dijeron que Julio estaba hablando contigo cuando sucedió.	They told me that Julio was talking with (to) you when it happened.
Quiero salir con ella, pero ella no quiere salir conmigo.	I want to go out with her, but she doesn't want to go out with me.

PERSONAL SPACE

Spaniards and Latin Americans tend to stand quite close to one another when they talk. You may find yourself feeling a bit boxed in by your new Latin friends. But from their perspective, standing close to you is an indication of

IF YOU'RE SO INCLINED

There is a third form of these "sigos": *consigo*. It means "with himself/herself" and is a combination of *con + se*. *Está muy enojado consigo mismo* = "He's very angry with himself"; *Llevaba consigo dos pistolas grandes* = "He was carrying (with himself) two large pistols." But at this stage, you'll be saying *con él, con ella,* and *con usted* much more often. Don't worry about *consigo* too much until you've moved beyond the contents of this book.

their concern and politeness. If you keep backing off, they might get the message that you don't like them or that you are cold and unfeeling.

Of course, if you feel threatened in any way, you should quickly move away and avoid eye contact. But in situations where you know you're among friends, you should be aware of this difference in personal space. It may take you a little time before you feel completely comfortable. But eventually, you may even find yourself preferring this Latin sense of closeness.

Lazy Practice

Notice the distance you keep when talking to people. Stand really close to your friends and see how they react.

ACTIVITY: ROLE PLAY

Choose a historical character who interests you. Learn some biographical information about him or her, and then give a short presentation (preferably, but not necessarily, to someone who speaks Spanish) pretending to be that person. So, if you want to pretend to be Christopher Columbus, say:

Buenos días, soy Cristóbal Colón. Soy italiano y descurbrí las Américas en 1492.

Once you have done this, you can stop pretending to be somebody famous and talk about yourself.

YOU'LL THANK YOURSELF LATER

In some Spanish-speaking countries (mostly South America), a man may be expected to kiss a woman on one cheek the first time they are being introduced (if the two are about the same age and social standing). Men may hug if they are good friends. However, it's always best to spend some time observing what the people around you are doing before you start running around hugging and kissing people.

Problem-Solving

No matter where you are, something will eventually go wrong. Either you get lost, lose or forget something, or fall ill. The dialogues in this chapter introduce some useful grammar and phrases that will help you to solve your problems (I hope). Study them carefully. And let's hope that nothing like this ever happens to you.

DIALOGUE: THE LOST WALLET

Brian is an Australian tourist in San José, Costa Rica. He has lost his wallet, and has arrived at the police station to report what happened. Study this passage carefully—it's probably the most difficult dialogue in the entire book:

Brian: Buenas noches, señor. Tengo una emergencia.

El policía: Dígame señor.

Brian: Resulta que he perdido mi billetera. Traía en ella todos los documentos importantes, el boleto de avión, las tarjetas de crédito, el pasaporte, la licencia de conducir, los cheques de viajero, y una cantidad de dinero en efectivo.

El policía: ¡Caray! Lo lamento mucho, señor. ¿Existe la posibilidad de que se trate de un robo?

Brian:	Bueno, no sé. No me asaltaron, y no me acuerdo de haber tenido contacto con nadie. Creo que se me cayó nomás cuando caminábamos por la calle.
El policía:	¿Con quién estaba usted y a dónde iban?
Brian:	Estaba con mi amigo Julio. Quería que encontráramos algo de comer. Íbamos a un restaurante cuando de repente vimos un puesto de comida en la calle y nos detuvimos para comprar algo rápido ahí.
El policía:	¿Y cuándo se dio cuenta usted por primera vez de que ya no tenía la cartera?
Brian:	Habíamos pedido que nos hicieran un sandwich. Cuando nos dijeron que pagáramos, me dí cuenta de que ya no la tenía. Eso fue hace aproximadamente quince minutos.
El policía:	¿Y en dónde la traía?
Brian:	En el bolsillo de atrás, donde también traía mis llaves. Pero las llaves las tengo todavía.
El policía:	Bueno, yo diría que existe la posibilidad de que se la hayan robado. ¿Estaba usted rodeado por mucha gente en ese momento?
Brian:	Sí, había varias personas esperando que se les diera la comida. Pero nunca pensé que me la pudieran haber robado sin que me diera cuenta.
El policía:	¿Se acuerda de haber sido empujado cuando esperaba por su sandwich?
Brian:	Pues, sí, ahora que me lo menciona, un muchacho me dio un codazo en la espalda.

IF YOU'RE SO INCLINED

The word for police station changes from place to place: *comandancia, comisaría, estación de policía, jefatura de policía, cuartel de policía.* You may want to ask the locals what they call a police station in their country. If you're in doubt, *estación de policía* will be understood by most everyone.

El policía:	Así lo sospechaba. A lo mejor, ese muchacho le sacó la cartera de su bolsillo en el mimso momento en que le dio el codazo. Habrá que hacer en informe. ¿Cómo se llama usted?
Brian:	Me llamo Brian Jones.
El policía:	¿De dónde?
Brian:	De Australia.
El policía:	Bueno, señor Jones, haré un informe. También le voy a buscar el numero de teléfono del consulado australiano. Permítame un momento … sí, éste es. Llame a ese número para infomarles de lo ocurrido. Debe comunicarse también con las aerolíneas y con los bancos emisores de las tarjetas de crédido y de los cheques de viajero. Dígales que el número del informe oficial es el 2437648. Con respecto al dinero en efectivo, temo que no hay mucho que podemos hacer.
Brian:	¡Qué desastre!

(a second police officer enters the room)

El otro policía:	Oiga, sargento. Acaban de entregar una cartera extraviada. Será de este señor australiano. Contenía su pasaporte con su foto y todo. (gives Brian the wallet)
Brian:	¡Ay, muchísimas gracias señor! Sí, es mía. Y el dinero también está todo aquí. ¡Gracias a Dios! ¡Qué suerte!
El policía:	Bueno señor Jones, parece que la emergencia se solucionó.
Brian:	Muchísimas gracias, señor. Usted ha sido muy amable. Espero que me disculpe por la molestia que le causé.

YOU'LL THANK YOURSELF LATER

In spite of what you may have heard, in most cases the police in Spain and Latin America will do whatever they can to help you. Unfortunately, their resources may be limited. Still, if something serious really does happen, you shouldn't be afraid to seek their help if you need it.

The word for "police" is *la policía*. However, if you're referring to a male police officer, you must say *el policía*. You may also refer to him as *el oficial* or *el agente*. Also, both *cartera* and *billetera* mean "wallet." *Billetera* is, perhaps, more universally understood (though not necessarily more common than *cartera*).

El policía: No se preocupe. Pero de ahora en adelante, le recomiendo que traiga sus cosas de valor en un lugar más seguro.

Translation:

Brian: Good evening, sir. I have an emergency.

The police officer: Tell me (what it is), sir.

Brian: Well, I've lost my wallet. It contained (I carried in it) all of my important documents, my plane ticket, credit cards, passport, driver's license, travelers' checks, and an amount of money in cash.

The police officer: Heavens! I am very sorry, sir ("I lament it"). Is there a possibility that it could have been a robbery?

Brian: Well, I don't know. I wasn't mugged, and I don't remember having contact with anyone. I think that it just fell (from me) when we were walking along the street.

The police officer: Who were you with and where were you going?

Brian: I was with my friend, Julio. He wanted us to find something to eat. We were on our way to a restaurant when all of a sudden we saw a food stand in the street and stopped to buy something fast there.

The police officer: And when did you first realize that you no longer had the wallet?

Brian:	We had asked them to make us a sandwich. When they told us to pay, I realized that I no longer had it. That was approximately fifteen minutes ago.
The police officer:	And where were you carrying it?
Brian:	In my rear pocket, where I also was carrying my keys. But I still have the keys.
The police officer:	Well, I would say there is a possibility that it was stolen ("to you it they may have stolen"). Were you surrounded by a lot of people at that moment?
Brian:	Yes, there were several people waiting for (the cooks to give them) their food. But I never thought that they could steal it without my realizing it.
The police officer:	Do you remember having been pushed while you were waiting for your sandwich?
Brian:	Well, yes, now that you mention it (to me), a boy elbowed me in the back.
The police officer:	Just as I suspected. Probably, that boy took out the wallet from your pocket at the same moment that he elbowed you. We'll have to (it will be necessary) make a report. What is your name (what do you call yourself)?
Brian:	My name is (I call myself) Brian Jones.
The police officer:	From where?

IF YOU'RE SO
INCLINED

Resulta que literally means "it turns out that," but in reality it's simply a filler that sets up an explanation. It's another way of saying "Well ... " and need not be translated.

Brian:	From Australia.
The police officer:	Well, Mr. Jones, I will make a report. I'm also going to look (for you) for the number of the Australian consulate. Hang on a second … yes, this is it. Call that number to let them know about what happened. You should also contact the airlines and the banks that have issued the credit cards and the travelers' checks. Tell them that the number of the official report is 2437684. With respect to the cash, I'm afraid that there isn't much we can do.
Brian:	What a disaster!

(a second police officer enters the room)

The other officer:	Hey, Sarge. They just turned in a lost wallet. I guess it belongs to this Australian gentleman. It contained his passport with photos and everything.
Brian:	Wow, thank you very much, sir! Yes, it's mine. And the money is also here. Thank goodness! What luck!
The police officer:	Well, Mr. Jones, it seems the emergency has been solved.
Brian:	Thank you very very much, sir. You have been very kind. I hope that you forgive the bother I've caused you.
The police officer:	Don't worry about it. But from now on, I recommend (to you) that you carry your valuable things in a safer place.

OK, I admit that Brian's wallet probably would never have turned up—money and all. But hey, nothing sells a book better than a happy ending.

The Lazy Way

QUESTION WORDS: INTERROGATIVES

You have already met most of these in previous chapters. Notice that these question words ("interrogative pronouns") have áccent márks on them. I'll explain why in a minute:

QUICK ☜☞ PAINLESS

¿quién?	who?; whom? (singular)
¿quiénes?	who? (plural)
¿qué?	what?; which? (sing. and pl.)
¿cuál?	which?
¿cuándo?	when?
¿dónde?	where?
¿cómo?	how?
¿cuánto?	how much?
¿cuántos?	how many?
¿por qué?	why?

You've seen other sentences with these question words before. Here are some more examples of how they can be used:

¿Quiénes estaban ahí en ese momento?	Who (plural) was there at that moment?
¿Con quién nos comunicamos en caso de una emergencia?	Whom should we contact in case of an emergency?
¿Qué tengo que hacer?	What do I have to do?
¿Dónde está la estación de policía más cercana?	Where is the nearest police station?

QUICK ✺ PAINLESS

The verb *querer* is *quisiera* in the past subjunctive. In addition to its normal grammatical uses, *quisiera* by itself is a great way to say "I would like ... " *Yo quisiera hacer un viaje a Londres* = "I would like to take a trip to London"; *Quisiera saber el precio* = "I would like to know the price." Use *quisiera* often; it's very polite.

¿Cómo era el hombre que le asaltó?	What was the man like ("look like") who mugged you?
¿Cuándo sucedió?	When did it happen?
¿Con cuál aerolínea va a viajar usted?	On (with) which airline are you going to travel?

Now, I know that you have also seen some of these words without áccent márks. This is because these very same words also serve as "relative pronouns." Don't worry about the grammar of it. It's really the same as in English. The áccent márks are there simply to help you differentiate between their two uses. The following English sentences should illustrate what I mean:

Whére do you live?

That's the house where I live.

Whó robbed you?

That's the guy who robbed me.

Hów múch did he steal?

I don't know how much.

Lazy Practice

Create sentences with questions asking who, what, where, when, and why. Use the previous examples as a guide and consult your dictionary for additional words.

THE PAST SUBJUNCTIVE

Remember the present subjunctive from Chapter 13? Well, get ready to meet the past subjunctive. The past subjunctive is used like the present subjunctive, only in the past! What I mean is, if you want someone to do something in the present, you use the present subjunctive: *Quiero que Juan lo haga* = "I want Juan to do it." If you wanted someone to do something in the past, you'd need the past subjunctive: *Quería* (imperfect past) *que Juan lo hiciera* = "I wanted Juan to do it." All the rules that you learned in Chapter 13 about the subjunctive

Past Subjunctive Endings for Regular *-ar* Verbs:

Ending:	Verb:	Example:
-ara	hablar	*hablara*
-aras	pagar	*pagaras*
-ara	contar	*contara*
-áramos	cantamos	*cantáramos*
-aran	pensar	*pensaran*

Past Subjunctive Endings for Regular *-er* and *-ir* Verbs:

Ending:	Verb:	Example:
-iera	comer	*comiera*
-ieras	vivir	*vivieras*
-iera	salir	*saliera*
-iéramos	entender	*entendiéramos*
-ieran	ocurrir (to occur)	*ocurrieran*

also apply to the past subjunctive. But now, the time or action of the sentence must have occurred in the past.

For regular verbs, the past subjunctives are formed by adding the following endings to the verb stem.

The verbs with irregular past preterites will also form irregular past subjunctives. Start with the *yo* form of the preterite verb, remove the last letter, and add the past subjunctive *–er* and *–ir* endings. Review the list of irregular preterites in Chapter 15 as needed:

hacer	*hice*	*hiciera*
saber	*supe*	*supiera*
poder	*pude*	*pudiera*
andar	*anduve*	*anduviera*
estar	*estuve*	*estuviera*
dar	*di*	*diera*

Ir verbs with stem changes in the present indicative will change to *"i"* in the past subjunctive tense:

pedir	*pidiera*
sentir	*sintiera*

El sargento mandó que la billetera se buscara.	The sergeant ordered the wallet be searched for.
El agente del banco me pidió que le ensenara mi pasaporte.	The bank agent asked me to show him my passport.
Me pidieron que me quedara en este lugar.	They asked me to stay here (in this place).

El ladrón dijo que todos se callaran.	The thief told everyone to be quiet.
Los del restaurante querían que nos fuéramos.	The folks in the restaurant wanted us to leave.

The verbs *ir* and *ser* look the same in the past subjunctive: *fuera, fueras, fuera, fuéramos, fueran.* You'll use these often, so you might as well learn them now. The context of the sentence will indicate which verb it is.

One of the most common uses you'll have for the past subjunctive is in "contrary to fact" sentences. When you say "if something were possible (but it's not)" or "if this were true (but it isn't)" you'll use the past subjunctive, even if the situation is going on currently. It's often used together with the conditional tense. Observe:

Si yo pudiera hablar el francés, ganaría mucho dinero.	If I could speak French (but I can't), I could make a lot of money.
Si estuviéramos en la Argentina, podríamos ir a la Tierra del Fuego.	If we were in Argentina (but we're not), we could go to Tierra del Fuego.
Si yo fuera presidente, crearía un nuevo sistema de seguro social.	If I were president (but I'm not), I would create a new social security system.
Si sólo fuera posible.	If only it were possible (but it's not).

Lazy Practice

Study the information in this section carefully. Try to create sentences that will help you to practice the past subjunctive.

QUICK ⊡ PAINLESS

Lo, our neuter pronoun, works with past participles to form "what (has whatever)" when the "what" refers to an entire set of events: *Lo ocurrido* = "what has occurred"; *lo hecho* = "what is/has been done;" *lo querido* = "what is/has been wanted." This is an easy way to get out of explaining all that happened every time.

DIALOGUE: *NO ME SIENTO BIEN:* "I DON'T FEEL WELL"

All other problems aside, no matter what happens to you, your health and safety are most important. You may have found your own corner of paradise, but if you get sick, you won't have much fun. If you're lucky, you won't have to seek medical attention, but you never know.

In this dialogue, Migdalia has come to the doctor in search of relief from her various ailments. She's quite the hypochondriac, so you'll get to hear about a number of different illnesses:

El médico:	Buenas tardes, señora.
Migdalia:	Señorita.
El médico:	Ay perdón, señorita. ¿Cómo se siente señorita?
Migdalia:	Ay, doctor, no me siento nada bien.
El médico:	¿Qué le pasa?
Migdalia:	Bueno, cada vez que salgo para hacer algo me enfermo.
El médico:	No me diga. A ver. ¿Cuáles son sus síntomas?
Migdalia:	Tengo hinchazón en la mano izquierda, ampollas en el pie derecho, y un sarpullido en la espalda. Y ando muy mal del estomago, doctor. Tengo dolores de cabeza y de la garganta. Me siento mareada e inquieta. Tengo mucha tos, y estornudo todo el tiempo. Creo que tengo también la ictiricia, la hepatitis, la alta presión, la diabetes, e inclusive el cáncer pulmonar. Ya va para dos días que tengo … usted sabe … la diarrea. ¿Usted cree que voy a morirme?

El médico:	Bueno, no sé, señora … digo, señorita. Déjeme examinarla primero. (The doctor examines her; she looks fine.)
El médico:	Bueno, no creo que se vaya a morir. De hecho, me parece que usted es una persona físicamente muy sana. Vamos a ver si no le podemos quitar lo de la diarrea. ¿De acuerdo?
Migdalia:	Sí, está bien.
El médico:	¿Quisiera que le prepare un té de manzanilla?
Migdalia:	¿Té de mazanilla? No puede ser. ¿En serio?
El médico:	No, señora … digo, señorita. Se lo dije en broma. Estudié la medicina en la Clinica Mayo en Minnessota y en el Hopsital de la Universidad de Stanford en California. Le voy a dar una reseta para unas pastillas. Se puede ir a la farmacia para comprar la medicína. Tome dos pastillas tres veces al día hasta que se sienta mejor.
Migdalia:	Bueno, y si todavía estoy mal, ¿qué debo hacer?
El médico:	Llame al consultorio para hacer una cita.
Migdalia:	Pues, espero que estas pastillas me hagan efecto. ¿Pero qué voy a hacer para las otras enfermedads que tengo?
El médico:	Conozco a un buen psicólogo.

Translation:

The doctor:	Good afternoon, Madam.
Migdalia:	Miss.
The doctor:	Oh, sorry, Miss. How do you feel, Miss?

YOU'LL THANK YOURSELF LATER

The definite article is used far more that the possessives when referring to parts of the body: *Me duelen las manos* = "my hands hurt" (literally "they hurt me the hands"). You can also say *mis manos,* but most people don't. There's no room for confusion, since the only hands that could possibly hurt you are your own (getting punched on the nose is a different verb).

QUICK ⬤ PAINLESS

Migdalia:	Oh, doctor, I don't feel well at all (*nada* here = "at all").
The doctor:	What's wrong?
Migdalia:	Well, every time I go out to do something I get sick.
The doctor:	You don't say. Let's see. What are your symptoms?
Migdalia:	I've got swelling in my left hand, blisters on my right foot, and a rash on my back. And I've got stomach problems, doctor. I have headaches and (pain in my) throat. I feel dizzy and uneasy. I cough a lot, and I sneeze all the time. I think I also have jaundice, hepatitis, high blood pressure, diabetes, and even lung cancer. It's been nearly two days that I've had … you know … diarrhea. Do you think I'm going to die?
The doctor:	Well, I don't know, Madam … I mean, Miss. Let me examine you first. (The doctor examines her; she looks fine.)
The doctor:	Well, I don't think that you're going to die. In fact, you seem to be a very healthy person, physically. Let's see if we can't take care of (remove) the diarrhea. Agreed?
Migdalia:	Yes, all right.
The doctor:	Would you like me to make you some chamomile tea?
Migdalia:	Chamomile tea? That can't be right. Are you serious?
The doctor:	No, Madam … I mean, Miss. I was just kidding (I said it to you in jest). I studied medicine at the Mayo Clinic in Minnesota

and at Stanford University Hospital in California. I'm going to give you a prescription for some pills. You can go to the pharmacy to buy the pills. Take two pills three times a day until you feel better.

Migdalia: All right, and if I still feel bad, what should I do?

The doctor: Call the office to make an appointment.

Migdalia: Well, I hope these pills are effective (on me). But what am I going to do about the other illnesses I have?

The doctor: I know a good psychologist.

REFLEXIVE VERBS: TALKING TO YOURSELF

When you wash yourself, talk to yourself, or ask yourself a question, your actions are considered reflexive: "I love myself." In other words, when the object or indirect object of a verb (in this case, "myself") is the same as the person doing the action (in this case, "I"), we have a reflexive construction. Thus, while "The dog bit Bob" is not reflexive, "The dog bit his tail (his own tail)" is.

When written as an infinitive in the dictionary, a reflexive verb will have a *se* stuck on the end:

lavarse	to wash oneself
levantarse	to lift oneself up (to stand)
preguntarse	to ask oneself
tocarse	to touch oneself
cuidarse	to take care of oneself
bañarse	to bathe oneself

It might be argued that most reflexive verbs aren't "reflexive verbs" at all, but simply reflexive constructions using regular old verbs. What makes them reflexive is that the INDOP (indirect object pronoun)—and sometimes just the DOP (direct object pronoun)—and the person doing the action of the verb are one and the same. Kick back and stop worrying about reflexive verbs. They're just a figment of some grammarian's imagination.

The Lazy Way

If you need to cry for help, yell *¡Socorro!* (English = "succor." Look it up if you need to.) Yes, *ayuda* also means "help," but somehow just doesn't sound quite as good as *socorro*: *¡Socorro! Me he caído y no puedo levantarme* = "Help, I've fallen and I can't get up!" By the way, Socorro is also a town south of Albuquerque.

Reflexive constructions use the same old INDOPs that you learned before, with only *se* being added for the third person. Reflexive infinitives referring to other people will have the appropriate INDOP stuck to it. So, *lavarnos* could also be reflexive if the people doing the washing are *nosotros.* Observe:

When conjugated, the *se* (or other object pronoun) is placed before the verb. Direct object promouns can also be added to the verb if it's not conjugated: *lavárselos.*

Many verbs that are reflexive in Spanish are not reflexive in English. However, the idea of yourself being the object is still understandable:

preocuparse	to worry (oneself)
emborracharse	to get (oneself) drunk
enfermarse	to get (oneself) sick
sentirse	to feel (one's state of being)
sentarse	to sit down (sit oneself down)
encontrarse	to feel (to find oneself)

The Reflexive Pronouns With the Verb *Lavarse:*

yo	*me*	me lavo	I wash myself
tú	*te*	te lavas	you wash yourself
él/ella/usted	*se*	se lava	she washes herself
nosotros	*nos*	nos lavamos	we wash ourselves
ellos/ellas/ustedes	*se*	se lavan	they wash themselves

imaginarse	to imagine (the images are in one's head)
preguntarse	to wonder (ask oneself)
llamarse	to be named (to call oneself)
enamorarse	to fall in love (not with oneself)

As always, here are some examples to show you what I mean:

Me siento muy bien.	I feel very good.
Tengo que irme.	I have to leave.
Me pregunto si eso va a ser posible.	I wonder (ask myself) if that is going to be possible.
Me llamo Daniel, y ella se llama Norma.	My name is (I call myself) Daniel, and her name is (she calls herself) Norma.
El hombre no quiso sentarse.	The man refused to sit down.
Me duelan las rodillas, y no quiero tocármelas.	My knees hurt and I don't want to touch (myself) them.
Nosotros queremos irnos.	We want to go.
Si tomas demaciado te vas a emborrachar.	If you drink too much you'll get drunk.

Now, you might think that this could all get pretty confusing, what with all these INDOPs and DOPs flying around. But it's usually not a problem. Just remember that when the subject of the verb (the person or thing doing it) is the same as the INDOP (or sometimes a DOP

QUICK **P** PAINLESS

The verb *dormir* means to sleep, but when it's reflexive (*dormirse*) it means "to fall asleep": *Siempre duermo bien, pero anoche no pude dormirme* = "I always sleep well, but last night I couldn't fall asleep." The verb *ir* means "to go," but *irse* means "to leave." *Fui primero al baño, y luego me fui del país* = "First, I went to the bathroom, then I left the country."

There are very few verbs that exist only as reflexive verbs. Remember: "Reflexive verbs" are simply reflexive constructions using "normal" verbs.

in short phrases), you're probably dealing with a reflexive construction. If things seem unclear, just use a subject pronoun (*yo, él, usted,* etc.) to make sure everyone knows who is doing what to whom.

ACTIVITY: BE PREPARED

Take a few minutes to list some things that might possibly go wrong during a trip to Spain or Latin America (you don't have to include being kidnapped by guerilla rebels if that sort of thing upsets you). It's always better to be prepared for the worst. Imagine scenarios in which you might find yourself where you would need to use your Spanish to solve a problem.

I have traveled extensively throughout Latin America without incident. Chances are you'll be fine. But the expression in Spanish for "Better safe than sorry" is *Más vale prevenir que lamentar.*

Las Fiestas: Celebrations

It's time to celebrate! You've arrived at the end of this *lazy* book with enough Spanish to paint the town *rojo.* Both Spaniards and Latin Americans find reasons to celebrate many events throughout the year—from saints, to independence, to the memory of their ancestors. Raise a glass to yourself and to these fun holidays. *¡Salud!*

SPANISH TEXT: *LAS FIESTAS DE MADRID*

Now that you're about to finish the book, it's time for you to try to understand a long text. Again, this is the real stuff. This text was written by a Spanish tourist bureau for Spanish speakers. Do your best to understand as much as you can. Believe it or not, you have been introduced to enough Spanish grammar at this point to understand this entire text with the aid of your dictionary. *¡Felicitaciones!*

Madrid es una ciudad muy alegre. Ofrece todo tipo de espectáculos propios de una gran capital. También tiene el encanto de conservar aún el sabor tradicional de "la

*villa", como se la llama. Y es cierto que en algún
sentido y en lo profundo de su alma Madrid sigue
siendo esa villa, esa ciudad de barrio que aún ofrece
toda la autenticidad de un pequeño pueblo.
Encantadora y versátil se presentará al visitante, si
tiene la oportunidad de saborear algunas de estas
fiestas que acontecen desde los primeros segundos
en que comienza el año:*

*El **Año Nuevo** comienza con el gran espectáculo.
Casi 40 millones de españoles estarán pendientes
cada año a la media noche del gran reloj de la
Puerta del Sol, que emitirá las tradicionales **12 cam-
panadas** para las que una gran muchedumbre, allí
congregada (y el resto de los españoles que lo
siguen por televisión), tomen las 12 uvas a su son,
durante los 12 últimos segundos del año. Este
momento marcará el inicio de la fiesta que se des-
pliega por toda la ciudad.*

*El **5 de Enero** tiene lugar la tradicional y vistosa
Cabalgata de los Reyes Magos, que desfila por la
zona de Hortaleza. Parece carnaval y representaran
la entrada de los Magos en la ciudad. Esta es también una tradición que se repetirá por numerosas
ciudades españolas.*

*El **15 de Mayo,** se celebran las **Fiestas de San
Isidro,** patrón de la ciudad, con numerosos festejos
típicos como verbenas, romerías y las mejores*

Yes, *fiesta* does mean
"party," but *fiestas* are
usually on a much
grander scale than a
mere get-together at a
friend's house. *Un día
de fiesta* may be a
national or religious holi-
day. For a smaller party
with friends, say *una
reunión* (although *fiesta*
would still be under-
stood).

corridas de toros del año. También se celebran conciertos de rock y jazz, teatro y ferias de artesanía.

Durante los meses de **Julio y Agosto** se celebran los **Veranos de la Villa,** campaña de teatro, cine, y espectáculos musicales organizados por el ayuntamiento. **Del 6 al 15 de Agosto** se celebra la **Verbena de la Paloma,** una de las fiestas más castizas de la ciudad, caracterizada por su colorido y el gran optimismo que se respira por la calle. En ella se resucitarán los típicos trajes de chulapa y del chulo madrileño, bailes, y los bellos mantones de manila, y lo mejor del folclore madrileño.

Septiembre, es la gran temporada de estreno en teatros, cines y espectáculos en general. Durante este més se celebran los **Festivales de Otoño** y la **Fiesta de la Melonera** en Arganzuela, cuyos origenes se remontan al siglo XVIII. **Del 8 al 12 de Octubre,** se celebra la **Fiesta del Pilar.** En **Noviembre** tienen lugar las tan diversas celebraciones de la tradicional **Almudena,** en contraposición con la **Fiesta Internacional de Jazz.**

Diciembre cierra el año con la exposición y venta de nacimientos y arboles de Navidad en puestos tradicionales situados en la **Plaza Mayor,** todo un espectáculo de luz y colorido con todo el encanto y romanticismo que acompaña a tan tradicionales fiestas.

QUICK ☙ PAINLESS

THE HOLIDAYS

Here's a list of some of the principal holidays celebrated in Latin America and Spain. Most are religious:

Miércoles de Ceniza	Ash Wednesday
Domingo de Ramos	Palm Sunday
Viernes Santo	Good Friday
Día de Pascua	Easter
Día de Todos los Santos	All Saints' Day
Nochebuena	Christmas Eve
La Navidad	Christmas Day
Noche Vieja	New Year's Eve
el Año Nuevo	New Year's Day

FIESTAS PATRIAS: INDEPENDENCE DAYS

Obviously, every Spanish-speaking country other than Spain was once a Spanish colony. Over the course of the nineteenth century, each gained its independence from the Spanish Crown. Sounds like a good reason to throw a party to me. Here's a list of the independence day holidays for Spain's former colonies:

Argentina	el 9 de julio
Bolivia	el 6 de augosto
Chile	el 18 de septiembre
Colombia	el 20 de julio
Costa Rica	el 15 de septiembre

QUICK ⬭ PAINLESS

Los puertorriqueños celebrate two special days: the November 19, the day Christopher Columbus discovered the island of *Borinquen* (now known as Puerto Rico); and July 25, the day the Puerto Rican constitution was signed. Many Puerto Ricans also celebrate the Fourth of July.

Cuba	el 20 de mayo
la República Dominicana	el 22 de febrero
el Ecuador	el 3 de octubre
las Filipinas (Philippines)	el 12 de junio
el Salvador	el 15 de septiembre
Guinea Ecuatorial	el 12 de octubre (1968)
Guatemala	el 15 de septiembre
Honduras	el 15 de septiembre
México	el 16 de septiembre
Nicaragua	el 15 de septiembre
el Panamá	
(from Spain)	el 28 de noviembre
(from Colombia)	el 3 de noviembre
El Paraguay	el 14 de mayo
El Perú	el 28 de julio
Uruguay	el 25 de augosto
Venezuela	el 5 de julio

PREPOSITIONS: TO, FROM, WITHOUT, IN FRONT OF, ETC.

A preposition is defined as an "invariable particle that unites two words or phrases establishing a dependant relationship between them." In plain English, a preposition is a short word or phrase that tells you where something belongs, is located, or how it is related to something else.

QUICK ☎ PAINLESS

You already know several Spanish prepositions. Here's a list to fill in the gaps. Some can take infinitives: *antes de comer* = "before eating." You should be able to translate the examples on your own:

Preposition:	Definition:	Example:
a	to	*al doctor*
alrededor (de)	around	*alrededor de mí*
antes (de)	before	*antes de comer*
cerca (de)	near	*cerca de mi casa*
con	with	*con las manos*
contra	against	*contra la pared*
de	of, from	*de mi familia*
desde	from	*desde la montaña*
debajo (de)	under	*debajo de la cama*
delante (de)	in front of	*delante de mí*
después (de)	after	*después de comer*
detrás (de)	behind	*detrás de él*
en	in	*en mi casa*
encima (de)	on top of	*encima de la mesa*
entre	between	*entre nosotros*
frente a	in front of	*frente a la casa*
hacia	toward	*hacia las montañas*
lejos (de)	far (from)	*lejos de aquí*
sin	without	*sin saber; sin tí*
sobre	over; about	*sobre la tierra*

GLUE WORDS: *PARA* AND *POR*

Of the many Spanish prepositions, *para* and *por* seem to cause more grief and confusion than all the others combined. Why? Because both are translated as "for" in English. So it's no surprise that many people have difficulty knowing when to use one and not the other.

   You have already seen *para* and *por* here and there in previous texts. *Para* and *por* are "glue words" because they hold a lot of things together, and if you can't use them reasonably well, your Spanish will start to fall to pieces.   Study the following examples to learn how to use *para* correctly:

Destination:

   Mañana saldré para Bogotá.

   I leave for Bogota tomorrow.

Use:

   ropa para niños

   children's clothes (clothes for children)

Purpose:

   una reunión para festejar tu cumpleaños

   a party to celebrate your birthday

Comparison:

   Para un inglés, usted baila muy bien.

   You dance pretty well for an Englishman.

Future time:

   La fiesta está programada para el próximo lunes.

   The party is scheduled for next Tuesday.

Tell it like it is:

   Para mí, éste es un evento maravilloso.

   This is a marvelous event for me. (in my opinion)

IF YOU'RE SO INCLINED

One device that you can use to remember how to use *para* is to think of "DUPCFT" = Don't Use Para Carelessly: Follow these Tips. These letters stand for Destination, Use, Purpose, Comparison, Future time, and Tell it like it is. (This one isn't mine. It's an old trick. You're welcome to improve upon it if you can.)

Now, for *por,* study these:

Motive:

> *Lo hacen por necesidad.*
>
> They do it out of need. (for necessity's sake)

Favor:

> *Voté por el otro candidato.*
>
> I voted for the other candidate.

Reason:

> *¿Por qué no vas al baile?*
>
> Why aren't you going to the dance?

Behalf:

> *Lo hice por mi patria.*
>
> I did it for my country ("native land").

Exchange:

> *Me dieron diez pesos por un dólar.*
>
> They gave me ten pesos for one dollar.

Time (duration):

> *Voy a estar en este pueblo por una semana.*
>
> I'll be in this town for a week.

Por is used to express the passive "by" and "by means of." It's also used where we would say "per," as in "per year." Observe:

La canción fue compuesta por mi amigo.	The song was composed by my friend.
Te enviaré el archivo por correo electrónico.	I'll send you the file by e-mail.
Me cobran diez pesos por hora.	They charge me ten pesos per hour.

THE OBLIQUE PRONOUNS: TO ME, TO YOU, ETC.

When *yo* and *tú* are governed by a preposition other than *con,* use *mí* ("me") and *tí* ("you"). Note the áccent márk on *mí* to distinguish it from *mi* = "my." These are known as oblique pronouns, and are quite common, especially with *a, por, para,* and *de.* The oblique pronouns for everyone else are the same as their subject pronouns: *a él, para ella, por ustedes, alrededor de nosotros,* etc.

Use the third person oblique pronouns (*a él, a ella,* etc.) or mention people by name (*a María, a los turistas*) to avoid confusion wherever the third person INDOP (indirect object pronoun) *se* is unclear. The oblique pronouns may also be used to emphasize the object or indirect object of a sentence:

Se lo dije a ella.	I told her.
Se lo dije a él.	I told him
Se lo dije a ellos.	I told them.
Se lo dije a Tomás.	I told Tomas.
¿Me vas a dar dinero?	Are you going to give me money?
¿Me vas a dar dinero a mí?	Are you really going to give ME money?
Te quiero.	I love you.
Te quiero a tí.	I love YOU (and don't you forget it).

MORE ABOUT *HABER*

As you've seen in previous examples, the helping verb *haber,* like other verbs, can legitimately take any tense or mood. Use *haber* to form the more complex "compound tenses." Usually your instincts will guide you as to what these mean, since we use very similar constructions in English. Take a look at the following examples:

La fiesta habrá terminado a esa hora.	The fiesta will have finished at that time.
Si yo hubiera ido a la reunión, te habría podido dar este regalo.	If I had gone to the party (but I didn't), I would have been able to give you this present.
Habiendo terminado su bebida, lanzó la copa hacia la pared.	Having finished his drink, he threw the glass toward the wall.
María lo habría hecho, pero no hubo tiempo.	María would have done it, but there wasn't time.
Es posible que no haya fiesta mañana.	It is possible that there won't be a fiesta tomorrow.
Habrá mucha gente para la reunión.	There will be a lot of people at the party.
No creo que Mario le haya dado un regalo a su mamá.	I don't think that Mario has given his mother a present.
No habían invitado a Juan, pero llegó a la reunión por su cuenta.	They hadn't invited Juan, but he showed up on his own.

Cuando celebraron mi cumpleaños, ya había cumplido 32.	When we celebrated my birthday, I had already turned 32.
Habíamos estado esperando durante tres horas cuando por fin llegó Miguel a la fiesta.	We had been waiting for three hours when, at last, Miguel arrived at the party.
Habrás estado celebrando esta fiesta toda tu vida, ¿no es cierto?	You've probably been celebrating this fiesta all your life, isn't that right?

HERE, THERE, EVERYWHERE

Again, some of these you've already seen. You'll need these to express "where" and to understand directions:

aquí	here
acá	here, over here (see sidebar)
ahí	there (in general)
allá	there (in general)
allí	there (more specific)
más allá	further on
derecho (adj.)	right ("las manos derechas")
izquierdo (adj.)	left
a la derecha	on the right
a la izquierda	on the left
derecho, recto	straight ahead
este lado	this side
el otro lado	the other side

YOU'LL THANK YOURSELF LATER

Both *aquí* and *acá* mean "here." In parts of South America (Argentina, Uruguay, Chile), *acá* is more common than *aquí*. Purists will tell you that *aquí*, however, is the preferred word. But you should still use *acá* with verbs of motion: *Vente para acá* (pronounced "vente paracá") = "Come over here."

TAN Y TANTO: SO, SO MUCH

The adverbs *tan* and *tanto* are used to say "so much" and "how much."

El examen fue tan dificil. — The test was so difficult.

Ay doctor, la cabeza me duele tanto. — Oh, doctor, my head hurts so much.

No le invites a Juan. Habla tanto. — Don't invite Juan. He talks so (too) much.

SUFFIXES: *-ITO, -CITO, -ÍSIMO, -AZO*

Spanish uses a number of suffixes to form new words and to alter the meaning of existing ones. You've already learned several of the most important suffixes: *-ción, -dad, -mente.* Here are a few more:

–ito and *–cito*

These are the most common diminutive suffixes. This means that they make the noun smaller or more delicate in some way: *gato* becomes *gatito* = "kitten"; *casa* becomes *casita* = "small house"; *poco* becomes *poquito* = "a little bit." Monosyllabic words that end in a consonant, and words containing diphthongs or that end in *–e*, usually take *–cito or -ecito: flor* becomes *florecita* = "little flower"; *bebe* becomes *bebecito* = "little baby"; *puerta* becomes *puertecita* = "little door." Notice that the ending must agree with the gender of the original noun.

-ísimo

This is a superlative suffix. It intensifies the meaning of a an adjective or adverb: *Te quiero muchísimo* = "I love you very much"; *Fue una tarea dificilísima* = "It was an extremely difficult task."

-azo

This suffix usually indicates a blow or hit with something: *un cabezazo* = "a butt with the head (soccer)"; *un palazo* = "a hit with a stick"; *Ella le dio un telefonazo* = "She hit him with a telephone." (This could also be a slangy way of saying "She gave him a phone call." Context, context, context!)

SOMETHING, NOTHING, SOMEONE, NOBODY

When you want to say "something," "someone," "nothing," and "nobody," you should use the following words. They are all invariable, and thus don't need to change for gender or number:

algo	something
nada	nothing
alguien	someone
nadie	no one

Don't forget that Spanish requires the use of double negatives. If you want to say "there isn't anyone," you're literally saying "there isn't no one" in Spanish:

IF YOU'RE SO INCLINED

To use suffixes effectively, you'll need extended practice reading and/or talking with Spanish speakers. If you're not careful, that new word you've proudly created by adding a suffix may convey numerous secondary meanings that you did not intend, or may just sound bizarre. Still, words such as *poquito* and *muchísimo* are pretty standard and can be used at any time. You may want to study the usage of suffixes in a good Spanish grammar book.

Hay algo ahí.	There's something there.
No hay nada aquí.	There isn't anything here.
Esta reunión es tan aburrida. No pasa nada.	This party is so boring. Nothing's going on.
¿No hay nadie que pueda arreglar esto?	There isn't anyone who can work this out.

A FEW MORE THINGS I WANT YOU TO KNOW BEFORE YOU'RE DONE

I'd love to make this list a mile long, but obviously, that won't be possible. So until they let me write *Learn Spanish The Lazy Way Part II,* these will have to do for the moment.

Cierto

The dictionary often defines this as "certain," but in usage, it's practically synonymous with "true." At the end of a statement, *¿No es cierto?* means "isn't that right?"

Gringo

You've probably heard the word *gringo* before as an insult, meaning Anglo-Saxon. In Mexico, it almost always means someone from the U.S.A., regardless of their ethnic background. But don't automatically assume that you are being insulted if someone calls you a *gringo,* especially if it's done in a courteous tone of voice. In some countries, it simply means an English-speaker, though in Argentina, a *gringo* could mean someone from Italy. The term is not used much in Spain.

YOU'LL THANK YOURSELF LATER

You already know that *pero* means "but." Now learn *sino. Sino* means "but rather." *No soy inglés, sino canadiense* = "I'm not English, but (rather) Canadian"; *Mis padres no hablaban el italiano, sino el portugués* = "My parents didn't speak Italian, but (rather) Portuguese." Use *sino* when the first part of your sentence is negative and you wish to make a correction to something stated or assumed. *Sino* as a noun means "fate."

On the Bus: *Controlar, Faltar, Bajar*

Controlar borders on being a false amigo, as it usually means "to check or inspect," rather than "to control." When tickets are reviewed on a bus, it's known as *control de boletos.* If the driver says *Necesito controlar su boleto,* he doesn't mean "I need to control your ticket" but simply "I need to check it to make sure you actually paid for this trip."

Faltar means "to lack or be wanting." It works a bit like the verb *gustar: Me falta dinero* = "I need money (money lacks me)." *Le faltan tres días todavía* = "He's got three days to go." If the bus you're on starts to leave without your friend, yell *¡Falta!* or *¡Faltan!* = "Someone's still missing!"

Bajar means "to get down," but from a vehicle, it means "to get off." If you want the bus driver to let you out, yell *¡Baja!* or *¡Bajan!* (not *"Bajo"*).

Beware of *Coger*

In Spain and most of the Caribbean, *coger* is *the* word for "to get, grab, or take." So, *Aquí se puede coger el autobus* = "You can get the bus here"; *Sonó el teléfono y Julia lo cogió* = "The phone rang and Julia got it." Seems easy enough. But in much of Latin America, especially in Argentina and surrounding counties (Mexico, too!), the verb *coger* has degenerated into a rather rude word for "sexual intercourse" and should be avoided. I need not comment on the gut-wrenching laughter you will provoke if you use *coger* in Argentina in the previous sentences. Please use *agarrar* instead.

Latinos tend to have a slightly different perception of time than Anglos. Arriving somewhere on time may mean being late by up to several hours. This is not necessarily true of public transportation or businesses. But if you are invited to a party and aren't quite sure if you should arrive on time or not, ask *¿A la hora en punto?* = "Should I arrive on time (sharp)?"

Enough Isn't Always Enough: *Bastante y Demaciado*

Bastante means "enough" and *demaciado* means "too much." But they can also both mean "a lot." So: *Me duele bastante la pierna izquierda* does not mean "My left leg hurts enough," but rather, it "hurts a lot." Also: *Juan tiene demaciado dinero* may mean "Juan has a lot of money," and not "too much money."

el que and *la que*

Remember that the articles *el* and *la* can also work a bit like pronouns. You saw this briefly before. When you know the gender of the thing you're talking about, and you need to keep talking about it, in some situations you can use *el que* or *la que* to avoid repeating the noun all the time:

Te rasco la espalda y tú me la rascas la mía.	I'll scratch your back and you scratch mine.
"Me duele el pie."	"My foot hurts."
"¿Cuál le duele?"	"Which one hurts?"
"El que está debajo de la rodilla."	"The one that's below my knee."

Make Time for *Hacer*

Time is "made" in Spanish: *Hace tres días que no duermo* = "I haven't slept in three days." Be careful not to fall into English syntax with phrases like *"no he dormido en tres días."*

YOU'LL THANK YOURSELF LATER

In Mexico, you'll hear the words *mero* and *puro*. *Mero* literally means "mere" ("He is but a mere boy"), but it is frequently used for "exact" or "real" as in *la mera verdad* = "the real truth" or *¿Dónde mero?* = "Where exactly?" The word *puro* means "pure," but in Mexico its meaning extends to "only" or "entire," as in *Tengo puras de harina* = "I only have flour (tortillas)" or *"Me trae puros problemas"* = "He brings me nothing but problems."

Nomás

Though considered substandard by purists, in Latin America you'll hear *nomás* ("no más") as an adverb meaning "just" or "only." *Es muy frágil. Lo tocas nomás y se te rompe* = "It's very fragile. Just touch it and it will break on you"; *Vaya nomás a la tienda y ahí lo va a poder compar* = "Just go the store and you'll be able to buy it there"; *Así nomás* = "Just like that (as easy as that)."

You Should Learn *Deber*

Deber means "should" or "ought to," and is followed by an infinitive: *Tú debes ir a la fiesta* = "You should go to the fiesta." But unlike its English counterparts, *deber* can also take the conditional or past subjunctive forms: *debería hacerlo, debiera hacerlo*. It's best to simply think of these as more polite ways of telling people what they should do: *Usted debería ir al concierto* = "You should go to the concert." You'll go crazy trying to translate these as "could should," "would should," and "might should."

More About the Articles

By now, you've probably noticed that the definite article is often used in Spanish when it isn't in English: *El español no es dificil* = "Spanish is not difficult"; *Me gusta el baile* = I like dancing"; *Me encanta la literatura española* = "I love Spanish literature"; *La democracia es un derecho humano* = "Democracy is a human right." As a general rule, the definite article is used with most abstract nouns, and other nouns that are not people or places. Some place names, however, are often seen with

The future tense can be used to express probability or wonder: *¿Quién será él?* = "I wonder who he is?"; *Será un turista alemán* = "He's probably a German tourist." The conditional tense does the same thing for the past: *¿Quién sería ella?* = "I wonder who she was"; *Sería una turista inglesa* = "She was probably an English tourist."

an article: *El Perú es un país muy diverso* = "Peru is a very diverse country." But usually they are considered optional with places. Never use the article with a person's given name: *"Llegó la María"* for "María arrived" is incorrect (although you may hear it in rural areas).

Pay Attention to *Fijarse*

Technically, the verb *fijar* means "to stick on" and can be used, like *pegar,* for adhering or posting things to walls and so on. But in a reflexive construction, *fijarse* means "to look at" or even "to consider." It's often used as a filler: *Fíjate que ya no tengo dinero* = "You see, I don't have any money left."

Volver a

Volver by itself means "to return." But a good way to express an action that will be repeated is to use *volver a: No vuelves a llamar* = "Don't call back"; *Vuelvo a intentar mañana* = "I'll try again tomorrow." *Volver en sí* means "to regain consciousness." You could also use the adverbial phrase *de nuevo: Llamé de nuevo* = "I called again."

Arrange to Use *Arreglar*

This verb literally means "to arrange," but can be extended to mean "to work something out" or "to fix things up." Use *arreglar* any time you need something repaired, fixed, worked out, or lined up: *¿Me podría arreglar un viaje a Galicia?* = "Could you fix up a trip for me to Galicia?"; *Voy a arreglar mis cosas* = "I'm going to get my stuff in order;" *Mi auto está descompuesto. Lo*

IF YOU'RE SO
INCLINED

Now and then you may see the words *cuyo, cuya,* and their plural forms. These mean "of which," "of whom," and "whose," and are mostly used in the written language: *un hombre cuyo caballo es veloz* = "a man whose horse is fast." Don't worry about *cuyo* in the spoken language, since there are always ways around it: *un hombre que tiene un caballo veloz* = "a man who has a fast horse."

voy a tener que arreglar pronto = "My car is out of commission. I'll have to fix it soon."

UNA ÚLTIMA PALABRA

Congratulations, you made it! I hope that this book has been useful to you. Not only did you get your feet wet, I'd say that you're in waist high. You now know enough grammar, vocabulary, and shortcuts to fill in the gaps on your own. *Que te vaya muy bien, y hasta la próxima.*

ACTIVITY: DINNER PARTY

Now that you're at the end of the book, invite all your friends over (and even a few people you don't like) for a big party with a Spanish or Latin American theme. Make Spanish and Latin American food, and give everyone a name tag with a Spanish name. Go to a party store and see if they have any *piñatas.* Turn up the stereo and blast the neighborhood with Spanish and Latin American music. You deserve to have a great time.

A COMPLETE WASTE OF TIME

The 3 Worst-Sounding Things in Spanish:

1. Saying *"mucho bueno"* and *"no problemo."* You should know why these are WRONG.

2. Not conjugating your verbs and trying to get by with infinitives all the time: *"Yo hablar español."* ¡NOT!

3. Being careless with *la concordancia* between your nouns and adjectives. Occasional mistakes are fine, but people will get lost if you don't at least try your best to make things agree.

More Lazy Stuff

A

How to Get Someone Else to Do It

By this I mean getting someone else to teach you Spanish. If you're considering returning to a classroom, check out what Spanish classes are offered at your local community college or adult learning center. Or, if you're really inspired, go back to school and major in Spanish.

You might also consider hiring a private tutor. Naturally, you'll have time and economic factors to consider before you decide to pay someone out of your pocket. Check the Yellow Pages first. Or run an add in the newspaper: "Wanted: Spanish tutor for private lessons." If there's a sizable college of university in your area, another possibility is to find a Spanish-speaking student who would be interested in making some extra money as a private tutor. But be sure to interview any candidates first to make sure that they are indeed able to explain the logic of what they are teaching you. If you ask: "Why does the verb change this way?" and the answer is "Just because," find a different tutor.

There are also excellent immersion programs in Latin America and Spain where you can live in a Spanish-speaking environment and receive language instruction from professionals. Contact the Spanish Department at a sizable university for details, or, as always, try surfing the Internet under "Spanish programs abroad" and similar queries.

If you're looking for someone else to actually do the writing or talking for you, you'll need to hire a professional translator or interpreter. But remember that quality translation and interpretation services are not cheap. If you are in a position to hire a professional translator or interpreter, shop around. Don't rely on bilingual people who may not have received higher education in both languages. Contact translation agencies, or surf the Internet under "translation/interpretation services."

B

If You Really Want More, Read These

BOOKS

There are literally hundreds of books in circulation about Spanish—far too many to list here. Many are excellent. Some are lousy. Check out what's available for free at your local library before you *gastar dinero*. If you plan to purchase a book, spend a few minutes reviewing it to make sure it suits your learning style. You might also consider browsing at **www.amazon.com** or at other book-related Web sites for more ideas.

Among the many texts available, here are a few resources that stand out in my mind as being clearly exceptional:

- *Cassell's Colloquial Spanish: A Handbook of Idiomatic Usage,* by A. Bryson Gerrard. 3rd Revised Edition, ISBN 0-02-079430-4, Macmillan, 1981.

  Ah, the book that changed my life! This used to be called *Beyond the Dictionary in Spanish*. I got hooked on it when I was in college. I might have given up on my Spanish had it not been for this little gem. While some of the information is now a bit outdated, this book will still do wonders for your Spanish and really have you speaking like a native. Not only is it full of great info, it's fun to read. I highly recommend it.

- *A New Reference Grammar of Modern Spanish,* by John Butt and Carmen Benjamin. 2nd edition, ISBN 0-8442-7088-1, Edward Arnold, 1995.

The Butt and Benjamin is one of the most comprehensive reference books on Spanish grammar currently available. If you plan on continuing your studies of this language, this book is a must.

- *El Pequeño Larousse Ilustrado 1999*. ISBN 9-706-07778-2, Larousse, 1999.

This dictionary/encyclopedia is written all in Spanish. Although it costs about $28, it's worth every *centavo*. You'll have easy access to information in Spanish about practically everything in one single volume. It's updated every few years. Buy the newest edition you can find. Your Spanish (and knowledge of the world) will improve by leaps and bounds. You can order it at most bookstores.

- *The Oxford Spanish Dictionary: Spanish English/English-Spanish,* by Beatriz Galimberti Jarman, Roy Russell, and Beatriz G. Jarman (editors). ISBN: 0-19-864510-4, Oxford University Press, 1994.

There are many excellent dictionaries out there, and everyone has their favorite. I'm rather partial to the Oxford. As a professional translator and interpreter, I have found this reference to be consistently superior in giving me the words, definitions, and phrases I need. The *HarperCollins Spanish Dictionary,* by Colin Smith (ISBN 00-627-0207-6, HarperCollins, 1997) is also quite good.

WEB SITES

As I've mentioned throughout this book, the Internet is one of the best places to find up-to-date information in and about Spanish. The best way to find Spanish-related Web sites is to search for "Spanish" or "Español" using your favorite search engine and then surf through the sites that are generated. At **www.altavisa.com** you can select Spanish as your target language.

There are hundreds of good Web sites that could be useful to you. Here are a few to get you started. I'm sure that you'll be able to find many more on your own. Remember that Web sites come and go and there is no way to control how long they will survive:

www.unc.edu/courses/span003/gram.html

www.el-castellano.com

ilisa.com/adverbs.htm

www.studyspanish.com/tutorial.htm

spanishculture.miningco.com

www.studyspanish.com/comps

MAGAZINES

Selecciones de Readers' Digest

Newsweek en español

PC Magazine (in Spanish)

Mecánica Popular (Popular Mechanics)

The list goes on. Contact the publishers to find out how you can subscribe to their Spanish publications. If your favorite mag doesn't publish in Spanish, write a letter to the editors and tell them that you want to read their publication in *español*. Eventually, they'll get the idea.

If You Don't Know What It Means, Look Here

Maybe a better title for this should be **"If You Don't Know What It Means, Look in Your Dictionary."** Still, here's a list of words to help you strengthen your vocabulary. Keep in mind that while lists such as these are useful, they are always incomplete. Please pencil in new words as needed.

Remember: if you don't know what something is called, just say: *esto* for "this," *eso* for "that," *estos* for "these," and *esos* for "those."

TRAVEL

airplane	*avión; aeroplano*
airport	*aeropuerto*
arrival	*llegada (llegar); arribo (arribar)*
baggage	*equipaje*
boarding pass	*pase de abordar; pase de embarque*
boat	*barco*
border	*frontera*

bus	*autobús; camión* (Mex.); *colectivo* (Arg.)
bus station	*estación de autobúses; central camionera* (Mex.)
car	*auto; coche; carro*
currency exchange	*casa de cambio*
customs	*aduana*
departure	*salida (salir)*
domestic	*doméstico*
flight	*vuelo*
flight attendant	*azafata* (fem.); *aeromozo; sobrecargo*
flight number	*número de vuelo*
How do I get to …	*¿Cómo se llega a …*
international	*internacional*
passport	*pasaporte*
road	*camino*
seat belt	*cinturón de seguridad*
smoking/no smoking	*fumar/no fumar*
street	*calle*
tariff	*tarifa*
taxi	*taxi*
ticket	*boleto*
town	*pueblo*
train	*tren (el)*
visa	*visa*

LODGING

bed	*cama*
blanket	*cobíja*
hot water	*agua caliente*
hotel	*hotel*
pillow	*almohada*
room	*cuarto; habitación*
sheet	*sábana*
youth hostel	*albergue*

PERSONAL ITEMS

brush	*cepillo*
comb	*peine* (masc.)
razor	*navaja; rasura* (Mex.)
soap	*jabón* (masc.)
toothbrush	*cepillo de dientes*
towel	*toalla*

CLOTHING:

dress	*vestido de mujer*
hat	*sombrero*
pants	*pantalónes*
shirt	*camisa*
shoes	*zapatos*
size	*talle* (fem.)
skirt	*falda*

socks	*calcetines; médias* (Arg.)
suit	*traje*
underwear	*ropa interior; ropa íntima*

BODY PARTS

arm	*brazo*
back	*espalda*
ears	*oídos* (inner); *orejas* (outer)
face	*cara*
fingers	*dedos*
foot	*pie*
hand	*mano* (fem.)
head	*cabeza*
knee	*rodilla*
leg	*pienra*
mouth	*boca*
neck	*cuello; pezcuezo*
nose	*nariz*
shoulder	*hombro*
teeth	*dientes*
toes	*dedos de los pies*

FOOD AND DRINK

A:

almonds	*almendras*
anchovies	*anchoas, boquerones*

apple	*manzana*
asparagus	*espárrago*
avocado	*aguacate* (masc.); *palta* (South Am.)

B:

bacon	*tocino*
banana	*plátano; banana; banano; guineo*
barbecue	*asado; al carbón; barbacoa*
beans	*frijoles* (Mex.); *porotos* (Argentina)
beef	*carne de res*
beet	*betabel; remolacha* (Spain)
bread	*pan*
bread (whole grain)	*pan integral*
butter	*mantequilla; manteca*

C:

cabbage	*repollo; col* (Spain)
cake	*pastel; torta* (Spain)
carrot	*zanahoria*
celery	*apio*
cheese	*queso*
cherry	*cereza*
chicken	*pollo*
cinnamon	*canela*
cookie; biscuit	*galleta*

corn	*maíz; choclo desgrando* (Argentina.)
corn-on-the-cob	*elote* (Mex.); *choclo* (Argentina)
crab	*cangrejo*
cream	*nata*
crepe	*panqueque*
custard	*flan*

D:

dinner	*cena*
duck	*pato*

E:

eel	*anguila*
eggplant	*berenjena*
eggs	*huevos; blanquillos* (Mex.)

F:

fat	*grasa*
fig	*higo*
fish	*pescado*
French fries	*papas fritas*

G:

garlic	*ajo*
grape	*uva*
grapefruit	*toronja* (Mex.); *pomelo* (South Am.)
grill	*parrilla*
guava	*guayaba*

H:

ham	*jamón; carne de cerdo*
honey	*miel*
hot (spicy)	*picante*

J:

jam	*mermelada*
jelly	*jalea*
juice	*jugo; zumo* (Spain)

L:

lamb	*cordero*
lard	*manteca*
lemon	*limón; lima* (Mex.)
lentils	*lentejas*
lettuce	*lechuga*
lime	*limón* (Mex.)
lobster	*langosta*

M:

mayonnaise	*mayonesa*
meat	*carne*
meatball	*albóndiga*
melon	*melón*
minced	*picado*
mustard	*mostaza*

N:

nut	*nuez*

O:

oil	*aceite*
omelette	*tortilla* (Spain); *"omelette"*
orange	*naranja*
oyster	*ostión; ostra*

P:

pancake	*torta; panqueque;* *"hotcake"* (Mex.)
parsley	*perejil*
peach	*durazno*
peanut	*cacahuate; maní* (South Am.; Carib.)
pear	*pera*
peas	*chícharos* (Mex.); *arvejas* (Argentina); *guisantes* (Spain)
pepper	*pimienta*
pepper (red)	*pimentón; chile* (Mex.)
pork	*puerco; cerdo*

R:

raisins	*pasas de uva*
raw	*crudo; natural*
red wine	*vino tinto*
refried beans	*refritos; frijolitos* (both Mex.)
rice	*arroz*

S:

salad	*ensalada*
salt	*sal* (fem.)

sauce	*salsa*
sausage	*chorrizo; salchicha*
shellfish	*mariscos*
shrimp	*camarón; gamba* (Spain)
slice/piece	*rebanada; trozo*
smoked	*ahumado*
soft drink	*refresco; soda; gasiosa*
soup	*sopa; caldo*
sour	*agrio; amargo* (bitter)
spice	*especia (fem.)*
spinach	*espinacas*
squash	*calabaza; zapallo* (South Am.)
strawberry	*fresa; frutilla* (South Am.)
string beans	*judías verdes* (Spain); *ejotes* (Mex.); *chauchas* (Argentina)
sugar	*azúcar (masc. or fem.)*
syrup	*almíbar*

T:

tea	*té*
tip	*propina*
tomato	*tomate; jitomate* (Mex.)
tripe	*tripas; mondongo*
trout	*trucha*
tuna	*atún* (the word *tuna* means "cactus fruit")
turkey	*pavo; guajalote* (Mex.)

V:

vanilla	*vainilla*
vegetables	*verduras*
vegetarian	*vegeteriano/a*

W:

watermelon	*sandía*

It's Time for Your Reward

No one ever said that learning a foreign language was easy. That's why it's important to reward yourself for all of your hard *trabajo*. Now it's time to kick back and relax. You've earned it!

Once You've Done This...	Reward Yourself With This...
Learned basic facts about Spanish	Have your favorite dessert for dinner
Learned spelling rules	Rent fun videos (in Spanish or English)
Learned numbers	Have breakfast in bed
Learned effective gesturing	Schedule a massage
Learned pronouns	Take a long nap
Learned cognates	Listen to your favorite music for a few hours
Learned nouns	Spend time with your favorite person, place, or thing
Learned adjectives	Mix up a pitcher of margaritas (the tequila is optional)

Once You've Done This...	Reward Yourself With This...
Learned verbs	Work on your favorite hobby or project
Learned new verb tenses	Go hot-tubbing
Learned the subjunctive	Have dinner at your favorite restaurant
Learned DOPs and INDOPs	Spend a weekend at a bed and breakfast or nice hotel
Finished this book	Buy something that you've always wanted

Where to Find What You're Looking For

Now you can do these tasks, too!

The Lazy Way

Starting to think there are a few more of life's little tasks that you've been putting off? Don't worry—we've got you covered. Take a look at all of *The Lazy Way* books available. Just imagine—you can do almost anything *The Lazy Way!*

Handle Your Money The Lazy Way
By Sarah Young Fisher and Carol Turkington
0-02-862632-X

Build Your Financial Future The Lazy Way
By Terry Meany
0-02-862648-6

Cut Your Spending The Lazy Way
By Leslie Haggin
0-02-863002-5

Have Fun with Your Kids The Lazy Way
By Marilee Lebon
0-02-863166-8

Keep Your Kids Busy The Lazy Way
By Barbara Nielsen and Patrick Wallace
0-02-863013-0

Feed Your Kids Right The Lazy Way
By Virginia Van Vynckt
0-02-863001-7

*All Lazy Way books are just $12.95!

additional titles on the back!

Learn French The Lazy Way
By Christophe Desmaison
0-02-863011-4

Learn German The Lazy Way
By Amy Kardel
0-02-863165-X

Learn Italian The Lazy Way
By Gabrielle Euvino
0-02-863014-9

Redecorate Your Home The Lazy Way
By Rebecca Jerdee
0-02-863163-3

Shed Some Pounds The Lazy Way
By Annette Cain and Becky Cortopassi-Carlson
0-02-862999-X

Shop Online The Lazy Way
By Richard Seltzer
0-02-863173-0

Clean Your House The Lazy Way
By Barbara H. Durham
0-02-862649-4

Care for Your Home The Lazy Way
By Terry Meany
0-02-862646-X

Stop Aging The Lazy Way
By Judy Myers, Ph.D.
0-02-862793-8

Get in Shape The Lazy Way
By Annette Cain
0-02-863010-6

Learn to Sew The Lazy Way
By Lydia Wills
0-02-863167-6

Train Your Dog The Lazy Way
By Andrea Arden
0-87605180-8

Organize Your Stuff The Lazy Way
By Toni Ahlgren
0-02-863000-9

Manage Your Time The Lazy Way
By Toni Ahlgren
0-02-863169-2

Take Care of Your Car The Lazy Way
By Michael Kennedy and Carol Turkington
0-02-862647-8

Get a Better Job The Lazy Way
By Susan Ireland
0-02-863399-7

Cook Your Meals The Lazy Way
By Sharon Bowers
0-02-862644-3

Cooking Vegetarian The Lazy Way
By Barbara Grunes
0-02-863158-7

Master the Grill The Lazy Way
By Pamela Rice Hahn and Keith Giddeon
0-02-863157-9